Judy Attfield leads an MA in Design History and Material Culture at Winchester School of Art. She has published extensively, contributing to John A Walker's *Design History and the History of Design*, Martine Segalen's *Chez-Soi: Objets et decors des creations familiales?*, and more recently to Pat Kirkham's *Gendered Objects*. An active member of the Design History Society, her current interests are in writing, criticism and historical methodologies with particular application to the material culture and consumption of popular everyday artefacts.

Pat Kirkham is Professor of Design History and Cultural Studies at De Montfort University, Leicester. She has published widely on design, gender studies and film, and her books include *William and John Linnell: Eighteenth-Century Furniture Designers*, *You Tarzan: Masculinity, Movies and Men* and *Me Jane: Masculinity, Movies and Women* co-authored with Dr Janet Thumin, *Harry Peach, Dryad and the DIA*, *The Gendered Object* and *War Culture* (co-edited with Professor David Thoms). Her major recent work is *Charles and Ray Eames: Designers of the Twentieth Century*, and she is currently work-ing on another husband and wife design partnership, that of Elaine and Saul Bass and their film title sequences which include those for *Cape Fear* and *The Age of Innocence*.

A View From the Interior

WOMEN & DESIGN

JUDY ATTFIELD & PAT KIRKHAM, EDITORS

First published in Great Britain by The Women's Press Ltd, 1989
A member of the Namara Group
34 Great Sutton Street, London EC1V 0DX

Reprinted with new material 1995

An earlier version of chapter 10 'Sexism in the Arts and Crafts Movement' by Anthea
Callen appeared in *Woman's Art Journal*, Tennessee, Vol. 5, No. 2, 1984/85. An
earlier version of 'A View from the Interior' by Alison Ravetz appeared in *Built
Environment*, Vol. 10, No. 1, 1984.

British Library Cataloguing-in-Publication Data
A catalogue record for this book is available from the British Library

ISBN 0 7043 4451 3

Typeset by AKM Associates (UK) Ltd
Printed and bound in Finland by WSOY

Contents

7

Illustrations

Acknowledgments

The authors would like to express their gratitude to the following: Mr T. Alderton, Mr and Mrs D. Anderson, Alan Beavons, Lindsay Boynton, Mrs I. M. Bodkin, Mr D. Bracey, Johanna Brenner, Brighton Polytechnic Library, City of London Polytechnic, City Museum and Art Gallery, Stoke-on-Trent, Andrew Clay, Sue Clegg, Susie Cooper, Gill Coveney, Mollie Crampton, Colin Cruise, Lys de Beaumont, Mr and Mrs J. Desormeaux, Dryad (Leicester), Ada Eardley, Electrical Association for Women, Judith Emmanuel, Mr and Mrs C. Evans, Michael Evans, Fawcett Library, Sharon Gater, Lady Gibberd, Ken and Doris Gleaves, Phil Goodall, Helena Graham, Tag Gronberg, Guildhall Library, Pat Halfpenny, Florence Hancock, Mr and Mrs V. Holden, Institution of Electrical Engineers, Joyce Jones, Eva Londos, Alex McCowan, Lynn Miller, Milne Museum, Museum of Modern Art, New York, Kathy Niblett, John Norris, Rosie Parker, Amelia Peck, Griselda Pollock, Sheila Rowbotham, Raphael Samuel, Cherril Scheer, Mary Schoeser, Jan Seed, Mrs D. Simmons, Stanford University Archives, Stanton Stephens, Star Wedgwood and F. Maitland Wright, Aubrey Stewart, Mary Stewart, Jackie Storey, Mrs D. Summers, June Swann at the Central Museum of Northampton, Leonore Symons, Eric Taplin, Mrs V. Taylor, Mrs B. Thompson, Mrs V. Tolley, Lyn and Len Toms, Warner & Sons Ltd, Ken Whaley, David Widgery, Wilton Carpets.

Introduction to the
Second Edition

Our original intention is putting together this anthology, first
published in 1989, was to present the subject of design history from
a feminist perspective.[1] The 'interior' referred to in the title was and
is intended as a metaphor for the archetypal feminine position
which we purposely set out to question. Although the interim
period has seen less published research than we had hoped, some
notable work has appeared in print,[2] helping to widen awareness of
the many contributions women have made to design as professional
designers and consultants as well as entrepreneurs and consumers.

Because design has popularly become associated with self-
conscious styling for the purposes of marketing products, it is often
perceived as trivial, particularly if compared to art. Our use of the
term is much broader; the kind of objects we are discussing here are
the very stuff which forms the environmental context, and therefore
the material culture, in which we live. We interact directly through
daily use with artefacts like clothes, cars, buildings, household
appliances and furniture at a much more intimate level than the
way we experience art. Because we encounter these things as
familiar in our day-to-day existence, design tends to become
invisibly absorbed into unself-conscious routines. Art, on the other
hand, calls attention to itself as unique and requires specialist
knowledge to be appreciated; it has to be sought in galleries or
museums where it can be viewed but not touched. Setting it apart
for contemplation lends art a special significance not associated
with familiar possessions such as chairs and shoes. Though clothes
may start out as highly visible 'designer' fashion, they soon merge
unobtrusively into everyday life, ending up outmoded and finally
discarded. Through the kind of ordinary things which fill our
wardrobes and inhabit our living rooms, design can become a focus
for the study of social relations.

So what does design tell us about the world we live in? Does it
form people's attitudes and reproduce patterns of gender dominance? Or is *it* formed by the shape of people's needs and desires?
What lies beneath that apparent veneer of triviality? The flowering
of scholarship in the cross-disciplinary area of women's and, more
recently, gender studies, has informed the study of design as an

aspect of material culture.[3] One of the projects of feminist and cultural research and writing has been to rescue the marginal and the so-called 'trivial' in order to study it within mainstream discourses. And it is to this broader spectrum of endeavour which we envisage this volume continuing to contribute.

As we approach the millennium and review the century that will soon lie behind us, it is more apparent than ever that careless technological development pollutes, and that only by maintaining sustainable growth and using fair trading practices will it be possible to avoid the exploitation of human and environmental resources. Design can no longer be regarded as politically neutral. Since the first edition of this book in 1989 there has been a greater recognition of the fact that the feminist critiques this volume offers can contribute to the mainstream of critical design practice and theory.[4]

We have not restricted the definition of 'design' to the confines of a professional occupation. One of the advantages of regarding it as an aspect of material culture is to reconsider the role of design as a site of social relations through which people interact with each other as well as with the environment. Feminist analysis has helped reveal the socially constructed nature of history and alerted us to the necessity of taking a decentred view that acknowledges cultural 'differences' more generally across class, race, sexuality and age, as well as gender. New developments in inter and multi-disciplinary studies has produced some of the most interesting possibilities for research in gender relations through the study of identity as objectified in what has been categorised as the 'androgynous object'.[5] The study of male/female design and art partnerships has also been reassessed through a number of case studies[6] which have suggested that such a relationship may be mutually supportive; yet while opening up opportunities for women it can also marginalise them. A feminist analysis can address women as agent, player, partner, beneficiary or colluder rather than always cast as the stereotypical victim.[7]

In Part One we see how a sensitivity to difference can throw light on topics as diverse as fashion and planning. The fascinating history of the stiletto heel discusses how a seemingly impossible design came to embody an image of femininity in the 1960s. We see how fashion for men has changed in the context of gender and class relations, how textile wrappings illustrates imperialist and sexist attitudes, and how architecture objectifies cultural dominance in a concrete form.

Part Two looks at two areas where women managed to gain a foothold – in textiles and pottery design. While among architects women continue to be in the minority, a particular concentration of female activity has been in domestic design. Architecture and planning has also been the area of design to which much feminist critique has been applied.[8]

Industrial design continues to be as male dominated as textile design is female dominated. In order to validate the work of women in the field of production it is essential to assert the importance of the hand-made object produced in the small workshop or in the home itself. Without this, and a consideration of crafts and anonymous design, much of women's contribution to design immediately disappears. This is clearly illustrated in Part Three where we see how the Arts and Crafts Movement both confined women to the conventional division of labour and at the same time gave them an opening to practise as professional designers. 'If You Have No Sons' shows how women's entry into the furniture trade was contingent on accidents of birth or marriage. The history of women's contribution to design through their participation in the early electricity industry illustrates how much women determined its success.

In Part Four the context is the home, with three case studies showing how a shift of analytical position can illuminate a different facet of women's relationship to design. They deal with practicality and rationality; the pleasures of consumption and popular taste; and the use women make of design to form their individual identities and their group relationships to the outside world.

We would like to thank again the contributing authors for their enthusiasm and scholarship that made the book what it is. We would also like to give a special mention in memory of Ros de Lanerolle, the original commissioning editor, who sadly died in 1992. There are many of us who owe her a great debt of gratitude for putting our work in print. It was her enthusiasm and belief in our project which helped make it a reality. We hope that readers will continue to enjoy the book, share in the pleasure we had in writing it and that it might inspire further research in the history of women and design.

Judy Attfield
Pat Kirkham
December 1994

Notes

1 The Design History Society (DHS) held the first conference on 'Women in Design' at the ICA in 1983, followed by 'Women and Design' at Leicester in 1985, 'Women Working in Design' Central/St Martins, London in 1986, 'The Cutting Edge' at the ICA in 1988 and 'The Crack in the Pavement:

Gender, Fashion, Architecture' at the Design Museum, London in 1991. Some earlier writing on the subject includes: Walker, Lynne, *Women, Architects: Their Work*, Sorella Press, 1984; Attfield, Judy, 'Defining the object and the subject . . . the perception of women in design history' in *Times Higher Education Supplement (THES)*, 1 February 1985, 'Feminist Designs on Design History' in *FAN (Feminist Arts News)* Vol. 2 (3), 1985, joint editor with Tag Gronberg *Women Working in Design: A Resource Book*, The London Institute, 1986, and 'Invisible Touch . . . what design history can gain from a feminist perspective' in *THES*, 19 June 1987; Buckley, Cheryl, 'Made in Patriarchy: Towards a feminist analysis of women and design' in *Design Issues*, Vol. 3 (2), 1987; 'FORM/female Follows FUNCTION/male: Feminist Critiques of Design' in John A. Walker, *Design History and the History of Design*, Pluto, London, 1989.

2 MacQuiston, Liz, *Women in Design: A Contemporary View*, Trefoil, 1988; *Women in Design* [exhibition catalogue in 2 vols] Design Centre, Stuttgart, 1989; Evans, Caroline and Thornton, Minna, *Women Fashion: A New Look*, Quartet, London, 1989; Buckley, Cheryl, *Potters and Paintresses: Women Designers in the Pottery Industry 1870–1955*, The Women's Press, London, 1990; Burkhauser, Jude (ed), *Glasgow Girls: Women in Art and Design 1880–1920*, Canongate, Glasgow, 1990; Seddon, Jill and Worden, Suzette, *Women Designing: Redefining Design in Britain Between the Wars*, University of Brighton, 1994.

3 Since the first publication of this volume, a considerable body of work has appeared which discusses artefacts and aesthetics as aspects of culture in which gender is central: Kirkham, Pat (ed), *The Gendered Object*, Manchester University Press, forthcoming, contains contributions by seven of the authors of this volume; Barnes, Ruth, *Dress and Gender: Making and Meaning*, Berg, Oxford, 1993; Battersby, Christine, *Gender and Genius: Towards a Feminist Aesthetics*, The Women's Press, London, 1989; Ash, Juliet and Wilson, Elizabeth, *Chic Thrills: A Fashion Reader*, Pandora, London, 1992; Craik, Jennifer, *The Face of Fashion: Cultural Studies in Fashion*, Routledge, London, 1994.

4 'Feminist Perspectives' in Whiteley, Nigel, *Design For Society*, Reaktion, 1993, pp. 134–57; Julier, Guy, *Encyclopaedia of 20th Century Design and Designers*, Thames & Hudson, London, 1993, pp. 79 and 212.

5 MacKenzie, Maureen A., *Androgynous Objects: String bags and gender in central New Guinea*, Harwood, 1991; Attfield, Judy, 'Playing with Gender: A case study of Barbie and Action Man, adult dolls for girls and boys' in op. cit. Kirkham, 1995.

6 Chadwick, Whitney and de Courtivron, Isabelle, *Significant Others: Creativity and Intimate Partnerships*, Thames & Hudson, London, 1993; Helland, Janice, 'The Critics and the Arts and Crafts: The Instance of Margaret Macdonald and Charles Rennie Mackintosh' *Art History*, Vol. 17 (2), June 1994; pp. 205–23 and 'Art Production as Cooperation: Collaboration among The Glasgow Four' in Kaplan, Wendy (ed), *Charles Rennie Mackintosh* [exhibition catalogue] forthcoming.

7 Kirkham, Pat, *Charles and Ray Eames*, MIT Press, Cambridge, MA, 1995; Seddon and Worden op. cit.

8 Wilson, Elizabeth, *The Sphinx in the City*, Virago, London, 1991; Greed, Clara H., *Women and Planning*, Routledge, London, 1994.

Part One
Images of Difference

1
Objectifying Gender: The Stiletto Heel

Lee Wright

This essay will focus on the notion of gender in relation to design. One reason for selecting the stiletto heel as a case study is that as an object it is seen as being exclusively female.[1] Even when worn by men it is with a view to constructing a female image. Gender specificity in object design exists on many levels. This essay attempts to equate the *process of making* with the *construction of meaning*. I will be discussing the stiletto heel in terms of its manufacture and production process alongside ideas concerning representation from its inception in the early 1950s to its demise as a mass fashion item a decade later.

The stiletto heel of the 1950s marks the culmination of an historical continuum: the high heel as representative of the female in footwear. At the same time it heralds a new era of shoe production and design. By focusing on this particular moment in the history of the high heel, this article identifies many of the issues concerning industrial manufacture in the 1950s, which, together with the particular social context of the period, explain the emergence of the stiletto as a new fashion item.

The stiletto is a particularly contentious case study in view of the interpretations which have caused its boycott since the 1960s. Feminists, in an attempt to express their reaction against traditional female roles, have often cast the stiletto as an object of exploitation, along with other items of clothing which appear to be inherently feminine. In the rejection of certain items belonging to the women's sartorial code, adoption of those thought inherently masculine has been sought: examples of the 1970s are flat-heeled shoes and dungarees.[2]

Using the stiletto as a focal point this study is part of a more general review which looks at how and why certain meanings become attached to objects and whether these meanings are inherent in the design criteria. An alternative reading of 'stiletto' may now be necessary in the light of a wider discussion in current fashion design of the manipulation of masculine and feminine aspects in clothing for both sexes. This reworking seems to centre on trying to redefine meaning rather than changing the form of clothes.[3]

The stiletto has been widely accepted as symbolising female subordination. It seems that this sort of theory is widely applied to female-gendered objects but not to those that are resolutely male. It would appear that the more 'female' an object, the more it is devalued. This implies that meanings are often based on an association already determined: that is, that *meaning* is subject to stereotyping, which results in the perpetuation of particular perspectives. With reference to gender it seems that all too often objects construed as male are equated with 'masculine' and are therefore active and assertive, while defining female is equivalent to 'feminine', indicating passivity and subservience.

Since the early nineteenth century conventional criteria of styling based on gender difference have been established in footwear. Before then, male and female fashions were closely allied in style.[4] The heel is the component of the shoe which has become the most visible expression of gender in that, in the nineteenth century, high heels became 'female' footwear and were disallowed in a male sartorial code.[5] Therefore, the high heel established itself as a part of female iconography and has since become a useful tool in the construction of a female image. The stiletto heel has evoked the most potent symbolism because, in design terms, it managed to reach the ultimate dimensions of its *genre*, combining thinness and height in a relationship never before attained. The stiletto is the peak of the career of the high heel, fulfilling all requirements of feminised styling at the same time as it *literally* reached its highest point. The extremity of such styling demands precipitated the technological innovation necessary to manufacture such shoes. In other words, the *idea* for the stiletto predated any means of producing it.

The stiletto was one of several objects created in the aftermath of the Second World War as deliberately feminine,[6] at a time when the role of women in society was particularly polarised. Much discussion has centred on the way women consumers were 'constructed' by specific traits in the design of clothes and other products. One can speculate on whether this was a conscious attempt to cast women in a more feminine mould or part of a less conscious social movement which objectified its ideals in a reinforcement of femininity.

Footwear cannot be isolated from fashion: it is an intrinsic element in the creation of a 'total look'. In this instance, the New Look launched by Christian Dior in 1947 provided the keynote in the design. Generally regarded as the most important fashion event in the immediate post-war period, the Corolle line, as the New Look was originally christened, became the fashion paradigm of the shoe industry. The high-fashion magazine *Harpers Bazaar* commented in May 1947:

> The New Look is a new shape and that shape follows the lines of the best possible figure, emphasising every feminine charm.

This reaction was one of many which stressed the expression of femininity as the prime motivating force in shaping the fashion of the time. Moreover, it stressed that the 'feminine' was determined by the female form itself rather than by an artificial form. It is obvious that the clothes were meant to be an extension of the female figure and *emphasise* it rather than *distract* from it.

The other essential ingredient was the need to appear contemporary. The creation of a 'new' design of a feminine nature was in contrast to the design philosophy of the Utility system, which was in operation during the war and for some time afterwards.[7] The Utility scheme was a system of rationed items specially designed to be functional and to save raw materials. Clothing had to be practical and durable and this led to forms of dress for women being based on menswear, which, since the nineteenth century, had tended to place novelty and fashion second in matters of design. Footwear manufacturers now used the stylistic guidelines of the new Paris fashions as a contrast to those of the Utility scheme.[8] This scheme emphasised function above any other design criteria, equating 'good design' with a non-ornamental style. A product which was lighter in weight would counteract the chunky practical Utility style, but the dilemma remained of how to oppose austerity plainness when new fashions were also demanding simplicity based on lack of ornament. However manufacturers resolved this, they were ultimately concerned with a concept of form rather than function in the late 1940s and early 1950s. The main issue was how to follow the French fashion dictate; as one journal put it in 1947,

> ... whether heels should reach a new extremity of height or a new low; which is the most flattering line for the ankle and interprets best the revival of flourishing femininity which characterises the recent fashion change.[9]

A year later this was still under discussion: 'Everything points to an even greater development of femininity . . .'[10]

Footwear manufacturers started trying to produce shoes that met these criteria, but it was a number of years before they finally came up with a satisfactory solution. Discussions centred on a tailored, refined shoe which gave the impression of lightness by means of a slender form.[11] The approach adopted was typical of the fashion industry. In order to appear 'new' the design had to be not just different from previous styles but a complete contrast to them.[12]

Objectifying Gender

9

The new spring shoes will be more delicate, more lady-like, more flattering than ever before. The heavy bulky shoe is definitely OUT.[13]

In contemporary language the term 'stiletto' is often used to describe a type of heel *and* the type of shoe to which it is attached – the court shoe. The two have become synonymous. The name originally given to the heel has, since 1953, become a generic title often used to describe this particular style and heel type. The reasons for this are basic to an understanding of the making and the meaning of the heel. The court shoe suited the New Look concept in that it was a tailored shape which followed the natural line of the foot. This slim-fitting form indicated and determined a lighter-weight product than Utility styles. It was not a new style, but its reintroduction after the war coincided with a refinement in last-making,[14] so it appeared updated even though it was a pre-war design. The plain court shoe shape, therefore, both *followed* and *broke* with the concepts of Utility footwear design. Just like the whole of the New Look the 'modernising process' was in some ways based on pre-war values. More importantly, its 'graceful' qualities apparently suited the new ethos determining what femininity looked like. While it moved sufficiently away from 1940s' styling to appear new and modern, it also inherited enough 1940s' characteristics to be seen not to break completely with tradition. A degree of continuity was important in helping the style to establish itself as market leader. By June 1951, the journal *Footwear* concluded that 'courts dominate the shoe market.'

In retrospect, we think of the stiletto as being of one type – a thin, tapering heel. In fact, this is the stiletto as it ultimately became rather than the one invented in the early 1950s. It was not a static design but a whole series of variations over a ten-year period. In these crucial ten years its design attempted to reconcile the demands of the dominant design philosophy, which emphasised simplicity above all, with the New Look femininity, which concentrated on styling. In order to answer the demands of fashion the heel changed in shape and construction from 1947, but by 1953 it had managed to establish a degree of resolution in its design (see Fig. 1.1). The court shoe shape, resolved prior to the heel, demonstrated the way in which femininity and modernity could be objectified. From 1953 the heel and toe took priority. The heel began as a two-inch thick but tapered shape which, by 1957, was gradually refined to the slender form we now recognise as a stiletto heel. The toe of the shoe underwent similar stylistic changes. The rounded toe of 1953 and before became sharper and eventually developed into an arrow-like point.

The choice of 'stiletto', the thin-bladed knife, to christen the heel is often thought to have originated from the invention of its metal core. The naming of a shoe from the style of heel was perhaps partly due to the fact that the shoe itself was very plain and the heel was therefore the focus of interest. When the *Daily Telegraph* published a photograph of a new heel called the 'Stiletto' on 10 September 1953, it was one of a number of terms denoting the *stylistic* characteristics and not an aspect of its manufacture.[15] The metal 'backbone' of the heel had not yet been invented! The heel of 1953 still used wood, the traditional material for heel construction. The 'spike', 'needle' and 'spindle' were all attempts to conjure up a name for a heel which was more tapered than ever before. Following the precedent set by the court shoe shape, the manufactures took elements of the 'Louis' heel, which was standard for a court shoe, but elongated and refined it.[16]

This produced a style of footwear which was impractical in a number of ways (see Fig. 1.2). The relative fineness of the heel meant that it would be difficult to walk on and that, with the pressure of walking, it could easily snap. Furthermore, the cut-away top of the shoe implied that it might not cling to the foot. But it was precisely this *appearance* of impracticality that made the 1940s' Utility styles look totally outdated.

As this shape of heel had never been seen before, a new name helped to identify it. Of all the names mentioned, some implied fragility, some implied strength and all suited the stylistic qualities. The stiletto seems to have prevailed at first because of its Italian association. 'Italian-ness' was a fashionable trend in the midfifties[17] and, along with the acknowledged traditional skill of Italian footwear manufacture in general, this helped to sell the product.

The problem for British manufacturers was how to make a commercially viable heel, one which would live up to its name and which looked like the fashion sketches. The initial experiments used wood as the reinforcement required to withstand prolonged pressure without breaking. By building a heel of interlocking pieces of wood, strength could be gained by a judicious use of the grain. Paradoxically, the heel which had consumer credibility in terms of wear was too heavy and clumsy to warrant the title of stiletto, while the one which did warrant the title by successfully reproducing the fashionable form did not stand up to wear. Pressure to produce the stiletto at this point seems to have come from the fashion industry, which continued to promote this airy, streamlined shoe. The demand was so great that in 1957, four years after the initial appearance of the stiletto in the *Daily Telegraph*, the perfect solution was still being sought.

Without much doubt the biggest single constructional

problem which the shoe trade has had to face in recent years has followed the trend in ladies' shoes towards even more slender heels.[18]

The motivation to continue with this seemingly impossible task was linked to the persistence of the *idea* of the stiletto. It was in the interest of the manufacturers to interpret the demands of fashion and the female consumer in a single, universal style which had the potential to dominate the market. In the 1950s a universal style was still possible, although the emerging youth commodity culture was beginning to break down such a dictatorial code of fashionable dressing. Perhaps the success of the stiletto was that its design allowed for variations. These variations were adopted by different consumer factions, but as a new product it was most popular with teenagers and women in their early twenties, anxious to ensure they looked modern and fashionable in a post-austerity era. It therefore became increasingly important to the shoe industry that a suitable method of production be found, which would be cost-effective and result in a heel which could endure protracted use and still look like a stiletto.

The pressure to create such a design caused shoe manufacturers to join forces and sponsor the Shoe and Allied Trades Retail Association (SATRA) to carry out research into the ergonomics of the stiletto heel. It had become clear that the wooden spindle heel would never be strong enough. A European solution pre-empted SATRA: in 1956 a plastic version with a metal strengthening core was shown at an Italian trade fair. Within a year a British heel component company puchased the UK rights and imported the machine process, which was based on the technique of injection moulding. From this point, the term 'stiletto' became the leader in the title stakes. The pointed shape that could now be achieved, together with the internal metal pin to sustain it, made the true meaning of the word directly pertinent.

In a sense, the plastic version can be seen as the second stage in the history of the stiletto, as it was only then that the concept for the design could be properly put into practice. It was four years since the shape had been created as the perfect solution to interpreting the feminine in shoe design, and ten years since the image had been drawn on paper. Now the manufacturing problem of combining style and form was finally solved. The new manufacturing process reinforced the newness of the product and gave the stiletto a permanent place in fashion vocabulary.

The plastic heel introduced a completely mechanised system of production in 1957 and ensured the stiletto's success by bringing it within reach of the lower end of the market. Ironically, this move created its own problem: how to produce a heel which could withstand any amount of wear. In high fashion the stiletto was a novelty item and, as such, worn only occasionally. The phenomenal retail success of the mass-produced version indicated that it was being worn far more, and in many situations not forecast by the manufacturers. What had previously been thought of as an evening shoe was now being subjected to much more rigorous use: women were wearing stilettos at work, when driving, running and catching a bus and for other everyday activities. The wide acceptability of the style did not mask the fact that the product still fell short of customers' expectations. While-you-wait heel repair kiosks appeared on every high street to service heels at a moment's notice. The volume of customer complaints encouraged SATRA to continue its research into what was then the relatively new field of plastics technology and chemical engineering.

It was not just the wearer who had cause for complaint: the minute heel-tip concentrated the wearer's weight so much that floors were often damaged beyond repair. The stiletto made news with stories like: 'The spike heels that English girls wear are ruining floors in factories, offices and dance halls . . .'[19] and 'Women's Stiletto heeled shoes are blamed for breaking up roads in Carshalton, Surrey . . .'[20] It was calculated that an eight-stone girl in stilettos exerted heel pressure of one ton per square inch.[21] This caused not only the banning of stiletto heels in various places from dance halls to aircraft, but also the redesign of floor surfaces. Bus platforms were altered: wooden boards were replaced with solid rubber matting in order to avoid the heels getting caught[22], and aircraft designers had to find tougher materials for flooring.[23]

In 1959 the plastic heel was evolving into its most exaggerated form – up to six inches high with a tiny heel-tip. This development parallels the 'sharpening' of the round toe into a point (see Fig 1.3). The arrow-like form of both heel and toe reinforced the idea of harmony of style between the shoe and heel, giving further cause for the title of stiletto to be used for the whole shoe. However, its antisocial reputation increased as it became more pointed, and worsened when the medical profession, confronted by an enormous increase in foot and posture problems, pronounced against the wearing of such footwear on medical grounds. SATRA investigated the effect of the stiletto on the body and found that continued wearing of the extreme form over a period of time could cause a variety of medical problems. Any style of stiletto caused the protrusion of chest and bottom and the development of calf muscles. The higher the heel, the more exaggerated the effect on posture thus increasing back problems; the more pointed the toe, the more pressure was put on the foot to follow an unnatural shape. This inspired as much moral as medical denigration: the body shape imposed by the stiletto was associated with an obvious display of female sexuality. In the early 1950s when the stiletto shape was being established, it was not seen as representing anything other than conventional 'feminine' attributes. Once the aspired-to shape was a reality, the meaning had changed, though the ideology of form had remained the same. It was more aggressive and seemed to be *breaking* with those early ideas of femininity rather than *conforming* to them. It seems that the stiletto in its various forms was by now so firmly installed in women's culture that no diatribe could prove strong enough to dislodge it. Indeed, its very notoriety coincided with an increase in sales in 1958 until 1962. One can speculate whether the new meaning was mapped on to the form or whether the form was continuing to be a representation of social relations of that era.

This is not to suggest, however, that all women wore stilettos of the more extreme variety. These were mainly worn by the younger generation in an attempt to break away from the style popular with their mothers. The wearing of 'winklepickers' (as this extreme variety was known) was often a defiant gesture against the establishment. Female youth culture was partly redefining itself on its differences rather than its similarities. As Angela Carter recalls in *Nothing Sacred*:

> When I was eighteen, I went to visit her rigged out in all the atrocious sartorial splendour of the underground high style of the late fifties, black mesh stockings, spike-heeled shoes, bum-hugging skirt, jacket with a black fox collar.[24]

The implication is that the stiletto was used by some women to represent dissatisfaction with the conventional female image and to replace it with that of a 'modern' woman who was more active and economically independent than her predecessors. The paradox is that, in retrospect, it has been labelled a 'shackling' instrument which renders women immobile and passive. It has also been stressed that the heels gave added emphasis to breasts and bottoms, which were features of the 1950s' cinematic female stereotype. While this is undoubtedly true, I consider it a more important factor that the stiletto did *not* symbolise the housewife. From 1957 the stiletto was associated with glamour, with rebellion: it represented someone who was in some way 'modern' and 'up to date', and, above all, someone who inhabited a world outside the home – a go-getter! Therefore, it may be more accurate to suggest that this stiletto symbolised *liberation* rather than subordination, despite the fact that high heels of any form were part of a stereotyped framework of what women wore. I suggest that stiletto-wearing in the fifties was part of a broader discussion of how to express the 'new woman' – one who was not content with pre-war values and traditional roles. In this sense it could be seen as *progressive* rather than *retrogressive*. The stiletto did not break with all the traditions of what is female in footwear, but it certainly took those traditions to their furthest point, especially when, in its most extreme form, it was used to symbolise a rejection of convention. It used what was acceptable to create non-acceptance.

The early stiletto could be said to represent traditional values. It was only as the shape changed that the meaning shifted and it therefore came to represent something other than its initial values. A crucial point to make is that the meaning became more radical at the same time as the style itself became more exaggerated. This reinforced its value as a commodity which represented women who were in the process of breaking with established female roles. The fashion industry of the fifties promoted the stiletto but the difficulties of production were such that the shoe industry would have welcomed a change in fashion dictates. However, consistent and increasing sales persuaded shoe manufacturers to continue. In this sense women were using consumer power to demand the production of the stiletto.

This exploration of an object which signified 'female' in the 1950s is not an attempt to prove that women were subordinate; it is rather a way of looking at how design works to objectify those characteristics which emphasised femaleness within the social context of that era. In a wider context, the objectification of gender traits of that decade seems to segregate the sexes rather than indicate the similarities. In later years, baggy clothes are an example of de-emphasis of the female form, disguising femaleness sometimes to the extent of making it look male. It has been said that this was a reaction against the fifties' stereotype which exaggerated those parts of the body which are female, and of course the stiletto played a part in this. Women have accepted too readily the notion that stilettos exploit women. By using male forms of clothing we are perpetuating the dominance of masculinity. Perhaps assertion of gender *difference* challenges the power relationship more effectively than any attempt to emulate what is seen as male. I am suggesting that power can be, and has been, represented in women's clothes if one explores ways in which 'femaleness' has been denoted.[25]

The exaggeration of gender attributes and an open display of gender difference has been labelled as exploitative when part of the female sartorial code. However, the physical changes imposed by the wearing of the stiletto need not be seen as an expression of submission. On the contrary, it exaggerated the existing physique by giving prominence to certain parts of the body and adding height. The body shape the stiletto creates depends on the shape and height of the heel. Again, the more extreme the stiletto, the more extreme physical prominence it gives. Given the suggestion that an overt representation of femaleness equals assertion, the most acute stiletto heel represents the most power. This is one example of the interdependence of form and meaning. The counter-argument, which says that the stiletto makes women less powerful by restricting their mobility, is secondary to the main issues concerning the stiletto in 1957. The stiletto put women on the edge of the dominance versus submission argument, but the fact that a fashion item could raise and explore those issues is significant and crucial to an understanding of women's role in the late fifties. I believe that from 1957 to 1962 the stiletto signified some liberation from traditional female values in object design. The sexual connotation was already established before the stiletto was invented, once high heels had come to symbolise the transition from adolescence to adulthood and had become the prerogative of women. The stiletto as the ultimate in high-heel styling served merely to crystallise what had already come to mean 'womanhood'. The purchase of a girl's first high-heels is often a signal of puberty and the onset of sexual maturity. The heel is used as a female rite of passage,[26] where the height of the heel indicates gradual progression towards maturity. The 'Kitten' stiletto of the early 1960s was devised for this purpose; the one-inch heel was the first step towards graduation. At the opposite end of the scale the stiletto could be so high that any pretence of function in terms of walking is lost. One symbolised sexual immaturity and a certain innocence, the other total maturity and sexual prowess. (Because the plastic construction of stilettos allowed for all these variations, the meaning became more strongly attached to the stiletto rather than any other type of high heel.) This is the point at which gender and sexuality become allied and the heel becomes an indicator of both 'female' and 'sex'. An example of this can be found in films of the fifties and sixties, where removal of stilettos was often used to imply a sexual encounter.

The stiletto is a 'grown-up' shoe in many senses of the word. By literally reaching new heights, combined with extreme thinness, it broke with the traditions of gender and form which initiated its production. That is, at first the stiletto was based on conventional interpretations of femininity. It was only later, when the basic form underwent certain stylistic changes, that a new set of assertive meanings was established. It seems, then, that in *one form* – the stiletto – there are *different meanings*, which originate from the polarities of the design. Therefore, at the point of design or production, not all meanings are set. In the case of the stiletto, some were 'in-built'. For example, the notion of femininity of the late 1940s was 'built' into the heel's design, but five years later both the meaning and the design had changed. I am unsure whether the object – the stiletto – came to represent particular ideologies or if representation created the need to change the object. In *Decoding Advertisements* Judith Williamson suggests the latter: 'Material things we need are made to represent other, non-material things we need . . . The point of exchange between the two is where "meaning" is created.'[27] Certainly, the stiletto in its more extreme manifestations went beyond the bounds of what was deemed 'acceptable' in that era – a crucial factor in the ability of the style to convey rebellion and dominance. This was based on the idea of the heel as a weapon to symbolise womanhood and its feminine attributes, and was put across in an aggressive, obvious manner rather than the subtle, passive way more commonly associated with femininity.

> I've been so mad at Johnny that I've gone for him with anything I could lay my hands on – a knife, a stiletto shoe, anything . . .[28]

The original motivation to produce a new type of attenuated heel survived the drawn-out development of the design and manufacture of the stiletto. The many methods devised all responded to a similar stylistic challenge, one which called for the invention of what could be termed a progressive product, a style which would announce its modernity and its affiliation to the feminine through a shape which could only be made possible through technical prowess. The stiletto mythology was completed in 1960 when the 'No Heel' stiletto appeared. The stiletto heel was so ingrained an image by this time that it no longer needed the very object that denoted it. The lightweight design of the heel had been ultimately achieved; it no longer existed! This novelty version, which appeared seven years after the stiletto's debut, served to make the point that both the technical and the stylistic challenge of the 'ideal' heel had been met.

The stiletto was devised and used to express femininity within the realms of what that meant in the 1950s. Therefore, it could be said that the ultimate form of the stiletto expressed extreme femininity in terms of its own traditions. It seems pertinent to raise the issue of whether we can criticise such overt expressions of the feminine in design as victimisation if we are basing our criticism on a male perspective. This negates the fact that expressions of femaleness can signify power and be objectified in ways other than masculine.

Notes

1 For example, Lisa Tickner writes that the stiletto 'isn't, and can't be, neutral; it is specifically female,' *Block*, No. 1, 1979.

2 This too has become a stereotype rather than an iconoclasm, as it was originally intended to be.

3 In an interview in *ID*, No. 45, March 1987, innovative fashion designer Vivienne Westwood comments: 'I've never thought it powerful to be like a second-rate man'. See early 1987 advertisements for fashion designer Katharine Hamnett.

4 Wilson, Elizabeth, *Adorned in Dreams*, Virago, London, 1985; Swann, Jane, *Shoes*, Batsford, London, 1982.

5 Platform shoes of the 1970s are the one exception to this rule.

6 Another example is the Hoover.

7 The Utility scheme ended in 1952.

8 *Utility Furniture and Fashion*, Geffrye Museum catalogue, 1974.

9 *Footwear*, February 1947.

10 *Footwear*, February 1948.

11 This impression reinforced dominant beauty ideals for women when 'a good figure' was equated with a slender form.

12 Konig, René, *The Restless Image*, Allen and Unwin, London, 1973. One of the few theoretical texts on fashion which seeks to explain how fashions are created.

13 *Footwear*, February 1948.

14 In 1948 a last – the form on which a shoe is made – was devised which created a more slender product; this enabled the snug fit of the court shoe, which is necessary for it to cling to the foot, to be increased.

15 Information based on an interview with Edward Rayne, makers of the 'Telegraph' shoe.

16 In a similar way to the last-making of the 'new' court shoe.

17 *Block*, No. 5, 1981. Dick Hebdige discussed the introduction of Italian design to the UK in the 1950s via the scooter.

18 *High Heels*, SATRA, July 1957.

19 *Shoe and Leather News*, 1958 (month unknown).

20 *Shoe and Leather News*, 3 July 1958.

21 *Shoe and Leather News*, 2 April 1959.

22 *Daily Telegraph*, 21 November 1959.

23 *The Times*, 5 August 1958.

24 Carter, Angela, *Nothing Sacred*, Virago, London, 1982, p.11.

25 Spender, Dale, 'Re-inventing Rebellion', *Feminist Theorists*, The Women's Press, London, 1983. I disagree with Dale Spender's comment that 'power is still a concept about which women have codified very little'.

26 Just as long trousers are sometimes used in a male rite of passage from child to adult.

27 Williamson, Judith, *Decoding Advertisements*, Marion Boyars, London, 1979, p. 14.
28 Hamblett, Charles, and Deverson, Jane, *Generation X*, Tandem Books, London, 1964, p. 94.

Further Reading

Barthes, Roland, *The Fashion System*, Jonathan Cape, London, 1985.

Brownmiller, Susan, *Femininity*, Paladin, London, 1986.

French, Marilyn, *On Women, Men and Morals*, Summit Books, New York, 1985.

Goodall, Phil, 'Design and gender', *Block*, No. 9, 1983.

MacKenzie, Donald, and Wajaman, Judy, *The Social Shaping of Technology*, Open University Press, London, 1985.

Molloy, John, *Dress for Success*, Warner Books, New York, 1975.
Parker, Roszika, *The Subversive Stitch: Embroidery and the Making of the Feminine*, The Women's Press, London, 1984.

2
Representations of Women and Race in the Lancashire Cotton Trade

Zoë Munby

This essay examines images of women woven and printed on the cloths which were manufactured in Lancashire for India and China, as well as similar imagery used in the advertising which accompanied those cloths. India and China were crucial markets for Lancashire cottons, yet ones with distinctive cultural requirements. The different imagery used by Lancashire designers for the two countries is discussed here to explore the ways in which patriarchal and colonialist ideas informed the trade; the use of images of women within this trade is a powerful record of the cultural impact of British industrialisation. The sources for the designs are collections of cloths, labels and trade-marks which survive in Britain. For this reason, and because a late-twentieth-century white perspective cannot do justice to the Indian or Chinese experience, this essay focuses on the reasons for the *development* of this imagery rather than on an assessment of its impact. The incorporation of racist and sexist imagery into products designed for use by the very people who were being represented is sufficient justification for this examination.

By the last quarter of the nineteenth century, competition from North America and Europe was forcing Lancashire to make a more concerted effort to extend existing markets and to develop new ones. India and China, where cotton was the main clothing material used and where, in different ways, Britain had political influence, were key targets.

Entirely plain, low-quality cloth had been sent to India from Lancashire from the early 1800s. India's own cotton industry had been weakened and then almost entirely destroyed by the combination of cheap imports of Lancashire cottons and fiscal measures imposed by Britain. From the 1850s these export goods were, in the majority of cases, heavily adulterated by sizing.[1] In some quarters it was felt, even leaving moral scruples aside, that the India trade was commercially endangered by the reputation it was gaining for bad quality and short measure. The period examined here, from 1870 to 1930, was one in which a section of the industry attempted to transform the trade. The types of cloths made for India continued to be of low quality but from the 1870s they were more diverse, with manufacturers adding new patterned cottons to existing ranges of plain cloths. These changes were, in part, a response to the need to increase trade. But to the problem of low quality was added that of designing for a culture with very different decorative traditions to those of Lancashire.

There were two methods of producing these patterned cloths: small quantities of the cloths sent to India were printed and this percentage increased in the 1870s.[2] There was also possible, by this time, manufacture on power looms of cottons with elaborate, large-scale, woven patterns. This created direct competition with the more expensive of the handloom-woven *saris* and *dhotis* produced in India, which could now be imitated cheaply in Lancashire factories. The printed cloths sent to India consisted mainly of indigo and 'Turkey' red cloths with stylised floral motifs imitative of India's own printed cottons.[3] The pattern-woven cottons were often produced with numerous variations on small geometric and floral motifs, similar to the cottons India had sent to Britain during an earlier period. But a number of manufacturers, as if entranced by the potential of the jacquard loom for producing large-scale intricate patterns, attempted figurative designs employing more adventurous subject-matter which would have been considered quite inappropriate for the home market. Animals – elephants, lions and other tropical beasts – were particularly popular, while the technological wonders of Western society, from sewing-machines to, later, airships, were other favourite subjects. There were also images of Indian and European peoples which explicitly suggested the colonial relationship between the two countries.[4]

The form these images took had many similarities with the advertising material which accompanied the cloths.[5] The last few yards of bales or 'bolts' of cotton for export were stamped with trade-marks and miscellaneous information as to the type and quality of cloth; similar information and images appeared in the form of 'tickets' – gummed, multicoloured labels. Where cotton was destined for non-European, non-industrialised countries, the images used on stamps and tickets were more strident, larger and brighter, conveying the necessary information in a form which was considered more suitable to the tastes of those outside the cultural orbit of the Western world.

These stamps and tickets, intended for use in sales displays to attract the eye of the buyer and then be discarded, had in practice a much more extended impact. The relatively simple styles of most of the cottons were positively enhanced by the intricate stamp impressions. In some cases, bolt ends were collected and sewn together to make a patchwork fabric whose dominant pattern consisted of the stamp rather than that of the original cloth. The tickets may well have been similarly preserved, for in a society where glossy, multicoloured paper printing had only recently become cheaply available, the quality and complexity of the printed tickets must have made a considerable impact.[6] Although evidence of the use of Lancashire goods is scarce, it seems probable that both tickets and stamped bolt ends were retained and valued for purposes other than those for which the Lancashire manufacturers intended them.

The subject-matter of the cottons, stamps and tickets were identical. When depicting people, the cheap quality of the jacquard cloth employed produced crude, caricatured figures; however, the stamps and tickets had the potential for more subtle effects. Europeans were most frequently shown in their powerful roles as members of the army or royalty, and the ever-recurring European women were Victoria and Britannia. By contrast, the Indian women featured were anonymous and were usually depicted as poor and passive, or as sexual objects, particularly on the tickets and stamps. The Indians were shown as primitive or subject peoples. This was achieved either by depicting them via racial caricatures and/or by showing them engaged in some 'primitive' or 'exotic' occupation: the men hunting with spears or snake-charming, the women spinning on simple hand-wheels although women were depicted at work far less frequently than men.

The 'humorous' or 'exotic' quality of the images of men made them suitable subjects for textile or advertising design, but images of women had, most commonly, to fulfil additional decorative criteria. The images of Indian women, with attractively arranged clothing and accessories, had, in particular, certain racial characteristics removed. Although dressed in Indian clothes, their faces, coyly smiling, were of the palest brown with features conforming to European ideals of beauty. This type ranged from the mildly provocative to more explicit images where Indian women were shown as sexual objects, with breasts or hips thrust forward, embracing a lover or posing on a bed (see Fig. 2.1). Today these images of Indian women appear familiar and unremarkable, because the combination of Westernised features with sexual objectification has been adopted in many fields of Indian graphic art in this century. A variety of Western visual sources over a long period of time have contributed to this style,[7] but Lancashire textiles of the 1870s onwards were a significant influence, circulating as they did among a wide spectrum of the Indian population. These ways of portraying Indian women may have also drawn on earlier Indian graphic traditions;[8] but it seems more probable that the mass importation of Lancashire cottons, with their attendant advertising material, served to introduce *new* ways of representing women into India itself.

British popular opinion was in no doubt as to Indian sexual mores. Liberal Imperial reformers of the early decades of the nineteenth century had justified the British presence in India as a civilising influence, frequently citing attitudes to women in Indian society, as exhibited in such practices as child marriage and *suttee*. The more sensual forms of Hindu art and literature were employed as evidence that Indian society was depraved. Apart from the writings of a few scholars, British society as a whole echoed the colonialist's confidence in the superiority, both aesthetically and morally, of British culture.

Indian religious art depicting sexuality and nakedness was clearly one source for the images of women which Lancashire exported. However, the use of such images in a secular context, mass-produced and commercially dispensed by an industry of the colonial power, led to images which were explicitly oppressive. Women were depicted not as sexually active and powerful deities, as in Indian artistic traditions, but as passively available – either alone, looking invitingly at the viewer, or passively accepting the advances of a male. Indian society already incorporated traditions of women's inferior role and male power, whether through marriage conventions or in religious and secular law, but these imported images suggested a *different* type of subservient and sexually available role for Indian women. This essentially foreign form of oppressive relationship was thus additional to existing patriarchal structures.

Such images were not part of Lancashire textile designers' everyday repertoire. The nude, in its classical form, was an easily available and familiar source, but as a vehicle for developing drawing technique and not as a decorative motif in commercial practice. A set of six cotton cloth designs of 1877, with border patterns of nudes taken from classical art, are evidence of the difficulties the Lancashire designers experienced in this area (see Fig. 2.2). Although this subject may have been intended to appeal to the supposed lasciviousness of the Indians, the incongruity of these cultural allusions, and the crude drawing of the figures, executed in low-quality weaving, produced images which were anything but alluring.[9]

If cheap, woven cotton cloth was not the ideal medium for conveying sensual imagery, then other techniques were used more powerfully. A well-documented instance was the series of black-and-white photographic tickets issued by a Manchester firm in the 1920s. Known to the firm by the collective name 'Lady Tickets', the series showed white women, semi-nude, disporting themselves in a variety of unlikely settings, beckoning or gesturing provocatively. The 'Lady Tickets' were one of the firm's most popular 'lines'. Although they were sold to cotton merchants and exporters

Representations of Women and Race 23

for labelling bales of cotton, they could be used in other ways. The firm still retains a file of correspondence indicating that these tickets were also sold in bulk to individuals in India who expressed an interest in specific pornographic effects.[10] It is significant that contemporary British assumptions of racial superiority were waived when the primary objective was to satisfy the tastes of the client, an Indian man. The white male ticket-maker and black male customer colluded in the creation of pornographic images of white women, who, in colonial India, were completely outside the social or emotional worlds of Indian men.

The clear message of the images incorporated into the products of the India trade is that the merchants, manufacturers and designers were content, in general, to convey the dominant British view of India, interpreted by designers from the accounts, commentaries and graphic records of Indian life which were available in Britain. The use of images of women and women's bodies to sell cloth was seen as particularly suitable for this market. Comparisons with the China trade suggest, however, that these images of women were not a universal patriarchal reflex, but were a specific, calculated and directed response to a market which reflected sexist and colonialist attitudes.

The cloths made in Lancashire for China clearly drew upon a concept of Chinese culture and society, as did the cloths for India, but from a Lancashire perspective China was a closed and largely mysterious society in the 1870s. The Chinese business community was virtually the sole point of contact between British and Chinese society, and apart from the trading ports controlled by foreign nations, Europeans were not encouraged to explore China. Much less Chinese fine and applied art was publicly available to designers in Britain than was the case for India, and this lack of familiarity, combined with a clichéd belief in the inscrutable nature of the Chinese character, led to a more circumspect attitude to the trade by the Lancashire industrialist.[11]

The main figurative cottons produced in Lancashire for the China trade were cotton 'brocades'[12] employing motifs such as blossom, chrysanthemums, bamboo, cranes, medallions and swastikas, all of which were commonly used in Chinese design. Images of Chinese people were less frequently used in the cloths sent to China, but they were common in stamp and ticket design. A significant difference between the China and India trade is suggested by two collections of designs for China where there is evidence of Chinese intermediaries being employed to supply designs or to select from existing ranges of designs. One Manchester ticket-maker's archives contain a collection of the sources from which their designers worked, which include preliminary watercolour sketches produced in China.[13] These consist of landscapes and interiors with static figures, drawn in conventional styles; very similar conventionalised portrayals of Chinese society are to be found in a volume of stamp 'impressions' which belonged to the Manchester exporters Sydney Hudson's. The Hudson designs date from around 1910–30.[14] They are particularly revealing as the volume was annotated by the firm in 1917, in consultation with, among others, their Chinese agent. This agent, known as a compradore, represented the firm's interests in China and played a part in determining designs. Each of the Hudson stamp designs was systematically examined and judgment was passed in the form of a note recording: 'The compradore thinks that . . .'[15] The compradore's assessment of the Chinese market is partly predictable: he did not approve of 'foreign' subjects such as tigers, camels, images of British life or any of the 'humorous' sketches. He chose subjects such as peacocks, eagles, carp or floral motifs, and only then if they employed stylistic elements from Chinese art.

He directed the firm away from politically sensitive subjects: the design showing a Chinese and a Japanese soldier raising their respective flags on a single flag-pole was 'not liked in China'.[16] More subtle grounds for selection become clearer when we consider three stamp impressions, clearly copies of Chinese originals, one showing a handloom weaver seated at a simple loom and two others showing boys ploughing with oxen in the paddy fields. Despite their stylistic loyalty to certain eras of Chinese art, they were considered unsuitable. A similar judgment was passed on the image of a Chinese woman dressed in a brief riding garment, astride a prancing horse (see Fig. 2.3). All four images were taken from a fine-art genre which depicted everyday Chinese life; it was presumably this informality and the focus of attention on the lives of humble people which was considered unsuitable for mass-production and widespread distribution. But in the case of the woman on horseback, this lively image was possibly also rejected because it was regarded as too sensuous and too independent. The compradore's most enthusiastic comments were reserved for a series of designs which depicted formal groups of Chinese dressed in elaborate costumes and posed statically as in formal portraits, with women and children standing respectfully behind the men (see Fig. 2.4). Incorporated into the stamps' borders are slogans:

> Perfect loyal. Perfect piety.
>
> Happy children. The whole family full of joy.
>
> Respectful joy makes happiness.[17]

The representations of Chinese women preferred by the compradore were similar to those found in other stamp, ticket and cloth designs. The women's faces, derived from stylistic elements in Chinese art, had only minimal indication of features; they were not shown as individuals but as doll-like figures. Their clothes were voluminous drapes, exaggerating this effect. The women were not important in their own right but were shown as elements in the correct representation of the family and society. These Lancashire images of Chinese women conformed to, and indeed were probably directly copied from, Chinese representations of a feminine ideal. Chinese women were depicted in their traditional place and only in relation to male power.[18]

The available sources for the China trade provide no evidence of the promotion of salacious or semi-pornographic images of women such as were used in India. Tickets produced in both an 'Indian' and a 'Chinese' version illustrate the closest the China trade appears to have come to accepting the risqué.[19] In each case a couple sits on a wall beside a fountain, the backdrop being onion-domed buildings to denote 'Indian' and pagodas to denote 'Chinese'. In the 'Indian' example the couple have their arms around each others' necks and the woman holds the man round the waist; their knees are touching and they are looking into each others' eyes. In the 'Chinese' example, apart from the woman's hand on the man's shoulder, loose clothing disguises whether or not they are touching; their knees are a respectable distance apart. The man's face is turned outwards and the woman appears to be looking past his left shoulder. This suggests an awareness of national sensibilities: it was realised that images which were considered slightly 'daring' by some British males would be offensive in China, yet they were considered appropriate for the India trade.

An Anglo-centric view of women, transferred to specific representations of Indian women, was a reflection of other political relations between Britain and India. India had been effectively administered from Britain since the eighteenth century and under direct colonial rule since the middle of the nineteenth centurey, so the idea that British and Indian needs converged was well established by this time. Although China was increasingly slipping under the economic and political control of a number of foreign powers in the late nineteenth and early twentieth centuries, it still maintained its own administration. It also retained a strong sense of independent cultural identity, despite economic and political dependency. Britain, amongst other countries, extorted lucrative trading terms in return for protecting the administration from internal reform and nationalist dissent. In doing this, the British were party to the retention of Chinese traditions of female oppression, such as foot-binding and polygamy, although they were prepared to condemn them on moral grounds.[20] If at this period China was able to resist Western forms of exploitative imagery, then the Hudson records also suggest that specifically Chinese manifestations of patriarchy could be substituted, and that Lancashire was a willing agent in this process. The interests of the Lancashire manufacturers and traders in China were clearly allied with the status quo; Lancashire cloths and advertising do not appear to have imposed preconceived notions of what was an attractive, saleable or suitable product, in the way they demonstrably did in India.

These fragmentary records of Lancashire's export trade, with the powerful representations of race and gender which they employed, are a clear statement of the breadth of colonial relations. Oppressive representations of women, linked to racial caricature and racially modified images, were potentially important means of cultural control. If they differed for different markets, what remained constant throughout was the power of the industry over the representation of women, and the representation of women without power.

Notes

1 The sizing of cotton warps, ostensibly a means of strengthening the yarn, was from the 1850s also used to increase the weight of the cloth, since for the export trade cloth was sold by weight rather than length. The size washed away in use, leaving a far flimsier cloth.

2 These were partly substituted for the cheapest plain cloths which were temporarily excluded by India's attempts to balance trade. In 1859 and again in the 1860s and 1870s the Indian administration attempted to impose a tax of 10 per cent on the cheapest Lancashire cottons, so as to reduce their trade deficit. They were ultimately unsuccessful as the Lancashire industry was able to mobilise politicians who overturned the legislation.

3 The printed export cottons have been studied where they survive in Lancashire business collections, but the following discussion of the imagery of the export trade is based on a detailed study of the weaving industry. The developments in cotton print design have not been explored in similar detail.

4 These included a variety of different scenes of Indian and British people symbolically arranged with the Indians either physically lower than the British or in some humble role in relation to the powerful white man.

5 The advertising consisted of 'tickets', which were coloured and gummed labels, and 'stamps', block-printed images used to complement the tickets. Both were applied to bales of export cottons as trade-marks and to indicate quality and technical details of the cloth. By the 1870s both had developed into very elaborate

forms; they decreased in use after the 1920s, along with the general decline in the Lancashire cotton trade. Jacquard-woven cottons and block-printed stamps were similar in requiring motifs which could be reduced to semi-linear designs; they were usually produced in a single colour. The tickets were, by the 1870s, produced by chromolithography and were more complex than the cloths or stamps.

6 Archer, Mildred, *Indian Popular Painting*, HMSO, London, 1977, pp. 159–62, discusses the development of the printing industry in India and provides evidence for the popularity of the products of the few Indian presses able to print in colour in the 1880s.

7 See particularly the activities of the East India Company and its sponsorship of artists and photographers in the eighteenth and nineteenth centuries.

8 Indian religious art portrayed women and men in a variety of symbolic and narrative scenes, often semi-naked, but within these traditions of representation women retained a powerful and self-possessed status.

9 This series of designs survives in the Registered Design collection in the Public Record Office, BT.43. 401/312038/315758.

10 D. Taylor and Co., firm's private collection.

11 The officials of the East India Company had been accumulating Indian art and artefacts from the eighteenth century; this collection was opened as a public museum in London in 1801, under the auspices of the Company, later the India Office. Part of the textile collection amassed by the Company was dispersed to the textile districts in the 1860s and 1870s. There was no equivalent focus for Chinese art and design in Britain, although a small quantity of Chinese material existed in the India Museum.

12 The technical term 'brocade' was used loosely in the Lancashire cotton industry to indicate any figured cotton.

13 D. Taylor and Co., firm's private collection.

14 S. Richards, private collection. The Taylor designs are undated but are also probably from the very late nineteenth or early twentieth centuries.

15 Sydney Hudson's impressions book, Richards' collection.

16 Ibid.

17 Ibid.

18 See also an unidentified pattern book, Lancashire Museums Service collection, Preston.

19 D. Taylor and Co., firm's private collection.

20 Various opposition movements had raised the issues of improving the position of women.

3
Tarting Up Men: Menswear and Gender Dynamics

Juliet Ash

Menswear has existed for the last 30 years, but until 1984 its presentation was subordinate to womenswear. Even during the sixties, when Carnaby Street revamped the made-to-measure tailor and Take 6 displayed Liberty-print shirts alongside maroon jackets and flared velvet trousers, it was only the young, hippies and LSD-doused Burroughs clones who invested themselves and their money in such extravagances. On the catwalks of Paris and in London, Cardin, Courrèges and Mary Quant mostly exhibited for women. Women's peasant dresses lasted well into the seventies, so that eventually even staid postmistresses in Suffolk villages were sporting heaving cleavages, tuckered little sleeves and floating mud-bespattered wrap-around skirts to the ankles at 11 o'clock in the morning.

Why 1984/5? What happened to menswear? In the way that women started talking about themselves as having been 'invisible' historically, culturally and politically in the seventies, so menswear started to be talked about in its own right in the realms of haute couture in 1984, in contrast to its previous 'invisibility'. Street fashion in Britain had come up with alternative male styles from time to time since the fifties: Bohemians had created Roman-toga-style extravaganzas during the early part of the nineteenth century and Beau Brummels and Oscar Wildes lavished attention on themselves as expressions of individual rebellion. Yet mainstream fashion in the last 200 years has stuck rigidly to the male supporting-cast role. From 1950 to 1980 men in fashion imagery were the besuited ghost-dancers behind the glittering ball gowns of the 'New Look' (which wasn't new in 1947, but had been developing from the 1930s), the shockability mini-skirt or the pensive midi. Alternatively, men were the unisexual playmate in casual sportswear swinging the beach-bag for the swim-suited belle on the catwalk. There were changes, but only in details: a pocket, a cuff, the width of the trouser-leg, the merging of two different fabrics, the loosening of the jacket. And mostly it was in upmarket publications like *Vogue Hommes* that an observer of the fashion world could have got an indication of these subtle nuances of change in menswear.

Then, in 1984/5 designers indicated a new direction for menswear. This time it didn't come from the bottom or necessarily from the young, although later it was to be interpreted by some old New-Men-styled socialists as 'not only a politics of gender, but one of generation'.[1] The fashion media caught on to Jean-Paul Gaultier's men in skirts (see Fig.3.1) and coined the phrase the 'New Man' to explain not merely a shift in dress but in consciousness also.

The dynamics of gender, age-old sexual conflicts and women's consciousness of inequalities were eradicated at a stroke. Male consciousness had been revolutionized in one year by one inflated image of ONE garment. But few actually wore the mini-skirt or sarong-cum-suit. And many young men's attitudes hadn't changed. Dress hadn't necessarily changed entrenched Yuppie or working-class male attitudes to breastfeeding, contraception, homosexuality and trade unions. The 'new' men's fashion magazines, which have followed the design innovations in menswear, even the recently launched *Arena* (the appendage to the *Face*, which emerged in Winter 1986) could still sport a compulsory female pin-up. Camera focused up the crotch, decently photographed in black and white, Lisa Marie lounges against pillows with mini pulled up to her thighs. She is sandwiched between Tommy Nutter checked suit for £375 and black cashmere crew-neck sweater at Harrods. What's changed since *Playboy*?

All that had happened were two things. First, in the design world gay male designers at last had the confidence to design flamboyantly for their own sex instead of tarting up women in hetero-induced fantasies to disguise their desire for their own gender; and young women designers were similarly gaining the confidence to design clothes for men, whether through an acknowledgment of the challenge that designing menswear presented or through sheer lust. Secondly, encouraged by the stylistic theories of Peter York and the monetarist practice of Margaret Thatcher, the Yuppies came, creating and having a market created for them. As house prices rocketed to accommodate the wealthy young execs. so the chain stores opened Next for Men, Principles for Men etc. Designer shops in South Molton Street, Bayswater, Kensington and King's Road in London also opened menswear sections. This market explosion reshaped masculine dress but did not revolutionise ideology. It is a fascinating development as far as it affects the opportunities for young designers; it indicates the constant shifts in the producing and consuming of clothes, and it undoubtedly makes men more lovely to women. As objects of desire in their beautifully cut clothes and their daring combinations of cashmere and denim, their eyes now glance away from the camera, affecting the eternal coyness of Lady Di in power. Fashion designers themselves would be the first to admit that clothes may transform our lives from the dreary, may intimate the dream but they shouldn't be elevated beyond their function to become catalysts of universal political and/or ideological metamorphosis.

But in 1984/5 the media, and fashion magazines in particular, tailed design. The New Man emerged. He was all things to all people. On the one hand, he was talked of as a reassertion of male aggression and supremacy, with his increased spending power; on the other, he was presented as passive, more 'effeminate' – an attribute inspired by gay men but now inverted as androgeny and asexuality. On the one hand, he embraced Rambo; on the other, he strutted in sarongs and tartan skirts. Design had pushed men's appearance to the limits, menswear *was* exciting, changing and 'new', and everyone revelled in the scoops. Yet fashion design is merely an indicator of possibilities and entertains its own internal and external limitations. It cannot even be a conclusive explanation of the world of appearances and its makers are often as inarticulate about ideas connected with gender as their interpreters are verbose. At least the *Face* was honest in its comment on the New Man in frocks:

> . . . the cynic favours the opinion that it's just another event in the fashion victim's diary: an obvious, ephemeral, reaction to Hard Times scruffiness.[2]

The article went on to describe Jean-Paul Gaultier's men in skirts 'epitomising the radical feminisation' – a term coined from the women's movement, meaning women separatists:

> men with long locks, brocade waistcoats and Jermyn Street velvet slippers . . . next to girls cropping their hair, slipping into Calvin Klein Y-Fronts and patent Doc Martens.[3]

The magazine *ID* presented this in an overtly sexual female visual: two women in pinstripe city shirts, boxer shorts and jackets, making love, leaning together in a *women's* toilet.

Behind the emergence of this seeming gender reversal, exaggerated to universal (as far as some media prophets were concerned), asexual, heterosexual proportions and synonymous with the re-establishment of the right-wing values of the covert sexuality of the pinstriped adorned female, lay a slow fashion-historical progression.

Rebellion in men's fashions was what the Teds did to the Edwardian frock-coat, what the Mods did with the mohair suit, what Punks did with men's hair. They were using fashion design for their own ends and aligned it to a search for politics, culture and an identity. Innovation in menswear was what Jean-Paul Gaultier did with the sarong and the mini-skirt and what women designers of menswear have done with the suit: the revealed concealment of the crutch in looser waistbands, freer upper leg and shorter jackets in, for example, Maria Conejo's designs.

The invention of the New Man as media type foresaw a genuine inventiveness and excitement concerning the design of menswear in the late eighties. But fashion journalists and others seemed to consider it valuable to interpret ideologically what was merely a design turn. In doing so the meaning of both design and men's aspirations became imbued with a plethora of ambiguous speculation.

What was more interesting than the New Man as fashion victim and consumer in 1984/5 was a development that was studiously avoided at that time by the media at large: the simultaneous advent of menswear designed by women designers, particularly in Britain . During the eighties many young women designers have started to branch out from the tradition of men and women designers designing more or less exclusively for women. The potential versatility of designing for both sexes has not escaped young women designers such as Caroline of The Geese in Manchester or even classic female designers such as Jean Muir, whose menswear appeared in *Vogue*, July 1986. This development culminated in the Autumn 1986 London fashion shows with the presentation of menswear and womenswear in most of the women designers' collections: for example, Ally Capellino, Wendy Dagworthy, Katherine Hamnett, Amanda Quarry and Elaine Challoner. This is less a result of the increasing body- and style-consciousness of men and more a sign of the increasing confidence of women designers with regard to their interest in and knowledge of the design traditions and limitations imposed on them when designing for men.

In practice, designing menswear embodies a subversion of conventional fashion design codes. Women designing menswear implies that it can be worn by women, since they were inspired to make it by enjoying the fabrics, the cut and the details. Menswear has traditionally been of better quality than womenswear, since menswear has fluctuated less in fashion terms and thus needed a higher standard in order to last longer. This provides a challenge for women designers in terms of the skills required to produce garments. But also, especially in Britain, the suit and its accessories provide another challenge for women designers in precisely how it can, in subtle ways, be subverted, ridiculed or made more flamboyant (see Fig. 3.2). One woman designer of menswear has used tie fabric round the edge of the collars of blazers, for example, and western boot-leg bows round the neck in conjunction with 'traditional' suits. Yet they need not be totally traditional. Padded shoulders were, in this case, inserted in the pinstripe jacket, while the hipster trousers and belt hung down to a mid-point, accentuating the crutch. Young women designers' inheritance of pragmatic feminism in this way replies strongly and originally to the more anxious critique of 'sexual objectification' launched by seventies' feminists against pornography and 'sexist' imagery of women. With the ideal man in mind (whether sexually desired by heterosexual women designers or merely appreciated in terms of the skilled cut of their garments by gay women designers), women fashion designers are beginning to dress men professionally, as men designers have dressed women for centuries. Together with this, women designers are revamping traditional male skills of tailoring and using accessories. The red felt bowler-hat, the tie-fabric collars and the pinstripe penis-hugging suit become signifiers of gender subversion, even sadism, in the hands of women. Alternatively, like the looser trousers mentioned earlier, the man's dressing-gown loses the sombre darkness of paisley or the short, velvet, tight fit of the Edwardian smoking-jacket to become a flowing-to-the-ground, loud, red-and-black print, freeing the body enfolded in fabric and unleashing a concealed potential for women's desires. The woman fashion designer has the potential to change both the gender dynamics of age-old designers' restrictions and the conventional adage that women are attracted to men's characters not their bodies.

The changing dynamics of menswear design had been effectively ignored until the media caught on to an obvious change in 1984. Yet it had already begun to happen in 1980. It started in an ironic way in the September 1980 issue of *Vogue Hommes*, in a review of the Paris winter collections entitled '*Les Collections vues par Carole Laure et Just Jaekin*'. A woman and a baby appeared, separately and suddenly, in the fashion pages. Up till then *Vogue Hommes'* fashion photography had contained static, full-frontal (highly covered) conventional men, on their own, in embarrassed stances with hands in pockets, eyes looking askance at the Emanuelle figure out of the frame. Suddenly Emanuelle herself appeared in the form of Carole Lauré, dressed as a man and taking a central position in the photograph. The men's attention was finally focused. They no longer needed to contemplate the horror of facing the camera lens or had to imagine the girl or boy of their dreams in the next photography studio. Even if they were gay models they could fix their eyes on a *real* narcissist – a woman. *Their* clothes were the reason for the photograph, yet the woman took centre stage. Men could return to their invisibility as long as women were there to take on the '*Déjeuner sur l'herbe*' role, even though fully clothed and in men's clothes. But what makes this different from previous imagery in *Vogue Hommes* is that women had entered a previously all-male enclave. Men were starting in 1980 to look to women for inspiration in the presentation of male dress and appearance, and this led to the beginnings of the effeminacy of structured menswear in the highest echelons of the fashion empire, the Paris collections.

Within the photographer's images a woman provided the supporting role, although not 'invisible', as traditionally men had been, but now, ironically, a pivotal focus for the image of menswear, not womenswear. The baby, hanging off the arm of a man in casuals, represented Peter York's 'mothercare man', 'sensitive nurturing quiche-eater'.[4] And in the *Vogue Hommes* of 1986, there are many children and babies to be seen with the male models. So men do everything now, even in the preserves conventionally allocated to women – the worlds of fashion and childcare. And women can do what only men used to be able to do: they can dress as men in a respectable sophisticated men's Paris fashion magazine. But I would suggest that although the imagery *can* be interpreted on a universal scale in terms of changing attitudes, it is more likely that, in the fashion world we are talking about, children are seen as an accessory to masculinity just as children in the seventies were accessories to the peasant-skirted female in the cornfields. The image of earth mother wasn't going to last once the *work* of rearing children started.

The possible objectifying of female desire, the emergence of sexually overt man, was to appear in the September 1982 issue of *Vogue Hommes*, with lavish displays of male flesh lounging in Calvin Klein underwear. But just as women narcissists have been fostered by imagery in the arts and media since time immemorial, so maybe this was a chance for male narcissism as much as for female desire. A retrenchment of gender-divided values underlies the seeming convergence of men and women's interest in the world of appearances and in particular in the representations of the fashion industry. If *Vogue Hommes* could present a changing image of masculinity in 1980 and 1982, then the male boom, the variegated imagery of masculinity, was to be an inevitability on the catwalks of 1984/5.

Wherever you looked, from *Tatler* and *Harpers* to the *Observer* and the *Guardian, Time Out*, the *Face* and *ID*, men were represented as clothes pegs for fashion ideas – old or revamped; exposed as beautiful bodies in Bruce Weber photography; and scorned by York for 'pushing the pram or wanting to cry'.[5] Their salaries were given new outlets in chain stores throughout the country devoted to mass-appeal male consumption. All this was typified in the new phrase 'male fragrances', borrowed from the twenties' *Art déco* period – a euphemism for male perfume.

To consider the sudden focus on masculinity is not to reveal a jealousy for such notoriety but to try and investigate what happened to the construction of men's clothes as part of a historical continuum rather than a masquerade of appearances.

The effeminacy of masculine appearance was to be universally talked about, but it remained virtually invisible on the streets. It was not a rebellion or confined to a particular sub-culture, gender proclivity or specific age-range. It indicated a desire for change but ran parallel to entrenchment culturally, ideologically, economically and politically. Class differences had widened so that chain stores (such as Concept Man and Next for Men) could attempt to popularise the haute couture trend but unemployment and low wages would ensure that many men would be unaware of these trends, or, even if they were aware of them, would be unable to afford the clothes while children were going hungry and the rent was still to be found. It was probably easier to stick to Rambo and more economically viable to become a 'casual', even if it did mean hunting around for the right labels.

The last historical period to espouse effeminacy, coopt male narcissism as an attribute of the establishment and attempt to popularise extremes of ornamentation in male dress was during the seventeenth and eighteenth centuries in England and before the Revolution of 1789 in France. As the court in England and France became more and more established during the seventeenth and eighteenth centuries, so the extremes of male dress increased (see Fig. 3.2). During the Jacobean period brilliant-red high-heels were fashionable for men and muffs were worn.

It makes one wonder whether male anorexics existed in the seventeenth century and why no one has written about the history of men's masochism with regard to fashion, especially as more and more is revealed about the sexual delights of middle-class female masochism during the nineteenth-century age of crinolines and corsetry.

Cromwell and the Roundheads attempted to curb the extravagances of aristocratic Britain, but with the defeat of the English Republic after Cromwell's death, aristocratic values returned with the Restoration and the court of Charles II. In terms of fashion, the Restoration took up where the Cavaliers left off, reintroducing long-skirted coats for men, making use of elaborate silks (whose production had been established by immigrant silk-weavers in Spitalfields in the 1580s) amd encouraging the growth of the periwig to the most ludicrous proportions. This was done in order to exhibit upper-class male wealth and status and to confront the sober dogmas of the Cromwellian period.

It was in the late eighteenth and early nineteenth centuries that the cleric, doctor and lawyer evolved *their* own distinctive hairstyle. The male (long-haired) wig became a symbol of establishment authority. Or, as Roy Porter puts it:

> Distinctions in dress were cameos of status and occupation . . . wigs, accessories and stuccoed cosmetics, modes of dress and undress, could reveal rank, age and even politics . . .[6]

The more weighty the wig, and particularly during periods of fashionably short hair for men, the more supposedly 'effeminate' the male appearance, the more power could be wielded by judges, doctors and solicitors. Although doctors' wigs were to fade, for both practical and fashionable reasons, Rembrandt's 'Anatomy Lesson' remains a magnificent testimony to the medical establishment's pomposity as the bewigged doctors arrange themselves around the corpse.

Dickens, in *Bleak House*, describes the law courts:

> Below the table, again, was a long row of solicitors, with bundles of papers . . . and then there were the gentlemen of the bar in wigs and gowns – some awake and some asleep . . . to see all that full dress and ceremony and to think of the waste and want, and beggared misery it represented.[7]

In France also Louis XIV's influence meant greater and greater emphasis on conspicuous wealth, symbolised by the men's wearing larger and larger hats, longer and longer wigs, more silk, ribbons, frills and ornamentation in the brocade used down the centre of a frock-coat or round the cuffs. Despite the fact that tailoring remained basically the same for all classes, the peasants, unlike the aristocracy, rarely wore skirts, and the upper-class effeminisation of masculinity was completed with elaborate use of cosmetics and 'painting'. The underlying seedy eroticism and debased culture of the eighteenth-century effeminate upper-class male is nowhere better exemplified than in the film *The Draughtsman's Contract*.

Vogue Hommes, not the most radical of magazines, admits that it was the rise of the 'sans-culottes' during the French Revolution that radicalised male dress and returned Europe to a more universal functionality:

> . . . on croyait qu'ils allaient nus. Diantre non. Ils étaient les seuls au contraire à porter des pantalons. Ils allaient donc 'sans culottes', c'est dire si le pantalon était d'un

vulgaire achève. Mais soit, notre homme au costume 3-pièces est déjà pantaloné . . .⁸*

So the suit was to continue from the French Revolution to the present day, going from strength to strength, changing in detail but never loosening its grip on the male form. The aristocratic male frock was effectively guillotined. The suit might espouse the frock-coat, as between the 1820s and 1860s, but the ornamentation of the seventeenth and eighteenth centuries was replaced by bourgeois utilitarian values, symbolised by the sober respectability and equally status-conscious suit or three-piece. Pleats in the waist of the trousers (or *pantalons*) would come and go, buttons would be replaced by cuff-links or hooks, lengths and breadths of jackets would vary, but the basic tailoring would remain the same. It even emerged in the fifties and sixties as the epitome of capitalist sobriety and male pecuniary power in the City of London, Wall Street and Tokyo. It re-emerged in the eighties as Yuppie garb, featuring 'The Duke of York' as star, as described in the *Face*, March 1983:

> Peter York – a pre-modern, prima fascist Prima Donna, perched on his pinstripes right down to his last cuffed detail. A miniature Mephistopheles mocking the majority . . .⁹

It was all too convenient for the media to turn to the concept of the 'New Man'; it was inevitable that it should occur after the 'New Woman' of the seventies, and it was inevitable that, in terms of a specialised fashion design dynamic, it should occur in 1984/5. But in reversing roles in appearance, even temporarily, it did little more than indicate possible changes in menswear design in the coming years. It did not mean that men would change their characters overnight or indeed that they wanted to, nor that women wanted them to. It may have meant only that some men would become more dress-conscious, and a lot of money would be made and spent on the 'new' market. As many fashion students have said: 'Where else was there to go? It's all been done before in womenswear.'

The New Man was an irrelevant invention because it took as fact the equation that exciting, more effeminate menswear equalled a change in men's consciousness. If anything, the initial extremism of

* People thought they went naked. Far from it. On the contrary, they were the only ones to wear trousers. So they were said to go without pants, which goes to show that trousers were badly thought of. This may be so, but it hasn't stopped our three-piece man being trousered.

men in skirts was a retrograde move, since it gave the appearance of men changing their roles in society from doer to decoration. It was inevitable that it would merely herald the more wearable, dynamic designs which were to occur in the late eighties. Gender norms are now being challenged by the clothing of men by women designers not merely by men donning a 'female' piece of apparel, the skirt. It is to the designers, the makers of the images, as much as to the products and consumers that we should turn for our inspiration.

The *Face* said 'maybe the New Man is just a fad . . . in the fashion world.'[10] But fads in the media operate as gross magnifications of rapidly changing seasonal trends in fashion design. Put the large lens of the media together with the little lens of haute couture and the combined effect is 100-fold enlargement. This apparent enlargement is so dramatic that the reader begins to feel *reality* has changed. It was a fad as far as journalists (the big lens) were concerned, but for women designers and haute couture (the little lens) menswear has become visible in its own right in collections, and this is a major breakthrough in design terms. But the 'ephemeral' vacuousness of the New Man of the eighties remains to be seduced by clothes designed by women for men.

The New Man of the eighties was and is *not* new, and neither is he rebellious, although he is stylistically colourful and exciting in a specialised haute couture sense. He is an off-shoot of an established élite who germinated from the catwalks of Paris, London and Milan and were cultivated in provincial chain stores up and down the country to take over from Burtons and Hepworths, with the intention of filling Nigel Lawson's coffers.

Women fashion designers still have a long way to go in moulding menswear, but they have their fingers on the buttons.

Notes

1 Mart, Frank, 'Images change: High street style and the new man', *New Socialist*, November 1986.
2 'Men's where', *Face*, November 1984.
3 Ibid.
4 York, Peter, 'Man-Ism', *Harpers*, November 1984, p. 212.
5 Ibid.
6 Porter, Roy, *English Society in the 18th Century*, Penguin, Harmondsworth, 1982, p. 166.
7 Dickens, Charles, *Bleak House*, Signet Classic edition, 1964, pp. 354–5.
8 'La véritable histoire de costume 3 pièces', *Vogue Hommes*, September 1984, p. 155.
9 Letter from Finnualla of St John's Wood, Letters Page, *Face*, March 1983.
10 'Men's where', *Face*, November 1984.

4

From Alcatraz to the OK Corral: Images of Class and Gender in Housing Design

Jos Boys

The ideas that architects and government decision-makers have had about 'proper' working-class family life and the role of women since the Second World War have affected public-sector housing design. Unfortunately these ideas don't have much in common with the everyday experiences of the different groups of women living in public housing. What, then, were these ideas about women, community and class? How have they affected the actual design of housing? How have they changed in the last 40 years? What impact have they made on the lives of women? Changes in the idea of community underlie the shift from the modern block of flats in public housing provision to more vernacular forms and styles in recent years. First, housing policy practice and design have been affected by a shift in ideas from the image of the working class popular in the 1950s as homogeneous, self-reliant and organised, to a re-emergence of conservatism in the 1970s and 1980s, where middle-class and 'respectable' working-class values of competition and individuality are seen to be combined, leaving behind a marginalised 'underclass'. Second, the impact of the changing images of the family has produced a shift from notions of a vigorous working-class street life and an emphasis on community to a concentration on individual family domesticity and privacy.

While these changes do reflect popular opinion about better housing, they oversimplify the realities of life for different groups of women in society. Such ideas attempt to use design as a solution for social conflicts (for instance differential class status or racism), economic inequalities in access to housing, and problems connected with the role of women in society. Here it will be shown that these design changes do not make underlying problems go away. However, design *does* affect the impact of these problems on different groups of women – often in ways unintended by architects and decision-makers.

The Working Class: An Ideal Community?

When architectural historian and critic Peter Reyner Banham reviewed the progress of a large public housing estate in Sheffield (Park Hill, built 1957–61) in 1973, he suggested that the scheme's continuing success (or at least lack of spectacular failure) was related to its design by architects 'who fiercely believed that the working classes are a very special breed of folk with a unique (Young and Wilmott) way of life that should be supported.'[1] Banham frequently cites the sociological studies of Michael Young and Peter Wilmott as a direct influence on architectural ideas about working-class families and their social behaviour.[2] While schemes like Park Hill were designed before Young and Wilmott published their research, the ideas about working-class people corresponded with the dominant threads in the political imagery of the new welfare state.[3]

First published in 1957, Young and Wilmott's book *Family and Kinship in East London* called for the retention of working-class people in inner city areas at a time when their dispersal to outlying suburban cottage estates was still a major plank of housing policy. Young and Wilmott's case study of Bethnal Green offered an affectionate account of a strong, stable working-class community maintained through support networks provided by women. In the study they look at the effects on social life of a move to a suburban estate, called Greenleigh. A chapter entitled 'Keeping Themselves to Themselves' highlighted female isolation in the home and an emphasis on status, competitiveness and material possessions – developments which Young and Wilmott found worryingly middle class.

There are now many criticisms of this study,[4] but at the time it appeared it seemed to have caught a popular mood, particularly among 'progressives', and it reinforced inter-war accounts of suburban estate life, such as Ruth Durant's 1939 study of Watling. Her research also described the problems of loneliness for women, the lack of facilities and the effects on men of long journeys to work, which tired them and reduced social life, with, as she says, 'fatigue and worry keeping the family at home.'[5] These descriptions of a lack of social vitality mirrored architectural criticisms of the visual monotony of inter-war speculative house building, suburban sprawl and council cottage estates, with what the architectural press called their 'prairie planning' and SLOAP (space left over after planning)[6].

Thus the scene was being set for a shift away from suburban development towards inner city flat building as the major public-sector provision by both Labour and Conservative governments through the 1950s and 1960s. First, the low-density suburban housing schemes of the 1930s and early 1950s were seen as socially boring; second, these new developments seemed to break up 'traditional' working-class communities; and third, their inhabitants were replacing a rich and informal social life with competitive and isolated individuality. The answer, then, was to provide more new housing within the cities themselves, in a way which *reflected* the 'natural' working-class community in its design. As Patrick Dunleavy shows,[7] these ideas were linked to other major political pressures: the unwillingness of outer area authorities to take inner city tenants in large numbers; the reintroduction of slum-clearance programmes in 1954, requiring a huge, complementary public rehousing programme specifically for *poor* working-class people; and the assumption that inner city housing *had* to be built at high densities.

This idea of 'community' was in fact a particular understanding, in its enthusiasm for both the urban setting and specifically working-class values. Others saw 'community' in a more traditional way as most 'naturally' present in a rural, village-like environment, with its assumed balance of social classes. Aneurin Bevan, Labour's Minister responsible for housing policy, told the Commons in 1949:

> . . . if we are to enable citizens to lead a full life, if they are each to be aware of the problems of their neighbours, then they should all be drawn from the different sections of the community and we should try to introduce in our modern villages what was always the lovely feature of English and Welsh villages, where the doctor, the grocer, the butcher and farm labourer all lived in the same street . . . I believe it leads to the enrichment of every member of the community to live in communities of that sort.[8]

Under Bevan's influence the 1949 Housing Act left out the term 'working class' and the public housing programme was for 'general' rather than 'special' needs, that is, for all social classes. In architecture and planning the appropriate spatial interpretation of this preferred social mix was, first, new and expanded towns, and, second, mixed development, that is, a combination of flats, maisonettes and houses with gardens, usually arranged as separate blocks in a parkland setting. To architects and politicians, mixed development symbolised harmonious social heterogeneity through its variety of visual treatments and housing types 'picturesquely' arranged in the landscape. It was also argued that some more desirable but expensive houses and gardens could be provided on costly inner city land by the savings made on building flats and maisonettes.[9] However, given the immediate post-war economic crisis, proposals for a general-needs housing programme were little more than a simplistic dream. As David McKay and Andrew Cox[10] note, despite the 1949 Housing Act, the underlying consensus across political parties was that inner city public-sector housing *was* for the working class, in particular the poorer sections of working-class people.

Among architects a series of parallel debates was taking place, with a shift from designs symbolising social mix to new images of the working class in particular. This shift was epitomised by a mixed-development housing scheme built by the London County Council at Roehampton between 1952 and 1959. The site of 130 acres, which was originally the grounds of a single estate laid out in the eighteenth-century picturesque landscape tradition, was now to be developed with a mixture of high blocks, four- and two-storey terraces and old people's dwellings at a density of 100 to the acre, and built in two stages, Alton East and Alton West. The architectural historian Nikolaus Pevsner describes the difference between these two sections, which highlights a more general change in attitude among housing architects in this period.

> ... there is a very noticeable change between Alton East and Alton West ... The earlier buildings are faced with pale-cream brick and have lively projections and recessions in outline. The earlier maisonettes and cottages have roofs of a gentler pitch. The whole combines perfectly with the picturesque plan, the winding streets and informally placed trees. It is architecture at ease. The later architecture is exacting. It is highly intelligent, concentrated, of great integrity, crisp and precise. The point blocks are completely flat in their elevation. Nothing must stick out. The maisonettes have flat roofs and windowless end walls and the slabs are extremely interesting but unquestionably ruthless in their rhythm.[11]

The first approach represented the 'humane' attitude, adapted from Scandinavian design and most common in early new and expanded towns such as Harlow, Stevenage and Crawley. The second approach became identified with the writings of English architects Alison and Peter Smithson and Team 10 (an international grouping of architects). Called 'Brutalism', it was concerned with avoiding the most mechanistic ideas of the earlier Modernists such as Le Corbusier. Like Young and Wilmott, the Brutalists showed considerable interest in the intricacies of 'human association'. However, they also wanted a more 'honest' approach to appearances – what Anthony Jackson refers to as 'a rougher gregariousness, supposedly more in character with working-class habits'.[12] As the Smithsons themselves write:

Brutalism has to face up to mass-production society, and

drag a rough poetry out of the confused and powerful forces which are at work.[13]

This 'rugged grandeur'[14] was seen as a modern version of the neo-classical housing design of Georgian London. It both continued the mathematical rationality of the style, with its emphasis on plainness and proportion, and had an 'ordinariness' similar to eighteenth-century 'mass-produced' terraced housing. This argument was used to justify repetitive units on a large scale, which were to stand symbolically for working-class unity, solidarity and egalitarianism. Simultaneously, a more rational, mathematical (and therefore more 'masculine') approach was being offered against the perceived 'cosiness' of the immediate post-war style of mixed development and the planning of new towns – what Banham calls 'the debilitating effects of the picturesque'[15] and Lionel Esher, 'a puritanical protest against the sentimentality, the effeminacy and the triviality of the Festival/New Town/Coventry style'.[16] There are echoes here of Richard Hoggart's description of working-class life as 'elaborate and disorderly yet sober: it is not chintzy or kittenish or whimsical or "feminised" '[17]

How, then, did ideas about the working-class community add to this notion of solid, unpretentious virtue in affecting housing design? The answer came in a new emphasis on the urban street, particularly in the development of wide access balconies known by architects as 'streets in the air'. At Park Hill, Sheffield (designed 1953–5, built 1957–61), this idea has its most fluent interpretation.[18] Here 3,500 people were housed in a continuous block overlooking the town centre. To the architects, Ivor Smith and Jack Lynn, the access decks were seen as a direct continuation of earlier urban housing and could solve the social isolation of women in both outlying estates and the high flat block by reintroducing street life. As Jack Lynn wrote:

> . . . centuries of peace and a hundred years of housing reform in this country have given us the open street approachable from either end and off which every house is entered directly by its own front door – a simple arrangement which gave complete freedom to come and to go, to meet or avoid whom we pleased.[19]

At Park Hill, this was translated into the following terms:

> Access to the dwellings themselves is by means of pedestrian street decks or Rows. At Park Hill, in place of the four-foot wide balcony serving every floor, promenade decks ten-foot wide, open to the air, are provided on every

third floor within the main building mass . . . The front doors to the dwellings open from the decks, which of course are much more commodious than the normal balcony and fulfil the function of 'streets' within the building, along which prams can be pushed and milk trolleys driven. Being covered from the weather and free from normal vehicular traffic they are ideal places for daily social contact.[20]

This underlying image of working-class community as street life therefore appeared to resolve the problem of women's isolation in the home by facilitating informal social contact. The overall appearance, with its symbolism of the (repetitive) unity and 'rugged grandeur' of working-class people, seemed to solve the problem of how to provide a large amount of public housing for the poor and do so cheaply. Thus within architectural debates problematic social and economic inequalities were dealt with in design terms with its resulting impact on the lives of different groups of women.

The Realities of 'Community'

Housing policy in this period was relatively simplistic, with both the Labour and Conservative parties supporting major public housing programmes, albeit for different reasons. Whilst Labour concentrated on public housing, Conservatives saw public provision as a short-term solution to replacing slums. Underlying these policies, however, was considerable agreement on a simple division between inner city flat building for very poor households and suburban housing estates for the better-off. There was little or no analysis of the dynamics of the housing market and the effects on it of government policy, or of the extent to which such housing provision was meeting the needs of different types of households. Both Conservative and Labour governments supported inner city public-sector flat building, with its emphasis on high flats and industrialised building methods, until Labour cut back on high flat subsidies in 1967. Architectural ideas about what forms were appropriate for the inner city working class fitted in with political demands for a mass-quantity, high-density housing programme. First, the shift away from an image of blocks in a parkland setting to blocks interconnected by high-level walkways set the scene (even if unintentionally) for a much closer packing of high blocks and no mixed development. Second, the resolutely urban and tough but 'ordinary' Brutalism enabled an easy slide into cruder finishes and a lack of detail or variety. Third, the connection between images of a homogeneous, egalitarian working class and repetitive units on a large scale provided an all too easy slippage into an acceptance of high-rise industrialised house building programmes whose designs were determined almost entirely by building contractors. Whilst the forms of housing originated in ideas about working-class community, much high-rise housing built in the boom between 1965 and 1968 was based solely on economics.[21]

The myth of a homogeneous and egalitarian working class was also directly contradicted by allocation policies. In the early post-war years, as Marion Roberts shows,[22] allocation depended very much on 'respectability', defined by high standards of housekeeping and the ability to pay rent regularly. With the reintroduction of the slum-clearance programmes in the early 1950s, many poor working-class households who were displaced were able to obtain a council flat or house previously available only to the more affluent, who could afford the rents on suburban estates. Most council allocation policies were clear. Households were 'respectable' or 'non-respectable' and were placed in 'good' or 'bad' property accordingly. Thus allocation reflected a different set of notions about working-class communities based on perceived social divisions *within* the class itself. Slum-clearance policies contained similar ideas. Slum clearance worked on a very different image of the working class to the one previously described.[23] At Park Hill, the old terraced housing had been cleared specifically to break up an area thought to contain working-class criminals. In 1963, Wilfred Burns, soon to be Chief Planner at the Department of the Environment and responsible for redevelopment schemes in Coventry and Newcastle upon Tyne, could write:

> In a huge city, it is a fairly common observation that the dwellers in a slum area are almost a separate race of people, with different values, aspirations and ways of living . . . One result of slum clearance is that a considerable movement of people takes place over long distances, with devastating effects on the social groupings built up over the years. But, one might argue, this is a good thing when we are dealing with people who have no initiative or civic pride. The task, surely, is to break up such groups even though the people seem to be satisfied with their miserable environment and seem to enjoy an extrovert social life in their own locality.[24]

With these assumptions, housing officials and politicians in the 1950s and 1960s saw some slum dwellers' resistance to flats as parochial and reactionary, took a rather sweeping approach to condemning both fit and unfit dwellings[25] and showed very little interest in the *actual* social mix, household type or income distribution in areas designated for slum clearance. Concepts such as 'community' or 'slum', then, obscured the realities of slum clearance and redevelopment and the complex effects they had on different groups of people. The new high-rise housing certainly lacked 'community' in the romanticised sense architects used, and in any case it was increasingly being divided by allocation policies into high-quality and 'sink' estates. This division threatened to define the degree of 'respectability' tenants had merely by the location and type of estate they lived on. Popular images of housing in this period certainly refused to agree with architects' images of 'rugged grandeur' and 'streets in the air'. Instead residents commonly chose nicknames from barracks, prisons and concentration camps such as Alcatraz or Colditz.

Yet underlying the sociological accounts of high-rise housing was the continuing search for this elusive working-class 'community' which had so influenced the work of both Ruth Durant in the 1930s and Young and Wilmott in the 1950s. This in turn makes it difficult for us, looking back, to assess the effects on women of a shift from poor-quality slum dwelling to 'modern' council houses and flats.

Pearl Jephcott's research on high-rise living in the late 1960s described the problems, particularly for women, of poor transport, inadequate or expensive local shops and lack of play space which Durant and Young and Wilmott had found in suburban settings.[26] To Jephcott, as to Durant, it was the combination of poverty with a particular built environment that produced difficulties. Poverty restricted choices in using the city. It meant less likelihood of a car or a nanny, little chance of using restaurants or theatres. Problems with inadequate lifts and an inhospitable housing environment could only make this worse, particularly for women with young children or the elderly, already restricted in their mobility.

But Jephcott's interviews also show a considerable enthusiasm by many tenants:

> Perhaps the fact that the new flat represents a rise in family social standards encourages people to keep themselves to themselves. Those met in the study certainly set a high value on the new privacy, even when they regretted losing certain features of the old intimate character of working-class life.[27]

Like the other sociologists, Jephcott regrets what she sees as a shift away from working-class community. Whilst her analysis considers poverty, her solution considers ways of 'improving' community through the provision of community centres and informal meeting places at lifts, etc., to 'enhance' social contact. Such notions are all too close to the ideas behind modern flat design in the first place. They fail to place high-rise housing in its wider political, social and economic context – both in terms of how it was provided and its effects on different women relative to their income, social role, race or mobility.

In the early 1970s working-class 'community' was discovered anew – this time in a nostalgic memory of slum areas, so recently vilified as the homes of criminal and non-respectable working-class people. Of course, the old slums were neither all supportive, friendly communities nor absolute dens of iniquity. Instead, they were a complex mixture where sheer poverty was the underlying force behind both mutual aid and petty thieving. But yet again we see the debate on housing contained by stereotyped images. Thus in the 1970s there was a wholesale shift in housing policy aimed at retaining existing 'communities'. Inner city housing rehabilitation and renewal (with an associated cut in public-sector housing expenditure), and a renewed emphasis on owner-occupation, began to create new patterns of housing form, tenure and use. That improving slum housing was forcing *out* low-income groups (the idealised working-class community) as rent levels rose and property became owner-occupied was ignored.

From Community to Territory

As early as 1961 an alternative imagery for high-density, low-rise estates was being developed: brick-clad estates around a series of 'garden' courtyards. Lillington Gardens in Pimlico, London by architects Darbourne and Darke (see Fig. 4.1) was the first major commission using this approach and was taken up by elements of the architectural press as a welcome return to middle-class values:

> [Darbourne and Darke] have begun 'changing the image' as we say. There are many sides to this subtle, yet decisive feat. There is, for example, the side which is concerned with knitting the new with the pre-existing non-municipal surroundings. Closely related to this is the side which aims to produce an image of organic growth, such as you get in free, unsubsidised communities in place of the image of planned-from-above, all-at-one-time. Then there is the side which is concerned with the individual unit. Under the impulse of collectivisation in the fifties, the home has become transmogrified and absorbed into something bigger than itself. Homes have become clutches of serviced cells. Slowly, in many aspects of this firm's work, these are being drawn back into a unity and you have the image of home once more . . . It could be argued that what they have done is to middle-classify the council house, but there is

more to their achievement than that. Their approach should be seen as an expression of the idea that the egalitarian society is more easily realised by building on the 'middle class' than it is by building on the old notion of the 'working class'.[28]

By the 1970s the popular consensus seemed to be that modern housing design did not represent a homogeneous and valued working class but state bureaucracy and facelessness. The new 'domesticity' of Lillington Gardens and its later versions, however, still meant large public building schemes retaining the access balconies and cheap municipal lifts of more explicitly 'modern' designs. Nevertheless, the new aesthetic it proposed became increasingly popular with local authorities and was referred to as 'neo-vernacular'.

In the early 1970s, Essex County Council produced design guidance for private developers, entitled *A Design Guide for Residential Areas*, which set out a sophisticated working of these ideas and had considerable popularity not just in East Anglia but in Britain as a whole. As John Punter writes:

> The Guide incorporated many established principles of townscape and urban design (scale, enclosure, static/ dynamic space, etc.) with more controversial ideas about the treatment of elevations (unity, restful/lack of repose, balance) and linked these with study of the local Essex vernacular tradition in house styles and materials . . . The Guide rapidly began to influence the design of new development, not least because it offered developers significant savings in land servicing and highways costs. While these were partly offset by the requirements of detailed design it was evident that, even in a period of recession, the neo-vernacular styles and compact layouts offered a differentiated product that appealed to the rural nostalgia 'village in the mind' mentality of many suburban owner-occupiers.[29]

Other authors continued to conflate these picturesque ruralesque arrangements with family life, privacy and domesticity. Meanwhile, high inflation was forcing both public- and private-sector house building into smaller and more compact housing both inside and out (see Fig. 4.2).

In his book *The Village in the City,* 1973, Nick Taylor argues, through a history of suburban development, that the suburban house is a 'natural' form for ensuring the sanctity of family life.[30] His emphasis on a whole series of virtues from the 'illusion' of ownership to the seclusion and intimacy of private garden space is very reminiscent of the Victorian bourgeoisie.[31] Unlike Young and Wilmott, Taylor believes that keeping yourself to yourself is a virtue for working-class people, here combined with a romanticisation of women's traditional roles and the 'feminine' in architecture. Of suburban houses built in the Queen Anne style at the turn of the century, for instance, he writes approvingly:

> It was style not merely bourgeois but feminine, being neatly domesticated in a manner appropriate to a generation which was at least giving women an opportunity to express themselves culturally.[32]

Ideas about the improvement of existing public-sector estates were concerned not with privacy *per se* but with a version of it: the concept of 'territory'. These ideas are best illustrated in Oscar Newman's book *Defensible Space*, originally published in 1966, and much more recently in *Utopia on Trial*, 1984, by Alice Coleman, which has been very popular with local authorities attempting to improve safety on their estates.[33]

Territoriality calls for the privatisation of as much space around dwellings as possible to enable its 'natural' surveillance by individual households. By this means 'intruders' can be recognised and questioned. To Coleman this means a reduction of all communal space, including the removal of children's play areas. While cynics might say that this approach simply enables local authorities to reduce their responsibilities for public area maintenance, to Coleman it has much deeper psychological consequences. She assumes a direct relationship between houses with gardens 'freely chosen' in the private market and acceptable social behaviour. 'Respectability' thus relates to housing design rather than to, say, income levels.

The notion of territoriality, however, unlike privacy, contains within it a new version of community. It implies that the social cohesion of a group is generated and maintained by keeping *non-group* members – strangers and potential criminals – *out*. In many schemes developed out of the neo-vernacular of Darbourne and Darke and the Essex Design Guide, influenced by popular interpretations of territoriality, architects have developed a symbolic language intended to indicate degrees of private and public property. Here certain kinds of spatial arrangements have the effect of drawing people in and others of keeping them out. As I have described elsewhere,[34] such ideas are based on a misunderstanding of social interaction and the relationship between social processes and the built environment. A concept such as 'territory' attempts to describe complex social, political, economic and environmental problems in universal, apolitical and symbolic terms, just as 'community' tried – and failed – to do in previous periods. Although the idea of 'territory' is supposedly neutral and above politics, it actually overlaps with political ideas in a problematic and obscuring way. For instance, design ideas about territory and defensible space have become interwoven with what Errol Lawrence calls 'common-sense racist ideologies'.[35] In the new Toryism, black households become synonymous with 'problem' families, partly because of poverty but also because of the linked ideas of 'inadequate family', 'criminal youth' and 'cultural deprivation' that surround black people in particular. The 'stranger' to be kept out can then be blurred with both the 'criminal' and the 'alien' presence conflated in racist ideas about young black males' propensity for crime. All of these images combine to appear threatening to the supposed homogeneity of society – that is, white society – at both national and local levels. And struggles over housing provision related to poverty, racism and the sexual division of labour (which affect any individual's access to housing and their use of the local environment) become merely 'crime prevention'.

In appearance, the improvement of estates again emphasises traditional design elements associated with an idealised rural family life. The overall imagery relies on the rural and domestic motifs of pitched, tiled roofs and wooden windows, panelling and fences, but in a way that is nevertheless different to both private-sector and earlier suburban public housing estates. As one tenant of a newly refurbished North London estate commented, 'It's like the OK Corral.'

Thus in public-sector housing there has developed an imagery of individuality and domesticity, with an emphasis on brick-detailing arranged picturesquely in a series of courtyards. This has been combined with an image of social respectability to be maintained by keeping strangers out. Again, the heterogeneity of working-class people is obscured and family life romanticised. What the effects of these resulting housing forms are on their occupants and on women in particular urgently need examining.

Class, Gender and Housing Design

This article has provided an outline of changing attitudes to the working class, to women and the family, and their effects on public housing design in post-war Britain. It is *only* on outline and does not deal with the complexity resulting from different individual interpretations, varying political and economic processes and differences in local conditions. Nevertheless, the evidence does seem to suggest that public housing designers justify particular housing forms by their perceived appropriateness to a particular image of working-class and/or family life. In the post-war period in Britain local and national housing policy has certainly reflected and reinforced these various stereotypes.

But for women, the ideas developed from such abstract notions as 'community' show little understanding of the everyday experiences of combining housework, employment and childcare, usually on low incomes. They show little understanding of the heterogeneity of working-class life and of problematic social relations within the working class concerning definitions of respectability and non-respectability, which often show themselves as racism, harassment, or marginalisation of 'problem' families.

Part of the problem, then, lies in the way in which architects and politicians relate social behaviour and physical design through universal and apolitical concepts such as community, territory or the 'inherent' respectability of a house with a garden. Physical forms then come to stand for a particular set of social relations in an unproblematic way, outside a particular political, social and economic context.

Many accounts of high-rise housing, for instance, accuse architects of 'environmental determinism', that is, of believing that physical form directly determines individual behaviour. Here, I have suggested that architects, rather than positing direct cause and effect, offer instead a blurring together of social and physical concepts so that each reflects and reinforces the other. This is not something they used to do with high-rise modern designs and now no longer do; it is still the underlying conceptual framework within which ideas about class and gender are placed. In this way many underlying contradictions in housing provision can be ignored or obscured: for example, the problem of improving housing standards for the poorest households without challenging the economics of the housing market, or of changing the material conditions of the home without considering its effects on the sexual division of labour, or of dealing with the complexity of economics and social relations in the provision of housing.

Instead, concepts such as 'community' or 'territory' stand for a much more complex social, economic and political process, where access to, and use of, housing is dependent on both economic position and social role (that is, an intricate mixture of class, gender, race, age, mobility, etc.) and where the availability of housing is dependent on the historical development of capitalist processes and patterns of state intervention.

Design based on the simple ideas described above hasn't made the underlying problems go away and can make them worse. Unless we can move beyond simplistic concepts of working-class family life, housing design will continue to exaggerate rather than ameliorate inequalities in housing provision and its use.

Notes

1 Banham, Peter Reyner, 'The Parkhill Victory', *New Society*, 18 October 1973.

2 In the *New Society* article quoted above, Banham writes, 'I was convinced that [by] grouping all the front doors of the apartments in to a street-type relationship, the deck would also promote patterns of 'community' that I, like the rest of my generation, had swallowed whole from those great mythmakers of our time, Wilmott and Young' (p. 154). He also refers to Young and Wilmott in his book *The Brutalism: Ethic or Aesthetic?*, Architectural Press, London, 1966, and 'Coronation Street, Hoggartsborough', *New Statesman*, 9 February 1962, p. 200.

3 See, for example, Laing, Stuart, *Representations of Working-class Life 1957–1964*, Macmillan, London, 1986, pp. 37–43.

4 Steedman, Caroline, *Landscape for a Good Woman*, Virago, London, 1986, p. 19.

5 Durant, Ruth, *Watling: A Social Survey*, P. S. King and Son Ltd, 1939, p. 118.

6 See, for example, Nairn, Ian, 'Subtopia', *Architectural Review*, June 1956, and 'Counter-Attack', *Architectural Review*, December 1956.

7 Dunleavy, Patrick, *Mass Housing in Britain 1945–1975*, Clarendon Press, London, 1981.

8 Aneurin Bevan, HoC Debate 426, 1949, Vol. 2126, quoted in McKay, David H., and Cox, Andrew W., *The Politics of Urban Change*, Croom Helm, Beckenham, 1979, p. 118.

9 See Robert Haynes, 'Design and Image in English Urban Housing 1945–1957', unpublished M.Phil thesis, University College, London, 1976. This describes the LCC's official adoption of mixed development and its support for building houses with gardens. In fact, the LCC built 13,102 flats and only 81 houses between 1945 and 1951. See Scoffham, E. R., *The Shape of British Housing*, George Godwin, London, pp. 59–78.

10 Mckay and Cox, op. cit., p. 119.

11 Pevsner, Nikolaus, 'Roehampton: LCC housing and the picturesque tradition', *Architectural Review*, July 1959, p. 35.

12 Jackson, Anthony, *The Politics of Architecture: A History of Modern Architecture in Britain*, Architectural Press, London, 1970, p. 159.

13 Smithson, Alison and Peter, *Architectural Design*, 1957.

14 Banham, op. cit.

15 Banham, Peter Reyner, 'Revenge of the Picturesque', in Summerson, John, ed., *Concerning Architecture*, WHO, London, 1968, pp. 265–73.

16 Esher, Lionel, *A Broken Wave: The Rebuilding of England*

1940-1980, Allen Lane, Harmondsworth, 1981, p. 60.

17 Hoggart, Richard, *The Uses of Literacy*, Penguin, Harmondsworth, 1986, p. 40. (First published by Penguin, Harmondsworth, 1957.)

18 This form of deck access was seen to improve on Le Corbusier's *rue intérieur*. Versions appeared simultaneously in the Smithsons' and Jack Lynn and Gordon Ryder's entries to the Golden Lane competition of 1952 and in Ivor Smith's AA thesis project; Park Hill was then based on these unbuilt schemes.

19 Lynn, Jack, 'Park Hill Redevelopment', Sheffield, *RIBA Journal*, December 1962, pp. 447–69.

20 Housing Committee of the Corporation of Sheffield, *Ten Years of Housing in Sheffield, 1953–63*, April 1962, p. 42.

21 See, for example, Dunleavy, op. cit.; McKay and Cox, op. cit.

22 Roberts, Marion, 'The Modernisation of Family Life? Sexual Divisions in Architecture and Town Planning 1940–1957', Town and Regional Planning, University of Sheffield, 1985.

23 Yelling, J. A., *Slums and Slum Clearance in Victorian London*, Allen and Unwin, London, 1986, pp. 153–4.

24 Burns, Wilfred, *New Towns for Old*, Leonard Hill, 1963, pp. 93–4.

25 Both these aspects are covered in some detail by Dunleavy, op. cit.

26 Jephcott, Pearl, with Robinson, Hilary, *Homes in High Flats*, University of Glasgow, Social and Economic Studies Occasional Paper, No. 13, Oliver and Boyd, 1971.

27 Ibid., p. 142.

28 Amery, Colin, and Wright, Lance, 'The Architecture of Darbourne and Darke', Foreword to exhibition catalogue, RIBA Publications, 1977, p. 8; exhibition held 17 May–29 July 1977 at the RIBA.

29 Punter, John, 'A History of Aesthetic Control, Part 2: 1953–1985', *Town Planning Review*, Vol. 58, No. 1, January 1987, p. 47. See also Forty, Adrian, and Moss, Henry, 'A housing style for troubled consumers: the success of pseudo-vernacular', *Architectural Review*, No. 167, 1980, pp. 73–8.

30 Taylor, Nick, *The Village in the City*, Temple Smith in association with *New Society*, 1973.

31 For a detailed account of the bourgeois development of the home, see Davidoff, Leonore, and Hall, Catherine, *Family Fortunes: Men and Women of the English Middle Class 1780–1850*, Hutchinson, London, 1987, particularly Chapter 8, 'My Own Fireside: The Creation of the Middle-class Home', pp. 357–96.

32 Taylor, op. cit., p. 54.

33 Newman, Oscar, *Defensible Space*, Architectural Press, London, 1973. Coleman, Alice, *Utopian and Trial*, Hilary Shipman 1984.

34 Boys, Jos, 'Women and Public Space' in Matrix, *Making Space: Women and the Man-made Environment*, Pluto Press, London, 1984, pp. 37–54.

35 Lawrence, Errol, in 'Just Plain Common Sense: The "Roots" of Racism' in *The Empire Strikes Back*, Centre for Contemporary Cultural Studies, Hutchinson, London, 1984.

Part Two
Women as Designers

5
Women Textile Designers in the 1920s and 1930s: Marion Dorn, a Case Study

Christine Boydell

Textile design today is often regarded as the province of women. One need look no further than our own colleges and polytechnics to see the large number of female students who dominate the courses, but this has not always been the case. It was in the 1920s and 1930s that many women first became involved in this field, and the majority of them who did so had good social connections and a secure financial background. There are few biographies of these women and even fewer publications attempting to locate them within the context of family and social background, personal relationships, education, the status of women in the design profession and the state of the textile industry. These are the issues pertinent to any history of women textile designers during this time.

One of the best known was Marion Dorn. Most of the information we have about her comes from contemporary journals and these can be used to construct a fully rounded biography that examines Dorn as a designer in her own right.

At present the literature on Marion Dorn is small and tends to take the traditional biographical form, where her work is predominantly explained or understood by reference to her personal life.[1] And it is only partly through her own talents that she is as well known as she is today; any mention is usually accompanied by reference to her colourful and romantic relationship with Edward McKnight Kauffer, one of the best-known graphic designers of the inter-war years.[2] A considerable amount has been written about Kauffer in recent years. Such is his 'star' appeal that it has proved difficult for design historians to evaluate Dorn's work on its own terms and to recognise her contribution. Even in a recent compendium of women designers, Kauffer still features prominently in the discussion of Marion Dorn:

> Born in San Francisco in 1899, Marion Dorn graduated from Stanford University in 1916 with a degree in education (graphic art). In Paris in 1923 she fell in love with the artist Edward McKnight Kauffer, whom she had first met in New York two years earlier. He left his wife

and young daughter and moved with Marion to London, where he had already established himself as a designer of advertising posters.[3]

Her relationship with Kauffer is often assumed to have been the major factor in her success as a designer. One of the most common assumptions when looking at a female designer whose partner was also in the profession is that the man assumes the primary creative role and that the woman must necessarily be influenced by him. Furthermore, a woman's physical appearance is often noted as a major factor. Anscombe records:

> Marion was a beautiful and talented young woman, and, with his help, was able to establish herself as a designer in London; as one friend commented, Marion 'could get away with murder' on account of her beauty and her relationship with McKnight Kauffer.[4]

Is her design work simply getting 'away with murder' or, as I would argue, as sensitive, innovative and successful in its own field as McKnight Kauffer's work was? Several general publications on design history choose to ignore Dorn completely, while including Kauffer.[5] Other women designers, such as Ray Eames, Margaret Macdonald Mackintosh and Marian Pepler, have been similarly treated. Most self-respecting design historians would no longer be so crudely biased, but the absence of women from these publications is indicative of the strength of the 'male genius' current which runs through so much art and design historical writing.[6]

Kauffer had been resident in Britain since 1914 and had a list of important and diverse commissions behind him.[7] He was obviously in a position to supply Dorn with useful contacts, but he did no more than provide the contacts that middle- and upper-class designers born and bred in Britain would naturally acquire through family and social contacts, so his influence should not be exaggerated.

When Dorn arrived in London in 1923 she became part of an exclusive set of artists, designers and writers, with friends such as the art historian Kenneth Clark and the writers Aldous Huxley, Harold Acton and the Sitwells. These people were her early clients and introduced her to future ones.

Most of Marion Dorn's professional contemporaries came from an educated middle/upper-middle-class background and the designs they executed tended to be for that market.[8] Dorn occasionally designed to commission, for clients such as the Savoy Hotel (1933–5), Claridges (1932) and Cunard's White Star Line (1935), as well as for friends such as Bryan Guinness (Lord Moyne), the writer Arnold Bennett, and the architect Oliver Hill. Many of her contemporaries also worked to commission, women such as Phyllis Barron and Dorothy Larcher, whose clients included the Duke of Westminster.[9] Unfortunately, it is not known how Dorn obtained her prestigious commissions for the Savoy, Claridges and Cunard. There is certainly no evidence to suggest that they came through Kauffer. Indeed, it was while Dorn was already working on the Dorland Hall exhibition in 1933 that Oliver Hill asked *her* to approach Kauffer about some work for that exhibition.

Education as well as social background needs to be examined in order to reveal the framework in which women designers, such as Dorn, became established within their profession. Dorn received her art education at Stanford University, California, in the Graphic Art Department, which catered for various types of student. Organised on a modular basis, the graphic art course could be taken as a major study with a programme including elementary still-life, linear drawing, lettering, landscape, organic form, perspective, design, handicraft, illustration, life drawing and an opportunity to follow the teachers' course.[10] Since Marion Dorn was recorded in the *American Art Annual* of 1919 as a painter, we can assume that she followed a course at Stanford that was fine-art based.[11] Many of her teachers were fine-artists, such as the Assistant professor, Henry Varnum Poor, whom she married in 1919.[12]

The majority of women who were designing textiles in Britain in the 1920s and 1930s had had some art training, whether it was in fine-art or craft. Several of these women had fine-art backgrounds,[13] while a smaller number had specifically studied textile design.[14] Occasionally designers were self-taught, and one, Marian Pepler, designed textiles after first training as an architect.[15] It is significant that many fine-art-trained women, after struggling to succeed as painters, actually turned to textile design as opposed to any other design area. Before the First World War it was rather difficult for women to train in craft or design areas, as these were traditionally associated with men. For example, in 1908, when the Female School of Art amalgamated with the trade-orientated Central School of Arts and Crafts, an opportunity for women to train in a wide range of crafts should have been available. However, many classes at the Central were restricted to trade students, who were usually male, and therefore female students were relegated to those areas regarded as appropriate for women – embroidery, textile design and illustration.[16] Alternatively they concentrated on fine-art, an area still dominated by successful male artists and teachers but deemed a suitable cultural, rather than professional, activity for women. By 1909 women were allowed to participate more fully in fine-art, being admitted into the life class.

The situation was similar in America. Middle- and upper-class women were being trained in the arts, while men were increasingly going into business or commerce, leaving art to become a female pursuit. By the 1920s about 20 per cent of art students in America were women,[17] but few concentrated on it professionally after leaving art school. While Europe was involved in the First World War, Americans saw their opportunity to climb out of the mire of copyism and snobbish allegiance to European, and particularly French, design. They encouraged greater alliance between art and industry and the use of museums as sources of inspiration for design. This was especially apparent in the area of textile design. The New York paper *Women's Wear* held an annual competition between 1916 and 1920 to design fashion fabrics for the textile industry and a supplementary competition was also arranged, the Albert Blum Exhibition of Hand Decorated Fabrics.[18] In the 1919 contest 12 out of the 17 top prize winners were women.[19] Many of the entrants for both contests were women who had previously trained in fine-art, such as Marguerite Zorach, Ruth Reeves and Marion Dorn herself. The large presence of women in these contests is indicative of their greater involvement in design associated with mass-production. Before the First World War, women designing on a freelance basis for industrial production were largely unheard of. This was also true in other areas of design, although it is significant that this early participation in design for industry should be associated with that particularly female preserve – fashion. Several women gained improved status from the competitions: Martha Ryther went on to work on a freelance basis for Mallinson and Belding[20] and Ruth Reeves for W. & J. Sloane.[21]

Marion Dorn, although educated in America, had a similar background to many of her British contemporaries in the design world. Her education can be favourably compared to the fine-art training of textile designers such as Josephine Cheeseman and Phyllis Barron at the Slade and Dorothy Larcher at Hornsey. What does seem to have set the two countries apart, however, were the opportunities open to women on the completion of their education. The American textile industry, in an effort to compete with European imports, encouraged the submission of work from freelance artists and designers long before British industry did so. Many of these designers were women, encouraged perhaps by the opportunity to profit from their art in one of the few areas open to them at the time.

Today there is general agreement that 'Marion Dorn was one of the most successful of a new generation of designers with a powerful new approach to the business of design.'[22] However, her success is usually seen as having been achieved in a vacuum. There has been no attempt, for example, to explain why Marion Dorn was regarded as a successful designer in her own day, or how the 'new generation of designers', both male and female, originated. This is of special importance to feminist design history, because the presence of female designers in the patriarchal textile industry of the 1920s was relatively new. Despite the Depression, this was a period of enormous opportunity for all designers. The imposition of tariffs in 1931 gave encouragement to designers working in Britain and to British manufacturers and it made possible the aspirations of the Design and Industries Association, which had been putting out propaganda on this issue since 1915. Furthermore, the Board of Trade's committee on Art and Industry, under Lord Gorell, recommended exhibitions to encourage good design, the formation of the Council for Art and Industry and the National Register of Industrial Designers.[23]

The ratio of male to female designers by the inter-war years was roughly equal. This was a situation peculiar to the textile industry. Other areas, such as furniture design, commercial art, architecture, industrial design, ceramics and glass remained the province of male designers, while 'less serious' activities such as embroidery were dominated by women. Furthermore women who worked in textile design usually concentrated on that area, diversifying within it, whereas the men who worked in textiles were, in the main, also involved in other areas of design. Only a limited number, of whom Ronald Grierson is an example, worked exclusively in textile design. Men were often known as painters, commercial artists and occasionally architects, and textile design was regarded as a secondary interest. For instance, Ben Nicholson, Paul Nash and Ashley Havinden were among those who were engaged as freelance textile designers on the strength of their reputations as fine-artists or commercial designers. Other male textile designers were primarily involved in textiles on the manufacturing side. Allan Walton, for instance, headed his own company, as did William Foxton and Alastair Morton.[24] It was much more difficult for a woman to be a successful painter or commercial artist, or a textile manufacturer, as these areas were dominated by men. Also fine-art-trained women who worked outside painting were restricted to areas where their talents were considered to be most appropriate, usually textiles or interior design.

There were three main areas of textile design in which women were directly involved in the twenties and thirties. The first was as freelance designers heading their own small companies or studios, where the designs were usually executed by persons other than themselves. For example, Eileen Hunter, a self-taught designer, ran her own company, Eileen Hunter Fabrics, from 1933 to 1939. Second, there was a large group of craftswomen/designers, such as Ethel Mairet and Elizabeth Peacock, who were weavers, and Phyllis Barron and Dorothy Larcher, who were blockprinters, who

Women Textile
Designers
61

executed their own designs in hand-craft techniques for limited production.[25] Finally, there were a small number of women employed as designers within manufacturing companies: Marianne Straub at Helios[26] and Theo Moorman at Warner & Sons.[27] The work of these women was usually marketed anonymously.

Although trained as a fine artist and describing herself as a painter, Dorn became involved in textiles around 1919, initially as a craftswoman/designer, but at the end of the 1920s and the beginning of the 1930s her textiles were being produced by manufacturing companies such as Wilton and Warner & Sons to her own designs, and by 1934 she had formed her own limited company.[28] As a craftswoman Dorn designed and produced batiks in the 1920s. Batik was a home-based craft which required relatively little capital outlay on tools and materials. It was also a fashionable design area in the 1920s, especially in Paris, where its chief exponent was Marguerite Pangon. Its popularity can be judged from the large number of exhibits at the International Exhibition of Modern Decorative and Industrial Arts in Paris in 1925.[29] In Britain Batik had several exponents, including Grace Digby, Jessie M. King and Cecile Francis-Lewis.[30]

The opportunities for free design offered by batik appealed to Dorn. It is probable that she was already working in this medium before arriving in London in 1923, as the technique was also very popular in America. She was a successful entrant in the annual *Women's Wear* design competitions, at which batik designs predominated.[31]

Dorn's batiks were illustrated in *Vogue* in 1925 and 1926,[32] and the accompanying text emphasised that she specifically designed for the spaces the batiks would occupy within a particular interior; the designs were, therefore, one-offs. The batiks themselves generally incorporated stylised figurative elements, such as animals or birds, or consisted of a large overall pattern with a design of foliage, ships, shells, figures or animals. Her designs were expensive: large panels retailed at 10 guineas, furnishing linens at 2 guineas per yard and silk shawls from 10 to 21 guineas.[33] These prices could be afforded only by a wealthy middle- and upper-class market, such as *Vogue* readers.

There were a number of important outlets for designers wanting to sell high quality craft work and many of these were run by women. The Three Shields Gallery in Kensington was opened by Dorothy Hutton in the early 1920s, the Little Gallery near Sloane Square, founded by Muriel Rose and Peggy Turnbull, opened in 1926, and Dorn herself sold designs at Modern Textiles, which was run by Elspeth Ann Little. These shops and others provided an outlet for designs and may have encouraged women to produce work once there was an opportunity to sell it.

Dorn's move out of craft production was an important development in her career. She began to diversify her products around 1926, when *Vogue* illustrated a rug designed by her.[34] When Dorn began to design rugs, she adopted both the geometry and the figuration of her batiks (see Fig. 5.1). She also drew upon European avant-garde painting: her abstract designs relied on the still-life paintings of artists such as Picasso, Braque and Léger. This can be seen in the rugs she designed for an exhibition with Edward McKnight Kauffer at Arthur Tooth & Sons in 1929.[35] These were conceived in terms of fine art, in that the design was contained within the frame like a painting, evidence of her early training.

Rugs, like batiks, had other fine-art connotations: they could be produced as one-offs or limited editions and signed to indicate authenticity, yet they could be made relatively cheaply. It should be noted, however, that Dorn's rugs were expensive when compared to the work of a designer like Marian Pepler. In 1936 Elizabeth Denby, a journalist, commented on a rug by Pepler retailing at £9/15s. and one by Dorn at £24: 2½ weeks income for a rug 10½ × 9ft.[36]

In the 1920s the various elements which made up an interior were increasingly seen as being important in relation to each other. Modernist architecture called for an interior which was simple, plain and sparsely furnished, yet the very austerity of this new interior lent itself to the subtle use of pattern in the shape of a painting or a modern rug on the floor. Indeed, the rug often became the focus of the room and 'attained . . . the pinnacle of its historic importance in the decorative scheme'.[37]

In Paris, the development of modern architecture was mirrored in rug design by Ivan da Silva Bruhns and Evelyn Wylde and highlighted at exhibitions such as the International Exhibition of Modern Decorative and Industrial Arts, 1925. It was within this framework that Dorn first produced designs for rugs. Rugs were increasingly illustrated in the quality art and design press, such as *Architectural Review* and *Studio*, and began to take on a high profile in artistic terms, which helped to put them on a par with fine art. This all added to the increasingly high status of the designer producing them, and Dorn was no exception.

Because of the similarities of rug design and modern painting, however, it was a design area dominated by men who had already become well known in other areas. Serge Chermayeff, for instance, was an architect and a designer of furniture and Ashley Havinden was a graphic designer like Kauffer. Yet the fact that rug design was also part of interior design, an area in which it was deemed acceptable for women to work, meant that women had relatively easy access to it. Once that access was obtained, women like Dorn could prove themselves alongside the well-established male commercial artists and architects. Indeed, it was Dorn and not Chermayeff or Kauffer who was referred to as 'the architect of floors'.[38]

By 1929, then, Dorn had moved from batik work to the high-status, high-profile area of rug design. This had everything to do with the art and architectural associations of the latter and nothing to do with the fact that it was a craft. When Marion Dorn and Edward McKnight Kauffer jointly exhibited rugs in 1929 at Arthur Tooth & Sons, the result was a string of commissions for Dorn and not for Kauffer.

One of the major factors which determined the appearance of Dorn's rugs was the kind of space which they were intended to furnish. This explains the major difference between her small rugs and large commissioned carpets. She saw the interior space as a unit in which the floor covering, furniture and textiles had a definite relationship to the ground plan and to each other. For example, the circular carpets for the lounge of Oliver Hill's Midland Hotel, Morecombe, were designed in tones of brown to complement the furniture and the Portland stone relief by Eric Gill. Furthermore, the directional design of waves is a clear reference to the seaside location. Most of Dorn's designs were hand-tufted by the Wilton Royal Carpet Factory, but in cases such as the Midland Hotel they were machine-made by H.M. Southwell.

Once she had made her name in rug and carpet design, Dorn was able to diversify in another textile area – printed textiles. In 1932 Warner & Sons, a long-established textile company,[39] began experimenting with screen printing, buying designs from various freelance designers, including Marion Dorn, Eileen Hunter, Louise Aldred and John Little. The development of this technology provided designers with the ideal medium for their work. The process offered greater scope for experimentation, as relatively short lengths could be produced with little financial risk. By contrast, other processes, such as roller printing, were initially expensive and large quantities of fabric had to be sold in order to recoup the initial outlay. Block printing, the other alternative, was both slow and expensive. Dorn's involvement with Warner & Sons began in the early thirties. It was not the first time she had worked with a large manufacturer, since her rug and carpet designs had involved close collaboration with companies like Wilton Royal. H.M. Southwell and Woodward Grosvenor. Dorn usually worked with Warner & Sons in one of two ways. She commissioned them to print designs, which were later marketed under her own name. In this case they charged her for the screen (or occasionally block), the printing and the fabric.[40] Alternatively, they sometimes used Dorn on a freelance basis, paying her royalties. On other occasions, however, she was commissioned to execute designs for a company

LOST

*N*O one would take a second look at Jo Arundel as you see her on the left. Her clinging collar hides a shapely neck and shoulder line. Her eyes are vague, her make-up insipid. The materials she wears — velvet, cloth, suede, patent-leather and braid—are merely confusing

☆

FOUND

A NEW personality, glamorous, exciting —with a changed hair-style and a new bonnet to make her sparkle. Her make-up now lends definition to the mouth and character to the eyes. Her suit emphasises the trimness of her figure, her improved posture makes her look vital and interested. And what a difference the shoes make! Now read the full story of Jo's transformation below.

THIS IS HOW A GIRL GETS CHIC

TEEN-AGER JO ARUNDEL presented herself as the first practical test for the team of experts. She wants to be an actress. She was, she said, in search of the chic and poise which would give her confidence to make the grade. . . . From dawn to dusk through one gruelling day the experts passed Jo from one to another. They studied, they criticised — and, finally, they groomed.

Her hair

The day began on a note of panic for Jo as Raymond approached her, scissors in hand.

But as he put the final touches to the sculptured hair-style he had chosen as a youthful frame for her features, Jo lost the hangdog look of a poodle which has just been sheared. There was a new,

excited sparkle in her eyes when we went to Rudolf for . . .

Her hat

Jo's faint murmur ("I've never worn a hat") gave place to a little gurgle of approval as Rudolf adjusted the Elizabethan Maid, scolloped bonnet he had designed specially to suit her. Next we went to see Miss Susan Hunt, who took over the question of . . .

Make-up

Jo's clearly defined, natural eyebrows were left severely alone. A touch of brown mascara was allowed (Jo is honey

fair). Experience ruled that make-up should be light and creamy; freshness is youth's golden rule. Any leaning towards heavy eye - shadow was smartly scotched.

Her suit

Maitli's choice, a beautifully plain blue grey, with a whittled-in waistline and slick, steep curve outwards over the hips.

Then off to Mrs. Newton-Sharp went Jo for . . .

Her shoes

She was given the very newest, taper-heeled calf shoes, with the new unblocked toes. "Simple and very suitable,"

she was told, and she hurried off to get . . .

Her fur

Mr. Tico chose a "hot chocolate" coloured seal. "Smooth, glowing, like youth's complexion," he announced. "With the taper line we can expect for Coronation year, a short, loose jacket is perfect."

Accessories

Jo wandered through the tiny Ali Baba cave of Mrs. Allan's glittering accessories. Drawer after drawer of long ear - rings, chunk bracelets, and necklaces were rejected.

With a single pair of gilt stud ear-rings and a tiny gold snake chain she was pronounced "complete." And Mr. Walmsley's pictures above, showing Jo Before and After the Fashion Court Treatment, provide the final evidence of success.

1.1
The plain court shoe (right)
complements New Look fashions
Sunday Graphic, 25 January 1953

THE HAZARDS OF THE 'STILETTO' HEEL

Photographed by CARL SUTTON

Doctors are already protesting that the 4-inch heel, with a tiny base, which has just reached London, at last, from Paris, will harm a girl's feet. Dressmakers welcome it, as it compels the wearer to take tiny steps. Unlike the new pointed toe, it cannot do much harm, if only worn occasionally. In any case girls will wear it.

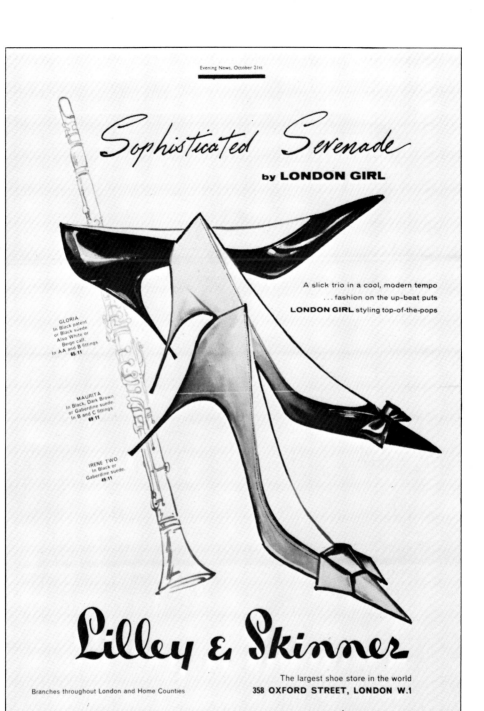

1.3
With the plastic heel,
stilettos reach new extremes
Evening News, 21 October 1959

2.1
'Ticket' or label used
on exported Lancashire cottons
Late nineteenth century

2.2
Woven border of sari or dhoti,
manufactured by Tamvaco & Co,
Manchester, 1877

2.3
'Stamp' trade mark of Sidney Hudson,
Manchester, 1917

3.1
Jean-Paul Gaultier's
macho knuckle-dusters and
mini-skirt for men

3.2
Katherine Hamnett's
subversion of the City:
duffle coat and pinstripe

3.3
Beribboned and bejewelled fop, 1663
From Francis M Kelly
and Randolph Schwabe,
Historic Costume 1140–1740, 1925

4.1
1961: reintroducing 'the image of home'
at Lillington Gardens, London

4.2
Compact housing with visual variety,
based on the 1970s
Essex County Council *Design Guide*

5.2
Marion Dorn, 'Fiddles', 1934,
block-printed linen
Warner & Sons Ltd

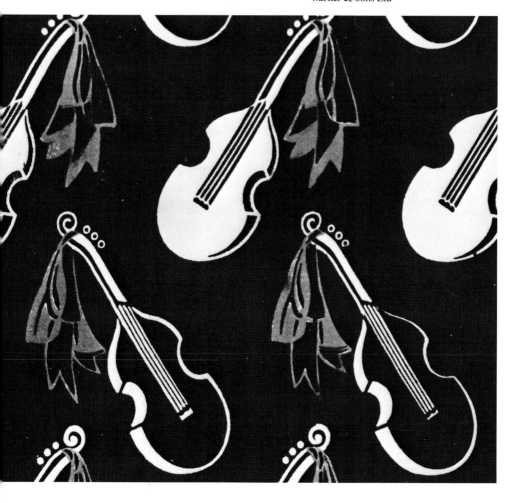

5.3
Marion Dorn, 'Acorn and Oakleaf', 1933,
screen-printed cotton
Warner & Sons Ltd

5.4
Marion Dorn, 'Greek Key', 1936,
power-woven wool and cotton
Warner & Sons Ltd

6.1
Freehand painter decorating
a Wedgwood vase in the
'Persian' pattern, 1926

6.2
Susie Cooper's earthenware
'Kestrel' hot water
jug with handpainted
leaf pattern, c. 1933

6.3
Susie Cooper's earthenware
'Kestrel' sugar bowl with
'Dresden Spray' lithograph
and handpainted shaded banding,
c. 1935

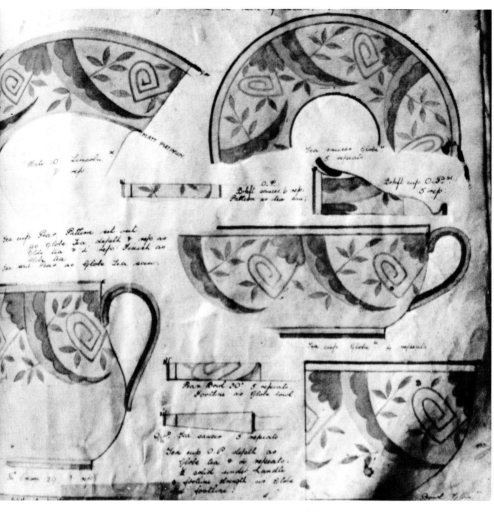

6.4
Millie Taplin's 'Winter Morn'
bone china tableware, c. 1934
Josiah Wedgwood & Sons Ltd pattern book

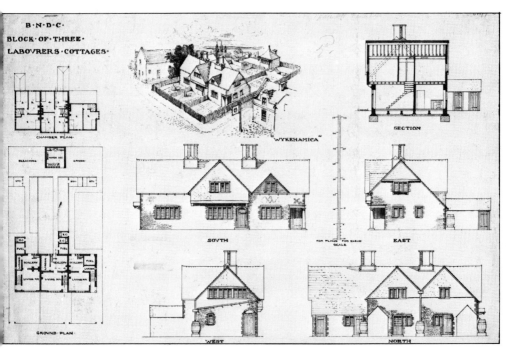

7.1
Ethel Charles design for three
labourers' cottages, 1897

7.2
Elisabeth Scott's
Shakespeare Memorial Theatre,
Stratford-upon-Avon, 1927–32

such as Gordon Russell Ltd which were then printed for that company by Warner & Sons.

Marion Dorn's designs for fabrics were determined not so much by her clients, as they were not usually done to commission, but by the technique, the cost and the stylistic trends of the period. For example, her designs for block-printed linens, such as 'Lily Leaf' and 'Fiddles' (see Fig. 5.2), designed in 1934 and printed by Warner & Sons, were simple, using few colours and characterised by small-scale repeats and bold outlines. Her designs for screen prints of the same year possess the same simplicity, as shown in the designs 'Anchor' and 'Cloudscape' both by Warner & Sons.

After 1934, Dorn tended to concentrate on design for the screen-print technique, which was finding favour with manufacturers like Warner & Sons, Old Bleach Linen and Donald Brothers. As her experience of designing for the screen increased, her designs became more sophisticated, requiring more screens, such as 'Acorn and Oakleaf' (see Fig. 5.3), 1935, a commissioned design for Warner & Sons. In the middle of the 1930s her screen-printed designs were dominated by leaves, flowers and animals, while in the second half of the thirties she increasingly used a more classical idiom. Examples of the latter are 'Hellene', 1935, a Donald Brothers' screen-printed linen with a design of Ionic capitals and ivy leaves, and, two years later, 'Column and Crown' (Warner & Sons) for the coronation of George VI. Her move to the classical idiom is an indication of her increasing experience of the screen-printing technique and a sensitivity to changes in fashion.

> She was leading when highly stylised patterns with one bold motif were the fashion. She is leading now when something more lyrical is desired . . . Lovely indeed is the free and flowing way in which she links up the romantic ruin of the temple within the loosely painted flower and the imaginatively drawn ribbons.[41]

Dorn's involvement with large companies like Warner & Sons offered her the opportunity to diversify further, into the area of weave design. Designing woven fabrics requires a sympathetic appreciation of the problems, possibilities and limitations of the machine; Dorn acquired these by working closely with Alec Hunter, the chief designer at Warner & Sons. Several visits to the mill in Braintree, Essex, meant that although she was not a weaving technician, she had a sound understanding of the capabilities of the machine. It was increasingly common for manufacturers like Warner & Sons to have a percentage of their total output concerned with exclusive ranges or 'modern' lines, for which freelance designers and artists were encouraged to design. Donald Brothers, for instance, had 'Old Glamis', their modern section, while Morton Sundour had 'Edinburgh Weavers'. In 1937 the latter introduced a range of 'Constructivist Fabrics', with designs by artists such as Ben Nicholson and Barbara Hepworth,[42] which highlighted the trend for commissioning designs from well-known modernist artists.

The opportunities for the textile designer to move, first, from a craft area to professional freelance status, and then to diversify within that area, were available and even encouraged in the 1930s. However, many women textile designers who became involved in industry on a freelance basis chose to specialise in one area only, usually print or weave. Marion Dorn, by contrast, used her experience and contacts with industry to further her career by producing in a variety of areas.

Her designs for woven fabrics were predominantly determined by the available technology. Early designs were hand-woven by weavers contracted by her, but through her connection with Warner & Sons and Alec Hunter she was able to experiment with designs for the power loom. The incorporation of figurative imagery was more difficult to accomplish in weave than in print, so many of Dorn's early designs are simple, such as 'Greek Key' (see Fig. 5.4) and 'Magnolia Leaf', 1936. But as the decade progressed they came to depend more obviously on the new technology. In 1937 she designed 'Hasta' for Edinburgh Weavers, in which a ground pattern of stylised leaves in linen and rayon is highlighted by leaves of a contrasting colour and texture in cotton. The design is an example of the collaboration between the factory designer, in this case Alastair Morton, and the independent designer, Marion Dorn. The quality of the cloth, with its different textures, was developed in the factory on the loom and then translated into the design by Dorn.[43]

Marion Dorn designed rugs, prints and weaves with continued success throughout the thirties. She exhibited printed and woven fabrics in the British pavilion at the Paris exhibition of 1937 and produced designs for John Perry Wallpapers. Her designs continued to be reproduced in *Architectural Review* and *Studio*. The result of this high profile in the art and design press meant that Dorn received more prestigious work, including a commission from Frank Pick at the London Passenger Transport Board to design moquettes for the upholstery on the underground trains.[44] Her success continued until her departure for America with Edward McKnight Kauffer, on the advice of the American Embassy, in 1940. She continued her career, although with less success, in the highly competitive field of freelance design in New York. She gained prestigious commissions, such as the design of a carpet for the Diplomatic Reception Room at the White House in 1960. She continued to design until 1962, when she retired to Morocco, where she died in 1964.

This study of the emergence of women textile designers in the

1920s and 1930s has concentrated particularly on women who worked in textiles on a freelance basis, an area in which Marion Dorn became successful and one in which an increasing number of women emerged in that period. Much of the information uncovered relates generally to women who were working at this time while some is specific to Dorn. Marion Dorn's success took place against the background of an increase in the number of women entering textiles as freelance designers and a growing number of women employed in professional work in the 1930s.[45]

Furnishing textiles are the items within an interior scheme which are most frequently replaced, as they are a relatively cheap method of providing a new look for a room. This, coupled with perhaps textiles' most important function, decoration, resulted in an ever-increasing demand for new designs. This demand was most often filled in the 1930s by freelance textile designers, many of whom were women. The increase was partly the result of an attempt by manufacturers in many areas to separate the design process from the rest of manufacture, and partly the result of their increasing awareness of the advantages to sales of advertising products by named designers. The design establishment of the time was also attempting to professionalise the practice of design in general, with the establishment of many societies and associations, and particularly with the formation of the Society of Industrial Artists in 1930.

The employment of freelance designers held many advantages for textile manufacturers. Their employment enabled them to respond more rapidly to stylistic trends and produce a greater variety of designs. It could also be argued that many designers preferred the greater freedom of freelance work. This greater freedom, along with the more socially acceptable idea of women working from the home or private studio, provided female designers with the opportunity to move away from craftwork.

It has been noted that one of the main functions of furnishing fabrics has been 'to personalise or humanise the space in which they are employed'.[46] This association of fabric with interior space and homemaking, and the involvement of women in the areas of interior and textile design reinforces the 'stereotypical idea of women as discerners of beauty in their "natural space" – the home'.[47] This idea of a 'suitable' area of occupation for a female designer is highlighted by the fact that many women who had partners also involved in art and design tended to be relegated to textile design, despite the fact that many of them had been trained as artists, while their partners specialised in more 'serious' areas. Marian Pepler is a good example. She trained as an architect but was encouraged by her architect/designer husband, R.D. Russell, to design rugs and carpets and to work as a colour and decoration consultant on furnishing schemes for Gordon Russell Ltd.[48] On the other side of the Atlantic there was Marguerite Thompson Zorach, who had studied painting in Paris and was married to fellow artist William Zorach. Occasionally they collaborated on designs for batiks, but by 1920 William was concentrating on sculpture while Marguerite worked on tapestry and embroidery.

Many of the women who practised freelance textile design did not need to do so for financial reasons, as they were often supported by partners who earned the primary salary of the household. This reinforced the idea of women as 'dabblers', or merely practising textile design as a hobby. However, looking specifically at Marion Dorn, this was not the case. Dorn was always financially independent of Kauffer. She had a small private income on which she relied at times, such as when she set up her own company, but certainly Kauffer was never in a position to support her financially.[49] Dorn's financial independence and her business-like attitude towards design resulted in her being taken seriously as a freelance textile designer.

Marion Dorn arrived in London in 1923 with certain advantages over her British contemporaries. Her education was similar to other women textile designers who had trained as fine artists, but the textile designer working in America had more opportunities to produce designs for industry than her British counterpart. Dorn's wide industrial connections with textile manufacturers in Britain were an extension of the opportunities open to textile designers in America before she left.

Notes

1 Mendes, V., 'Marion Dorn: Textile designer', *Journal of the Decorative Arts Society 1890–1940 UK*, Vol. 2, 1978, pp. 24–35.
2 Marion Dorn lived with Kauffer from 1923 to 1950, when they married. However, during the fifties they lived separately. Kauffer died in 1954.
3 Anscombe, I., *A Woman's Touch: Women in Design from 1860 to the Present Day*, Virago, London, 1984, p. 172.
4 Ibid.
5 Bayley, S., *The Conran Directory of Design*, Octopus Press, London, 1985.
6 Parker, R., and Pollock, G., *Old Mistresses: Women, Art and Ideology*, Routledge & Kegan Paul, London, 1981.
7 Haworth-Booth, M., *E. McKnight Kauffer: A Designer and His Public*, Gordon Fraser, London, 1979.
8 Eileen Hunter is a good example of a textile designer from a middle-class background who set up her own company to design printed textiles in the thirties.

9 Gaylard, M. O., 'Phyllis Barron and Dorothy Larcher: Textile designers and block printers', *Journal of the Decorative Arts Society 1890–1940 UK*, Vol. 3, 1979, pp. 32–9.

10 Courses of Instruction, Stanford University Archives, California.

11 'Who's Who in Art', *American Art Annual*, Vol. XVI, 1919.

12 Henry Varnum Poor became an important potter in the 1920s. See Boswell, P., *Varnum Poor*, Harper & Brothers, New York, 1941.

13 Eva Crofts and Josephine Cheeseman are examples of women with fine-art backgrounds.

14 Barbara Hayes and Helen Sampson both studied at the Central School of Arts and Crafts.

15 Allwood, R., and Laurie, K., *R. D. Russell, Marian Pepler*, Inner London Education Authority, London, 1983, p. 28.

16 Callen A., *Angel in the Studio: Women in the Arts and Crafts Movement 1870–1914*, Astragal Books, London, 1979, p. 45.

17 Slatkin, W., *Women Artists in History*, Prentice-Hall Inc., New Jersey, 1985, p. 115.

18 Crawford M. D. C., *The Heritage of Cotton: The Fibres of Two Worlds and Many Ages*, Fairchild Publishing Co., New York, 1941, p. 203.

19 *Women's Wear Daily*, Fairchild Publishing Co., Vol. 18, No. 5, 1919, p. 1.

20 Schoeser, M., *Fabrics and Wallpapers*, Bell and Hyman, London, 1986, p. 51.

21 Davies, K., *At Home in Manhattan: Modern Decorative Art, 1925 to the Depression*, New Haven, Conn., 1983, p. 99.

22 Thackeray, A., 'Marion Dorn and Carpets in the Thirties', *Leisure in the 20th Century*, Design Council Publications, London, 1977, p. 14

23 Marshall, H. G. Hayes, *British Textile Designers Today*, F. Lewis, Leigh-on-Sea, 1939, p. 324.

24 Scottish National Gallery of Modern Art, *Alastair Morton and Edinburgh Weavers*, HMSO, London, 1976.

25 Gaylard, op. cit., p. 33.

26 Schoeser, M., *Marianne Straub*, Design Council Publications, London, 1984, pp. 48–70.

27 Bury, H., *Choice of Design*, catalogue, Warner & Sons Ltd., London, 1979, p. 59.

28 *Cabinet Maker*, June 1934, p. 250. It was fairly unusual at this time for women to form limited companies.

29 *Reports of the Present Position and Tendencies of the Industrial Arts as Indicated at the International Exhibition of Modern Decorative and Industrial Arts, Paris, 1925*, Department of Overseas Trade, London, 1925, p. 70.

30 Francis-Lewis, C., *A Practical Handbook of Batik*, Francis-Lewis Studio, London, 1924.

31 Crawford, op. cit., p. 203.
32 'New furnishing fabrics', *Vogue*, May 1925, pp. 50–1, October 1925, p. 48.
33 Mendes, op. cit., p. 24.
34 'Some rugs of today', *Vogue*, September 1926, p. 61.
35 'New design for Wilton rugs by E. McKnight Kauffer and Marion Dorn', *Studio*, Vol. 98, 1929, pp. 35–6.
36 Denby, E. M., 'Everyday things for whom?', *Trend in Design for Everyday Things*, Vol. 1, 1936, p. 51.
37 Todd, D., 'Marion Dorn: Architect of floors', *Architectural Review*, Vol. 72, 1932, p. 109.
38 Ibid.
39 Bury, op. cit.
40 Dartford Print Books, Warner & Sons Archive, Braintree, Essex.
41 *Studio*, Vol. 119, 1940, p. 183.
42 Scottish National Gallery of Modern Art, op. cit., p. 6.
43 Read, H. E., *The Practice of Design*, Lund Humphries, London, 1946, p. 27.
44 Marx, E., 'Fabrics for hardwear', *Architectural Review*, February 1944, pp. 53–5.
45 Woolf, V., *Three Guineas*, The Hogarth Press, London, 1938, p. 180.
46 Schoeser, op. cit., p. 7.
47 Buckley, C., review of *A Woman's Touch* in *Feminist Arts News*, Vol. 2, No. 3, p. 17.
48 Allwood and Laurie, op. cit., p. 27.
49 Haworth-Booth, op. cit., p. 93.

6
Pottery Women: A Comparative Study of Susan Vera Cooper and Millicent Jane Taplin

Cheryl Buckley

Both Susie Cooper (b.1902) and Millie Taplin (1902–80) worked as designers in the North Staffordshire pottery industry between the wars. Although they worked in the industry in different capacities, one as a designer in a self-managed business, the other as a designer in an internationally renowned company, as women working in a male-dominated design profession they confronted similar obstacles. Susie Cooper began working for the pottery-decorating firm A. E. Gray and Co. Ltd in 1922, before she formed her own company, Susie Cooper Pottery Ltd, in 1929; she continues to work today. Millie Taplin began working for Josiah Wedgwood and Sons Ltd in 1917 and continued there until her retirement in 1962. Both women were active as designers when the pottery industry and women's role within it were undergoing change. The issues which dominated the North Staffordshire pottery industry between the wars were, as we will see, to have implications for the roles that women designers were able to play. These issues included the position of women in pottery production, the importance of design as a tool for regenerating the pottery trade and the relevance of design education to the industry.

Underlying this discussion will be an examination of how women designers' roles were defined and confined by patriarchy, and the way that their work has been subsequently acknowledged by design historians.[1] Within the pottery industry only certain aspects of design were considered suitable for women: Susie Cooper was able to break down this gender division, whereas Millie Taplin's position as a designer was prescribed by it.

The roles Susie Cooper and Millie Taplin played were not unique. Women had worked as designers in both the eighteenth and nineteenth centuries with firms such as Minton, Doulton and Josiah Wedgwood, although they worked primarily as designers of surface decoration.[2] During the nineteenth century this area of design became more acceptable for women with the formation of Minton's and Doulton's Art Pottery studios, which offered reputable employment to young middle-class women.[3] This type of designing was considered appropriate for young ladies because it was clean and it took place in the respectable surroundings of small studios detached from the main manufacturing processes. China painting, as it was known at the time, could be viewed as an extension of Victorian ladies' accomplishments as it required many of the skills which women were considered to possess 'naturally' such as delicacy, dexterity and patience.[4]

By the end of the nineteenth century, women were established as designers in the pottery industry, although their roles were circumscribed by a gender division within the field of design. This was reinforced by a strict female stereotype which delineated acceptable modes of behaviour for young, middle-class women. These perceptions of female artistic skills still permeated the pottery industry when Susie Cooper and Millie Taplin were training to be designers between 1915 and 1922. They were compounded by labour divisions within the pottery industry at large, which was organised along lines of gender, and to a lesser extent according to craft skills. Divisions on the basis of gender stemmed from the commonly held view that women were better suited to certain types of work as a result of their biology.[5] The introduction of female labour into jobs previously considered to be male preserves focused debate on women's role in the pottery industry. The male unions began to call for this role to be strictly limited to those areas seen as suited to female skills. This meant jobs which placed women in a subservient position to men – as their assistants or in jobs which were at the finishing end of the production process and were considered to require the stereotypical female attributes of dexterity and patience. The manufacturers, however, were keen to break the power of the craft unions by employing semi-skilled women workers, who were non-unionised.[6]

The debate about women's role in the industry intensified during and after the First World War. As male conscription increased, more and more women took over jobs which had been done by men before 1914. Until this point, the trade unions were still undecided in their attitude to female labour, even though there were 2,000 female members of the National Amalgamated Society of Male and Female Pottery Workers (NASMFPW), which had been formed in 1906 from the numerous craft unions. However, during the First World War, as it became apparent that women were doing men's jobs but being paid only half the wage, the National Society of Pottery Workers (NSPW), which superseded the NASMFPW, fought successfully for equal pay on behalf of women doing men's jobs. By 1919, the NSPW had 25,000 female members, which represented 50 to 60 per cent of women workers in the industry at that time.

The sexual division of labour, although to some extent undermined by the introduction of new machinery and the labour changes necessitated by the First World War, still dominated the pottery industry during the inter-war period. Women workers were to be found at all stages of production, although at the clay end they rarely worked independently of male overseers. It was at the finishing end of the production process, and especially in the decorating shops, that skilled women's work was to be found. Here, women were trained, as they had been in the nineteenth century, as china decorators. The roles which Susie Cooper and Millie Taplin were able to play in the pottery industry were shaped by both the traditions of the china decorators of the nineteenth century and the continuing operation of the sexual division of labour.

Women's employment prospects as designers were also governed by the economic health of the inter-war pottery industry and the attitude to design of the pottery manufacturers. The North Staffordshire pottery industry between 1919 and 1939 was not unlike its nineteenth-century predecessor. Many firms continued to specialise in one area, such as sanitary earthenware, sanitary fireclay, tiles, jet and rockingham, and general earthenware and fine china. The industry was still dominated by the small to medium-sized unit, which comprised 82 per cent of all pottery factories (or potbanks, as they are more commonly known) and employed under 300 workers. In most pottery companies, financial and managerial control resided with the founding family.[7] This practice extended from the small potbanks, such as the one set up by Susie Cooper, to the large, internationally known companies, such as Josiah Wedgwood and Sons Ltd. The small companies tended to produce a restricted range of products for a distinct market; the larger ones, which often employed as many as 1,000 workers, produced a wide range of wares, aimed at different markets.

The inter-war years were an uncertain and difficult period for pottery manufacturers and their workforce. Indeed, unlike the rest of British industry, which showed fairly modest growth between 1907 and 1933, there was a fall in output in the pottery industry.[8] Optimism, which had been created by the boom immediately following the end of the First World War, proved unfounded. Pottery exports failed to reach pre-war levels and in fact both foreign and home markets were threatened by foreign competition. The Wall Street crash had an immediate and overwhelming effect on the large companies like Wedgwood, whose market for the ornamental jasper and lustres was primarily North American. The problems of the pottery industry were intensified by strong local competition between manufacturers which, when combined with foreign competition, served to push prices down.

To offset these difficulties, manufacturers adopted various strategies, all of which had serious implications for the workforce, pottery manufacture and design. To reduce labour costs and lessen manufacturers' dependence on craft skills, new technology was introduced which allowed the widespread employment of cheap, unskilled female labour. Some of the large companies turned to Taylorism, which was the theory of scientific management proposed by Frederick Taylor. This was a system of improving worker efficency by finding the optimum method for each job. The aim was to minimise wasted effort on the part of the worker by carefully planning and designing the production process and tools. In addition to this, a formal managerial system was implemented. Against this background of economic uncertainty, manufacturers attempted to reverse the advantageous work conditions and wages won by the union immediately following the First World War.[9] In 1923, the employers unilaterally reduced wages by 10 per cent. In a period characterised by high unemployment, the union was weak and unable to resist the employers' actions, and this set the tone for the next decade.

New methods of stimulating trade were considered by pottery manufacturers; one of these was improving the quality and design of pottery. Numerous lectures and discussions were organised by the Design and Industries Association and the Ceramic Society, on themes such as the relevance of art to industry, the relationship between design and machinery, and the role of the pottery designer.[10] Instrumental in the organisation and intellectual direction of these debates was Gordon Mitchell Forsyth (1879–1952). In 1920 Forsyth had been appointed Superintendent of Art Education for the City of Stoke-on-Trent and the Principal of the City Schools of Art. One of his first tasks had been the reorganisation and rationalisation of art schools in the Potteries. This he had done by making Burslem, which had the best facilities, the centre for day classes, Longton the centre for preparatory classes, Hanley for design and Stoke for modelling and sculpture.[11] At the outset he was keen to align the art schools with local industry, because he believed that 'it was only by art that the pottery industry would gain fresh ground and find new fields to conquer.'[12] Forsyth gained considerable support in his efforts from the pottery manufacturers, who rightly saw the art schools as providers of new talent which would be ready-trained in the techniques of the industry.

Active participants in the debates about design were Major Frank Wedgwood (1867–1930), director of Josiah Wedgwood and Sons Ltd from 1916 until his death in 1930, and Albert Edward Gray (1871–1959), founder of the pottery-decorating business of A. E. Gray and Co. Ltd. In the first 30 years of the twentieth century, the Wedgwood company had made a conscious attempt to change the traditional nature of its market and products.[13] This latter development had come about chiefly through their contacts with Alfred (1865–1960) and Louise (1882–1956) Powell, who began designing for Wedgwood in 1903. Wedgwood showed that it was interested in progressive design, and this was reinforced in 1926 when a freehand painting studio was opened at Etruria and run by Millie Taplin. This marked a clear response to the increasing demands for hand-painted ware, which was paralleled by the activities of Gray's. By 1914, Gray's ware was advertised as being of 'excellent workmanship and delicacy of design'.[14] Unlike Wedgwood, A. E. Gray and Co. Ltd was not a manufacturer of pottery. However, Edward Gray was active in the debates about pottery design which took place under the auspices of the Ceramic Society; in fact, in 1917 he had urged this society to establish a separate art section.[15] During the 1920s and 1930s, Gray was an employer of the art-school-trained freehand paintresses, who were thought to be ideally suited to hand-painting the company's ware. This was due to gender stereotyping which ascribed greater dexterity in handling loaded brushes of paint and more skill in producing delicate, detailed decoration to women. Susie Cooper's introduction to the pottery industry came at A. E. Gray's; it was in this role that she learned many of the decorating techniques which she was to develop later in her own company.

Within the pottery industry there was a subtle shift of emphasis in attitudes to design in these two decades. In the 1920s, although threatened by foreign competition and diminishing export markets, it was still possible for pottery manufacturers to export their expensive hand-made products; the North American market was especially lucrative. For these products, the hand-paintresses used a variety of decorating processes, such as lustre, enamel, gilding and printing. After the Wall Street crash in 1929 and its devastating effect on the British economy, pottery manufacturers found themselves without a market for their products. Of necessity, they looked to the home market and they examined their product ranges in relation to this less lucrative, though potentially substantial, market. Both Josiah Wedgwood and Sons Ltd and the new company which Susie Cooper formed in 1929 followed this pattern.

The parallel careers of Susie Cooper and Millie Taplin as designers in the North Staffordshire pottery industry provide an interesting insight into the factors which determined the role of women in design in Britain between the wars. Designers' roles generally in the pottery industry were governed by specific factors which originated from within the industry. The reputation of some companies rested on the high quality of their products and as a consequence they stressed the important part played by designers. In these, large sections were established to facilitate the activities of the designer. In other companies, design was seen as peripheral and designers were employed to copy the successful products of rival manufacturers rather than to initiate independent work. Roles varied according to the size of the company, the type of products made and the attitudes of the manufacturer. Through a comparison of their roles, it is possible to see that other factors were important when the designer was a woman. Particularly crucial were class and family background, which in the case of these two women were different.

Susie Cooper, like most other women who worked as designers in the pottery industry at this time, came from a middle-class background.[16] Her father, who died when she was 11 years old, had worked in the family farm and wholesale vegetable business and had intended taking over the farming side of it. Susie, who was the youngest of seven children, was educated at a local school until the age of 11 and after this she attended a private school in Hanley. Her mother, who was a Sunday-school teacher at Hill Top Chapel in Burslem, was relatively enlightened, encouraging her daughter to go to evening classes at Burslem School of Art and to consider working for a living. To begin with, Susie took both art and cookery classes with a friend, although it was not long before her talent in art was recognised by Gordon Forsyth, who encouraged her to apply for a scholarship. This she did, and by gaining a scholarship she was able to begin her day-time studies at Burslem School of Art, probably in 1919. She spent three years at Burslem and was trained within the newly organised art-school system initiated by Forsyth. Her move into the pottery industry had not been planned. In 1922, she sat an entrance exam for the Royal College of Art but proved to be ineligible because she was not employed in industry. Entry was restricted to people who were already working in industry because the college's aim was to develop skills acquired through practical training as well as to teach new ones. It was in order to gain industrial experience that Gordon Forsyth arranged for her to work with the pottery-decorating company A. E. Gray and Co. Ltd.

The route taken by Millie Taplin at Wedgwood was quite different. Her background was working class; her father was employed in the pottery industry as a caster with the company of Whieldon Sanitary Pottery. She was brought up with her two younger brothers in a terraced house in Boothen, in the heart of the Potteries. Her mother worked for a while when the children were old enough for school, although this was from necessity not by choice. Millie attended the local Church of England school until the age of 13, after which she went to work in a millinery shop. She left within a month when she won a scholarship to Stoke School of Art after being proposed for this by her old school. At the same time, one of her teachers gave her an introduction to the pottery firm of Greens of Fenton as a liner. This involved painting gold lines on cups and saucers, and for this she was paid half a crown a week, a wage which reflected her trainee status. Growing increasingly impatient with this job she moved to Minton's, where she learned to paint the well-known 'Rose', 'Pansy' and 'Forget-me-not' designs. In 1917 she started work at Josiah Wedgwood and Sons Ltd as a hand-paintress, while continuing her classes for three or four nights each week. Like Susie Cooper, Millie Taplin benefited from the training provided by the Potteries art schools; she was taught 'still-life painting, plant drawing and pottery painting'.[17] Her working-class background meant that Millie Taplin had to work to contribute to the family income; art-school training had to be undertaken in her own free time.

When Susie Cooper went to work for A. E. Gray and Co. Ltd in 1922, she found herself in a company which had established a characteristic style of ware. According to Kathy Niblett 'from 1913 . . . the use of enamelled lithographs declines and freehand painting becomes prevalent', thus revealing 'a desire on the part of A. E. Gray to promote the artistic skills of the Potteries'.[18] A year after her arrival a new range of lustre, Gloria lustre, was introduced; this had been produced by Edward Gray in collaboration with his friend Gordon Forsyth. This particular ware, which was brightly coloured and hand-painted, was intended to be both ornamental and functional. By 1924 Susie Cooper had achieved the status of designer and to coincide with this a special named backstamp was produced for all ware designed by her. Gradually, Susie Cooper began to develop bold and highly colourful designs based on abstract and floral patterns for the freehand enamel paintresses. In October 1929, with words of warning from Edward Gray that she would only last eight months, she left to set up her own company. As she has said more recently: 'it was of course taboo for women to go into industry in those days. But I knew what I wanted to do.'[19]

The hand-painted wares developed by Alfred and Louise Powell were becoming increasingly popular in Wedgwood's market; these were initially based on revivals of hand-painted designs from the original eighteenth-century pattern books. Contrasting with these traditional patterns was a range of freehand patterns which were also produced by the Powells; these were adapted either to the Wedgwood earthenware shapes already in existence or to the new shapes which had been specially manufactured for the Powells. Most of the Powells' designs which were put into production were for earthenware with lustre decoration of bronze and silver. With their Arts and Crafts background, the Powells eschewed many of the mass-production processes which were crucial to Wedgwood's survival in the 1920s. Their continuing role in the company was dependent on the commercial success of their designs, but it was left to Millie Taplin to adapt their intricate and complex patterns to the skills of the freehand paintresses.

It was from this collaboration with Alfred and Louise Powell that Millie Taplin's career at Wedgwood began to develop. Her training with the Powells was put to good use when she was asked to form a handcrafts department in 1928. A year later this was merged with the hand-painting department and Millie Taplin was put in charge. The designs produced under the auspices of this department included the Queensware lustres developed by the Powells, the ornamental and functional earthenware in the Islam-inspired Rhodian and Persian patterns, introduced by Wedgwood in 1920 and 1926 respectively, and Millie Taplin's own designs (see Fig. 6.1). These included 'Buds and Bells', 'Papyrus', 'Spring', 'Summer', 'Autumn' and 'Sun-lit'. The last is a typical example and was designed for Cane ware, c. 1930. Like the hand-painted designs of Susie Cooper, it is boldy patterned, with a combination of abstract and stylised flower motifs in bright, strong colours like orange, green, red and blue.

To broaden her knowledge of art and design, Millie Taplin began making regular trips to London to see exhibitions and visit museums, and her youngest brother, Eric, remembers her first trip to Paris, which was a source of great excitement to him and the rest of the family.[20] Apparently her parents didn't attempt to hold her back, although her lifestyle was hardly typical for a young working-class woman in the Potteries.

Both Millie Taplin and Susie Cooper were well established as designers by the early 1930s, one with an increasingly important role in one of the most prestigious pottery manufacturers in Britain at that time, the other in her own company with finance from her family. On her twenty-seventh birthday, Susie Cooper embarked on her career as independent manufacturer. From the outset, she planned to design pottery shape as well as pattern: an impossibility at the decorating firm of Gray's. The finance for her company came largely from her family; with her brother-in-law, Jack Beeson, as partner, in the autumn of 1929 they found a small factory in Tunstall where they could rent space. On one of the painting floors of the George Street pottery, Susie Cooper established the facilities needed to hand-paint ware. Within three weeks, following the Wall Street crash on 29 October 1929, the creditors of the pottery foreclosed on the loan which had kept her landlord's firm solvent and as a consequence she was without premises. Not to be put off, she began to look for other suitable premises and in the spring of 1930 she was once again ready to start production, at the Chelsea Works in Moorland Road, Burslem, in space rented from Doulton's, at that time one of her suppliers of blank pottery. In the *Pottery Gazette and Glass Trade Review* of April 1930 it was reported that:

it is only rarely . . . that one comes across an instance of a pottery artist – and particularly a lady – who has the confidence and courage to attempt to carve out a career by laying down a special plant and staff on what must be admitted to be something suggestive of a commercial scale.[21]

From the outset, the Susie Cooper Pottery Ltd was noted for its modern design. Early designs were very simple and included 'Polkadot' and 'Exclamation Mark', both of which were produced in a single colour on cream-coloured earthenware. Another popular design was 'Wedding Ring', which was made up of concentric shaded bands of colour. More complicated patterns based on floral motifs included 'Nosegay' and 'Briar Rose'. She has since said that many of these designs resulted from her need to create designs which could be reproduced perfectly by her paintresses.[22]

Paintresses started working for Susie Cooper at the age of 14 and they were trained by her initially to grind colour and to apply it on to blank ware. Gradually, they acquired greater skill, which could then be passed on to new trainees. Florence May Hancock went to work for Susie Cooper as a bander in January 1938 at the age of 15. As a trainee she earned about five shillings a week; then, after two years, she went on to piece-work and earned about 17 shillings a week.[23] Banding was one of the decorative techniques which Susie Cooper employed in her designs. It could take various forms, including shaded, solid, narrow, flat and wash-banding, and it could be combined with other decorative techniques. Later in the 1930s Susie Cooper combined it to good effect with lithographs.

Following the considerable interest which Susie Cooper's designs generated at the 1931 British Industries Fair, Harry Wood, another of her blank ware suppliers, offered her new premises in his factory, the Crown Works, on Newcastle Street, Burslem. Susie Cooper was keen to take up this offer, as she preferred Wood's blank shapes to those of all her other suppliers. She wanted to develop a close relationship with a manufacturer, hoping that eventually she would be able to get her own shapes produced. Confirmation of Susie Cooper's early success came in 1932, when the Queen ordered a breakfast-in-bed set and a jug from her display at the British Industries Fair. In the same year, Harry Wood agreed to manufacture shapes to Susie Cooper's own designs; these were to be produced in an ivory-bodied earthenware. The names of these new shapes, whose outlines were reminiscent of stream-lined bird forms, were Kestrel and Curlew (See Fig. 6.2). With the introduction of these new shapes Susie Cooper began to achieve her ambition, as reported in the *Pottery Gazette and Glass Trade Review* of August 1935,

Form, decoration and even texture in the Susie Cooper
ware are part of a considered scheme; it is not merely a
case of sticking a decoration on to a pot regardless of
context . . .[24]

With her new shapes in production, Susie Cooper began to
develop suitable surface decoration. Hand-painted patterns like
'Crayon Lines', 'Spirals' and 'Beechwood' were developed, although with increasing production, the demands on the paintresses'
time were becoming too great. It was in response to this problem
that Susie Cooper turned her attention to lithographs. In April
1933 she had attended and contributed to a debate organised by the
North Staffordshire branch of the Society of Industrial Artists on
'Lithographs as a Means of Pottery Decoration'. It was claimed at
this debate that 'most of the time of the lithographic transfer
printers had been taken up in the past in producing cheap, gaudy
imitations . . .'[25] Susie Cooper argued for cooperation between the
pottery and lithograph manufacturers, claiming 'that it was no use
the lithographer bringing out lithographs produced by an artist who
knew nothing at all about the manufacturing processes'.[26] She
produced watercolours of proposed designs, which she then took to
a lithograph manufacturer for the artist to make interpretations.
Once she had established a source of satisfactory lithographs, she
combined them with hand-painted decoration, such as shaded
bands, dots and stripes to produce designs like 'Endon Border',
'Dresden Spray', 'Iris' and 'Clematis'. (See Fig. 6.3). All of these
designs had hand-painted decoration combined with lithographs of
such high quality that it is almost impossible to distinguish them
from fine hand-painted designs.

Susie Cooper's involvement in the debate about lithographs
highlights her increasing confidence in her role as pottery manufacturer. In September 1932 she was elected to the Council of the
Society of Industrial Artists' North Staffordshire branch and she
became an active participant in both its debates and those organised
under the auspices of the Ceramic Society and Design and Industries
Association. As an employer she was fair though exacting.[27]
Between 70 and 100 people worked for her company in the late
1930s; these included freehanders, lithographers, aerographers,
biscuit-workers and kiln-loaders and there was a small printing
shop. The company was thriving, with a turnover of a quarter of a
million pounds by the financial year 1939–40. Susie Cooper was
involved with the company at every level. She produced about 200
new designs a year; in the meantime she was involved in the
day-to-day running of the company, taking part in recruitment,
work organisation, promotion and marketing.[28] At busy times she
would even get involved in packing ware.

From the outset, Susie Cooper identified a distinct market, which she believed to be professional, with little money but plenty of taste. At the time, it was argued that 'she has found, if not actually created, a market for her productions!'[29] One of the things she did was to discern a growing market for smaller sets of pottery rather than the massive dinner sets of the Edwardian era, she believed that 'the drastic changes that have come over the domestic life of many people warrant the provision of smaller and better-balanced services.'[30] To this end she introduced new combinations of ware such as a 15-piece dinner set, a breakfast-in-bed set and an early morning set.[31] In the mid-1930s, the cheapest early morning set which had banded decoration retailed at five shillings in shops like Peter Jones, Selfridges, John Lewis, Waring and Gillow, Harrods and Heals.

Susie Cooper took the marketing and retailing of her products very seriously. She had a London outlet in her own showroom at Audrey House, Holborn, advertised regularly in the trade journals and exhibited at the annual British Industries Fairs and at most of the major design exhibitions in the 1930s. This included the Dorland Hall exhibition of 1933, the British Art in Industry exhibition at the Royal Academy of 1935 and the Paris exhibition of 1937. For all these exhibitions, she designed display stands which were described as 'totally unlike anything else . . . imaginative and at times a trifle audacious'.[32]

In terms of manufacturing, the Susie Cooper Pottery was a small- to medium-scale unit whose production was closely tied to the design skills of its owner. In turn, any new designs were introduced with the paintresses' skills in mind. New decorating developments were accommodated with relative ease within the factory organisation, which was flexible. Susie Cooper found the business arrangement she had made with Harry Wood when she took up space in his Crown Works factory to be ideal. He agreed to produce blank ware (eventually to her own design), so that she was able to concentrate on the decoration of ware and the business organisation of her company. Wood also benefited, as Susie Cooper produced several shape designs for his company, including 'Wren' and 'Jay', which were introduced in the mid-1930s. Added to these were two new shapes which she designed for her own company in 1937 and 1938, 'Falcon' and 'Spiral'. Good design was central to Susie Cooper's aims. She wanted to combine 'low cost with good design' and believed that 'the pottery manufacturer should cost his products to cover production costs not design.' She argued that 'the difference costwise in producing very poor design and very good designs in the pottery industry is negligible – therefore it is the duty of manufacturers to produce the best that they can'.[33] Her pottery was dependent on simplicity in both shape and decoration.

Modernity was the essence of her approach to design. This can be seen in both the streamlined shapes and the innovative decoration she developed in the late 1930s.

The reporters for the two major trade journals of the pottery industry, the *Pottery Gazette and Glass Trade Review* and the *Pottery and Glass Record*, discerned in Susie Cooper's designs a 'feminine' style. In their reporting of the various trade fairs where she had exhibited, they made much of this. In 1932 it was claimed that 'Miss Cooper is a lady who designs from the standpoint of the lady.'[34]

There was a grudging acceptance in other articles that 'the woman's point of view . . . counts for a good deal – in domestic pottery design at all events.'[35]

The Wedgwood company of the 1930s was very different to that of the 1920s, and as a consequence Millie Taplin's role as a designer underwent a change. The need to reorganise the company became urgent in 1930 following the slump in exports and the death of the chairman and managing director, Major Frank Wedgwood. When a young management team, headed by Josiah Wedgwood V, a qualified economist, took over the running of the company in 1930, the previous years' total sales were £158,000, with a net profit of £7,000.[36] According to Josiah Wedgwood V, 'the Etruria works at that date was little changed from the time of Josiah I.'[37] The new management team was made up of Hensleigh Wedgwood, who joined the New York branch of the firm, Tom Wedgwood, who had responsibility for buildings and plant, and Norman Wilson, who was works manager. In 1934, Victor Skellern joined the company as art director to complete the new team. First on the agenda was a programme of modernisation, which began with the introduction of an earthenware glost tunnel kiln, installed in 1930. This oil-fired kiln was developed by Tom Wedgwood and Norman Wilson. Other new developments included flow-line rubber belt production, a quick-drying kiln, many new glazes, such as matt and satin ones, and new wares, such as the translucent pink bone-china which was introduced in the early 1930s.

The aim of modernisation was to enable Wedgwood to compete in the mass-production markets by producing medium-priced tableware. Inevitably, there was a shift in emphasis away from the more complicated hand-painted work which had been done in the 1920s towards simpler shapes and decoration. At this point, Millie Taplin found herself part of a company structure which was quite different to the paternalistic organisation of Wedgwood in the two preceding decades. Wedgwood's new management had imposed a rationalised management structure, with departmental managers and supervisors. Millie Taplin was part of the design section, in which she designed to a brief in accord with company policy determined by its art director, Victor Skellern. He coordinated the activities both of the chief company designers, who, in addition to himself, included Millie Taplin, Star Wedgwood, Keith Murray and Louise Powell, and the freelance designers, who were increasingly introduced as the 1930s progressed.

In its search for a new market, Wedgwood's design and marketing began to overlap with that of Susie Cooper. Like Susie Cooper, the Wedgwood team involved itself in the debates that focused on the pottery industry and they also showed ware at the same exhibitions in order to publicise their new ranges.[38] In 1936 a special Wedgwood exhibition was staged at the Grafton Galleries; it was 'the first public display of the results of recent experiments at Etruria'.[39] These experiments produced a new body, called 'Alpine Pink', which was a self-coloured translucent china.[40] Other wares on display were white fine china, queensware, coloured earthenware and the moonstone and matt designs of Keith Murray. Of the designers of domestic tableware, Millie Taplin contributed the most with 11 designs, including three for the new 'Alpine Pink' body.[41]

Millie Taplin was an important designer at Wedgwood's during this period and she produced a whole range of designs in response to Wedgwood's new policy. All her designs, and indeed those of her colleagues at Wedgwood, were hand-decorated; lithographs were not properly introduced into Wedgwood until the late 1940s. Millie Taplin's Wedgwood designs at the British Art in Industry exhibition of 1935 at the Royal Academy were favourably reviewed in the trade press. Her design 'Green Lattice' won fulsome praise from a severe critic who had attacked ware which was more concerned with aesthetics than practicality. He described Millie Taplin as 'a talented young lady who actually operates at the factory, and of whom it has been said that she is concerned not with art *on* industry, but art *in* industry'.[42]

Wedgwood's sexual division of labour restricted women to design of decoration. Millie Taplin, therefore, was only involved in surface-pattern design at Wedgwood, unlike her male colleagues Victor Skellern and Keith Murray, who also designed shapes. This segregation was due to two factors: first, women were denied experience of forming ware, because of the sexual division of labour which excluded them from skilled jobs in the clay end of manufacturing; second, the legacy of nineteenth-century perceptions of female artistic skills meant that pottery-decorating was thought to require skills which women possessed as part of their nature. Millie Taplin's position in a design team at Wedgwood's gave her little freedom to break out of this 'feminine' stereotype, especially given that her female colleagues were also designers of decoration. This contrasts strongly with Susie Cooper, who could design both shape and decoration because she was able to define her own role in her own company. At first Millie Taplin 'lived and dreamed Wedgwood', but during the 1930s she felt increasingly disillusioned with her lack of progress in the company, something she attributed to her poor educational background.[43] Unlike Skellern, who had won a Royal College of Art scholarship, and Keith Murray, who had trained as an architect, she had no professional qualifications. It was in order to increase her professional status that she became a member of the Society of Industrial Artists in 1934. She also felt some friction with both designers, because Skellern officially approved her designs and Murray unofficially carried much weight in decisions on design.

In 1934 the *Pottery Gazette and Glass Trade Review* noted 'a host of new ideas emanating just now from the Wedgwood studio'.[44] The most striking feature of Wedgwood's product range at this time is that domestic tableware dominated over ornamental wares. Except for Keith Murray's vases, lamps and bowls in matt glazes and John Skeaping's animal figures, the 1936 Grafton Galleries catalogue was filled with domestic tableware at moderate prices. Millie Taplin's contributions to this reveal the extent of her design work, which ranged from stylised floral patterns, such as 'Winter Morn' and 'Falling Leaves', to abstract and geometric designs, such as 'Moonlight'. (See Figs. 6.4 and 6.5). She designed for several different decorative techniques, including banding, gilding, ground-laying, lustres, stencilling and hand-painting. Wedgwood's china shapes, such as the 'Globe' (designed about 1935 by Norman Wilson), were simplified but not as overtly modern as Susie Cooper's, and as a consequence they have a traditional feel. The decoration does, however, show the influence of 1930s' fashionable taste, with its subdued colours and stylised, abstract motifs.

The work of Susie Cooper and the Wedgwood design studio were frequently referred to in the trade journals, in periodicals like the *Studio* and in books on pottery design written in the 1930s.[45] The designs of both won praise from Nikolaus Pevsner; special mention was made of Susie Cooper's lithographs and Keith Murray's designs for Wedgwood.[46] Indeed, Murray's work was the most frequently mentioned. Gordon Forsyth in *20th Century Ceramics*, 1936, suggested that 'the employment of Flaxman by Josiah Wedgwood has its modern equivalent in the work of Keith Murray.'[47] The trade journals tended to be more critical and asked questions about the practicality and ease of production of the designs of both Susie Cooper and Keith Murray.[48] Their work was easily identified because it was stamped with their names. This was a technique adopted by manufacturers who were keen to emphasise the importance of design and the role of the designer. Although

Wedgwood used this strategy in their sales literature, Murray was the only designer at that time to have his own backstamp. The designs of both Murray and Cooper had a high profile with the Modernist writers of the 1930s. In their designs, Pevsner and his supporters could discern the themes of the Modern Movement: the use of modern shapes and patterns, and an interest in advanced processes and technology. It is a paradox that the matt glazed ware designed by Murray and frequently illustrated in key design texts of the 1930s as being an exemplary machine product was advertised in the *Pottery Gazette and Glass Trade Review* as being 'thrown and turned by hand to get the finish and strength that the design warrants'.[49] High on the Modernists' list of criteria for 'good' design was the integration of shape and decoration. In his book *Art and Industry*, 1935, Herbert Read defined the good designer as an abstract artist or sculptor who brings unity to form and decoration. Clearly, in her design work, Millie Taplin was unable to meet this essential requirement to qualify for the label 'good designer' and thereby gain entry to the Modernist histories of 1930s' design.

It is clear from an analysis of pottery design in Britain in the 1930s that neither Keith Murray nor Susie Cooper were by any means typical, and that Millie Taplin, Star Wedgwood, Louise Powell and even Victor Skellern were effaced as designers at Wedgwood by Keith Murray's great popularity with the small but powerful group of writers who set about determining the nature of good design across a range of manufacturing industries. More recently, historians have perpetuated this process by defining pottery design in Britain between the wars in terms of Modernism.[50] This was not the case. Pottery design was dominated by eclecticism, with most manufacturers producing a variety of designs including all types of traditional, *Art nouveau*, Regency and *Moderne* styles. Only a few manufacturers were concerned with Modernism as a distinct theory, and even then their responses were restrained by the economic conditions of the period.

Susie Cooper and Millie Taplin fared differently in the accounts of 1930s writers on design. In the trade journals both women were consistently acknowledged, but in the key design texts Susie Cooper figured prominently while Millie Taplin was ignored. The framework for our contemporary knowledge of their work has been determined primarily by the accounts of this latter group of writers who espoused the values of modernism. As feminist design historians, it is crucial that we challenge these partial accounts; otherwise we will leave intact a design history which overemphasises Modernist design made by men.[51] It is important that we seek out other forms of documentation such as oral history sources, contemporary trade journals, and alternative accounts, which widen our understanding of the work of women designers, and that we examine design as part of a complex system which is responsive to social, economic, political and cultural change. Central to the formulation of a feminist design history is an understanding of patriarchy and the way that this has defined gender, femininity and the sexual division of labour. The roles of Susie Cooper and Millie Taplin as designers in the North Staffordshire pottery industry between the wars are an illustration of many of these themes. Both women worked within an industry which was dominated by labour divisions originating in gender; each had to negotiate her position as a designer in relation to this. For different reasons both were defined or confined by the label 'feminine'. Their opportunities in the pottery industry were tied to a whole set of overlapping issues, including their class backgrounds, the nature of their design education and its relevance to pottery manufacture, the economic health of the pottery industry, manufacturers' attitudes to design and the roles open to women in the industry. Susie Cooper established an independent identity within the male-dominated territory of the North Staffordshire pottery industry. She was a successful business woman and designer. Millie Taplin was without financial support in her role as designer, but within Wedgwood she established herself as one of its foremost designers. Both women made careers in the industry and worked a minimum of four decades. Their work provides an example to women designers today.

Notes

1 Patriarchy as a concept has been defined by various feminist theorists. An early definition is to be found in Millett, Kate, *Sexual Politics*, Abacus, London, 1972, p. 25:

> Our society . . . is a patriarchy. The fact is evident at once if one recalls that the military, industry, technology, universities, science, political offices, finances – in short, every avenue of power within society is in entirely male hands.

The central problem with this definition of patriarchy is that it is a universal and trans-historical form of oppression which is being described. It presents specific problems for a Marxist feminist approach which is located in historical analysis. A useful definition of patriarchy which attempts to overcome this problem of universal oppression is outlined by Pollock, Griselda, in 'Vision, voice, and power: Feminist art history and Marxism', *Block* 6, 1982, p. 10:

> Patriarchy does not refer to the static, oppressive domination of one sex over another, but a web of psycho-social

relationships which institute a socially significant difference on the axis of sex which is so deeply located in our very sense of lived, sexual identity that it appears to us natural and unalterable.

2 For more information see Rose, Peter, *Hannah Barlow: A Pioneer Doulton Artist, 1851–1916*, Richard Dennis, London, 1985; Rakow, Mrs Leonard S., 'The feminine touch at Wedgwood', in the Proceedings of the 12th Wedgwood International Seminar, held at the Smithsonian Institution, Washington, 1967.

3 Callen, Anthea, *Angel in the Studio: Women in the Arts and Crafts Movement 1870–1914*, Astragal Books, London, 1979.

4 Women wrote on this subject in the nineteenth century. See, for example, Lewis, Florence, *China Painting*, Cassell & Co. Ltd, London, Paris and New York, 1884.

5 For a full discussion of this in relation to the contemporary pottery industry, see Sarsby, J.,'Sexual segregation in the pottery industry', *Feminist Review*, No. 2, Winter 1985, pp. 67–94.

6 Women were largely un-unionised because they were unskilled and therefore ineligible to be members of the craft unions. As craft jobs became deskilled with the introduction of new machinery in the late nineteenth and early twentieth centuries, female membership of unions was resisted because it was feared that women would take men's jobs.

7 Whipp, Richard, 'The art of good management: Managerial control of work in the British pottery industry, 1900–1925', *International Review of Social History*, Vol., XXIX, Part 3, 1984.

8 Machin, D. J., and Smyth, R. L., *The Changing Structure of the British Pottery Industry, 1935–1968*, Department of Economics, University of Keele, Newcastle-under-Lyme, 1969.

9 These consisted of the abolition of the 'good from oven' agreement, which had meant that ware had to be in perfect condition after its removal from the kiln and, as a consequence, defective ware was the workers' responsibility and its cost deducted from their wages; the introduction of a 47-hour week with fixed working hours; and the scrapping of stoppages from workers' pay to cover lighting, sweeping, printers' mixing and hot water.

10 For example, Nash, Paul, 'Design', *Pottery Gazette and Glass Trade Review*, 1 May 1925, pp. 767–70; Chermayeff, Serge, 'Modern art from the designer's point of view', *Pottery Gazette and Glass Trade Review*, 1 December 1932, pp. 1504–7; Price, J. F., 'Machinery and pottery design', *Pottery Gazette and Glass Trade Review*, 1 March 1935, pp. 363–9.

11 Haggar, Reginald, *A Century of Art Education in the Potteries*, Stoke-on-Trent, 1953.

12 Forsyth, Gordon, 'Art: Its effect upon the pottery industry', *Pottery*

Gazette and Glass Trade Review, 1 August 1921, p. 1220.

13 For more information see Batkin, Maureen, *Wedgwood Ceramics 1846–1959, Richard Dennis, London, 1982;* City Museum and Art Gallery exhibition catalogue, *Wedgwood of Etruria and Barlaston*, Stoke-on-Trent, 1980.

14 City Museum and Art Gallery exhibition catalogue, *Hand-painted Gray's Pottery*, Stoke-on-Trent, 1982, p. 14.

15 Ibid.

16 For more detail on the importance of class background, see my article 'Women designers in the English pottery industry, 1919–1939', in *Woman's Art Journal*, Fall 1984/Winter 1985.

17 Lodey, Joy, 'A flower was picked and a famous pottery design was born', *Six Towns Magazine*, September 1963.

18 City Museum and Art Gallery exhibition catalogue, *Hand-painted Gray's Pottery*, Stoke-on-Trent, 1982, p. 20.

19 In conversation with author, March 1983.

20 Eric Taplin in conversation with author, April 1985.

21 'Buyers' notes', *Pottery Gazette and Glass Trade Review*, 1 April 1930, p. 593.

22 In conversation with author, March 1983.

23 In conversation with author, September 1986.

24 'Buyers' notes', *Pottery Gazette and Glass Trade Review*, 1 August 1935, p. 975.

25 'Lithographs as a means of pottery decoration', *Pottery Gazette and Glass Trade Review*, 1 June 1933, p. 701.

26 Ibid., p. 713.

27 Florence May Hancock in conversation with author, September 1986.

28 Snodin, Su, 'Susie Cooper: diverse designer', *Antique Collector*, August 1982, pp. 52–5.

29 'Buyers' notes', *Pottery Gazette and Glass Trade Review*, 2 April 1934, pp. 467–8.

30 Buyers' notes', *Pottery Gazette and Glass Trade Review*, 1 October 1932, p. 1251.

31 A breakfast-in-bed set included tea cup and saucer, sugar and creamer, teapot, covered muffin dish, cruet, toast rack, egg-cup, marmalade and butter pots. An early morning set included two cups and saucers, sugar and creamer, teapot and two biscuit plates.

32 'Report on the British Industries Fair', *Pottery Gazette and Glass Trade Review*, 1 April 1932, p. 489.

33 In conversation with author, March 1983.

34 'Buyers' notes', *Pottery Gazette and Glass Trade Review*, 1 October 1932, p. 1249.

35 'Buyers' notes', *Pottery Gazette and Glass Trade Review*, 1 August 1935, p. 975.

36 Wedgwood, John, *A Personal Life of the Fifth Josiah Wedgwood*

1899-1968, Josiah Wedgwood & Sons Ltd, Barlaston, 1979, p. 10.

37 Ibid.

38 These were Dorland Hall in 1933 and the Royal Academy in 1935.

39 Grafton Galleries, op. cit, p. 1.

40 Self-coloured means that the colour is in the body of the clay so that it is permanent.

41 Grafton Galleries, op. cit.

42 'Report on the British Art in Industry exhibition at the Royal Academy', *Pottery Gazette and Glass Trade Review*, 1 February 1935, p. 216.

43 Eric Taplin in conversation with author, April 1985.

44 'Buyers' notes', *Pottery Gazette and Glass Trade Review*, 1 October 1934, p. 1207.

45 For example, Trethowan, Harry, 'Modern British pottery', *Studio*, Vol. 106, 1933, pp. 181–8.

46 Pevsner, Nikolaus, *An Enquiry into Industrial Arts in England*, Cambridge University Press, Cambridge, 1937.

47 Forsyth, Gordon, *20th Century Ceramics*, The Studio Ltd, London, 1936.

48 'Report on the British Art in Industry exhibition at the Royal Academy', *Pottery Gazette and Glass Trade Review*, 1 February 1935, p. 216.

49 Wedgwood advertisement in *Pottery Gazette and Glass Trade Review*, 2 April 1934, p. 438.

50 See, for example, The Open University, *British Design*, A305 course, 1975, and also Arts Council exhibition catalogue, *The Thirties. British Art and Design before the War*, Hayward Gallery, London, 1979. In her recent book *Ceramics*, Bell and Hyman, London, 1986, Frances Hannah explores the issue of Modernism in Britain from a more critical viewpoint.

51 The most recent account of Susie Cooper's work is a major catalogue published to accompany the exhibition of her work held first at the Victoria and Albert Museum, London, and then at the City Museum and Art gallery, Stoke-on-Trent, in 1987. See Eatwell, A. *Susie Cooper Productions*, Victoria and Albert Museum, 1987.

7
Women Architects

Lynne Walker

Many women in Britain today are actively involved in a range of activities and positive initiatives related to architecture. They participate in the creation of the built environment through the design process as architects, planners, engineers and designers and contribute to its production as builders, quantity surveyors, construction workers and, most numerously, as consumers of architecture, users of buildings and the spaces around them.

The work of women architects represents the full range of contemporary professional practice and includes the public sector, private practice and housing associations, while feminist architects concentrate on projects which give priority to women's needs. Although architecture remains a male-dominated activity with **2,502 women currently registered as architects to 25,298 men (about 9 per cent), women in professional practice have made major** contributions to some of the best-known contemporary buildings: the Open University (Jane Drew, completed 1977); the Joseph shops in West London (Eva Jiricna, 1984 and 1986); Heathrow Airport Terminal 4 (Ann Gibson of Scott, Brownrigg & Turner, 1985); the Manchester Crafts Village (Gillian Brown of the Manchester City Architects Department, 1982); the Thames Barrier (Jean Clapham, GLC Architects Department, 1972–8); and the pedestrianisation of South Molton Street (Iona Gibson, 1977). And there are feminist architects, or, more precisely, women who are architects and feminists and who emphasise 'the primary importance of changing the existing design process so that women are involved in decision-making at every stage',[1] who choose to work with women whose interests are not normally represented in the design process – ethnic minorities, disabled and working-class groups – to provide building types which are intended specifically to serve these groups' needs – for instance, health centres, nurseries and women's training centres. Feminist cooperatives, such as Matrix and Mitra and the Women's Design Service (WDS), an information and resource centre, work collectively and challenge conventional design philosophy, which they see as overlooking women's interests in the built environment.

Matrix's architecture is grounded in their study of architectural history and their research into women's past role and position in architecture, which they wrote about in *Making Space: Women and the Man-made Environment*, 1984. But they wear this learning lightly, designing low-key, well-planned and comfortable environments, working together with the client group. Often under-resourced, one of Matrix's best-known buildings, the Jagonari Women's Educational Resource Centre, designed with the Asian women's group Jagonari, was well-funded by a grant of £600,000 from the GLC and brings to a larger scale the best qualities of their earlier projects and buildings. Conscious of its context, which is next to a listed historic building, and with security a major consideration, this substantial four-storey brick building with a two-storey crèche across the courtyard at the rear was designed 'to have an Asian feel about it but . . . to avoid the symbolism of any particular religion'.[2] The dignified and eclectic Whitechapel Road front has a shaped gable, onion-domed flèche and is metal-grilled, for decoration and security, while the carefully planned interior is light and spacious with a reassuring atmosphere of comfort and safety, essential to an Asian women's building in a neighbourhood where racist attacks are commonplace.

With contemporary practice as the starting-point, I want to look back to the late nineteenth and early twentieth centuries at the role and position of women who, as architects and designers of buildings, were active agents in challenging patriarchy, which limited women's activities to the home and unpaid domestic duties. In fact, many of the women who took part in architecture as designers during this period – Harriet Martineau, Agnes and Rhoda Garrett, Ethel and Bessie Charles and Elisabeth Scott – identified themselves with the Women's Movement. The contemporary corollary of this precedent is that women's present under-representation in the design process can only be altered by similar resistance and struggle.

After a brief introduction, I shall first examine the relationship between architecture and patriarchal assumptions about women's role and position in society, from the emergence of the organised Women's Movement around 1850 to the design of the first major public building by a woman in this country, in 1927. Important debates about the nature and value of a woman's role in this period in the context of architecture centred around the campaign for married women's property rights, women's access to professional training and the entry of women into the Royal Institute of British Architects (RIBA). These issues are significant because they generated overt expressions of cultural assumptions and norms which reveal the socially constructed nature of attitudes to women.

The Amateur Tradition

Before the nineteenth century there were two routes to becoming an architect: through the building trades or through an amateur interest in architecture. From the seventeenth century until the end of the nineteenth century, women worked mainly in the amateur tradition, which until the nineteenth century was associated with the aristocracy and upper classes, without having its later pejorative, feminine connotations.

Although it was exceptional for unmarried women to be apprenticed to the guilds which were allied to building, such as carpentry and masonry, married women in the seventeenth century did sometimes receive their husbands' rights and privileges, and widows of carpenters could take apprentices and have 'practical control'[3] of the business. As in carpentry, in architecture some women also practised in succession to their husbands. After the death of her architect husband Elizabeth Deane (1760–1828), for instance, completed the Naval Dockyards and Works on Haulbowline Island, Cork (1822), efficiently carrying on the family firm, which was joined in 1806 by Thomas Deane, her eldest son, who was 'aided by his mother's great ability'.[4]

However, in the seventeenth and eighteenth centuries architectural design by women was, it seems, exclusively associated with the upper class, which had the time, money and leisure for essentially amateur pursuits. For the sufficiently well-off, architecture was a domestic activity and was therefore appropriate to women, because it could be practised completely within the confines of the family estate, which might provide not only the site but also the building materials and workers. Lady Wilbraham, who designed Weston Park (1671), a country house in Staffordshire, guided by Palladio's *First Book of Architecture*, is an early but typical example of a woman architect working in the amateur tradition.[5]

During the Enlightenment, educated women were taught drawing, mathematics and surveying, which gave them an excellent preparation for architecture. For aristocratic women, the design of buildings was seen as an extension of these approved ladies' accomplishments, which in the eighteenth century were often expressed in shellwork rooms and grottoes done in the company of women friends and female members of the family. For instance, in the 1740s the Duchess of Richmond and her daughters devised and executed the decoration of the Goodwood Shell House, which was the result of their serious and expensive avocation.[6]

Upper- and middle-class women in the nineteenth century combined their interest in architecture with a desire to improve the condition of their estate workers. This, in addition to the benevolent end of providing better accommodation, contributed to the consolidation of the position of the landowning classes. George Eliot's Dorothea in *Middlemarch*, who built 'good cottages' for farm labourers to the architect, J. C. Loudon's designs, may have been inspired by Louise, Marchioness of Waterford, artist, friend of Ruskin and founder of the model village of Ford in Northumberland.[7]

This combination of philanthropy and building within the amateur tradition was significant for women architects. Estate improvements, in one instance, led to projects for large-scale public works – an entrance to Hyde Park Corner and a Thames Embankment promoted by Elizabeth, Duchess of Rutland.[8] Nevertheless, more typically, women of education and means practised the twin motives of philanthropy and building exclusively in the domestic sphere. After studying architecture while travelling on the continent for ten years, the cousins Jane (d. 1811) and Mary (d. 1841) Parminter built a chapel, school and almshouses in Exmouth for their foundation to promote the conversion of Jews to Christianity. This complex of buildings was joined to a thatched polygonal stone house, A-la-Ronde (1794), by a garden, all designed by the Parminters.[9] In their house, much of the Regency-style furniture and the interior decoration in patterns of shells and feathers was also designed and executed by them in the eighteenth-century mosaic fashion favoured by lady amateurs.

By 1850 the enormous pool of untrained, single women was recognised as a social and economic problem. Suitable employment had to be found that would be appropriate for what were perceived as women's special feminine qualities, which were not to be polluted by the commercial world and, as Anthea Callen has pointed out, would not weaken male dominance or threaten to undermine the patriarchal order of Victorian society.[10] Married women whose position was particularly invidious often also undertook useful but unpaid employment to preserve their respectability as 'ladies'. In the mid-Victorian period, the approval of middle-class women's mission to the poor gave many of them experience beyond the home, and architecture, although it remained an exclusively male profession until the 1880s, became an area of acceptable activity for middle-class women if it was combined with philanthropy.[11]

One of the earliest and most prominent campaigners for women's rights in Victorian Britain, Harriet Martineau, designed her own house, with a concern for philanthropy which was typical of the nineteenth century but highly uncharacteristic of most private house-builders in that period. She wrote in her *Autobiography* about her efforts to reform the payment of building workers. She was strongly opposed to 'the pernicious custom of the district to give very long credit, even in the case of workmen's wages', and one of her intentions in building her own house 'was to discountenance this and to break through the custom in my own person'.[12]

The other building type which, with domestic architecture, was thought appropriate for women to design was a church or chapel, especially if built as a memorial to a family member. This activity reinforced the idea of women's supposedly superior moral and spiritual nature; their traditional caring role could be expressed in the design of memorial churches and these, like most domestic architecture designed by women before the end of the nineteenth century, were first and foremost monuments to the family. They were for the family's use, designed as an unpaid private pursuit, thought to be comfortably within the domestic sphere, but they nevertheless gave women opportunities to design buildings and established precedents for participation in professional practice. Sara Losh, for example, designed the highly individual and imaginative St Mary at Wrey, in the Lake District, as a memorial to her sister, Katherine (consecrated in 1842).[13] Like the eighteenth-century Parminters, her travels on the continent led her to an appreciation of architecture (in her case, early German and Italian Romanesque), which she treated in a completely personal way, untrammelled by architectural fashion.

The memorial motive and benevolence were combined by Mary Watts in the Mortuary Chapel which she designed for the remains of her husband, the painter G. F. Watts, and executed with her class of the Compton Home Arts and Industries Association, which she had established for the improvement of local young men and women. This provided meaningful, paid employment in the craft-based terra cotta industry. The Watts Chapel was a focus of Arts and Crafts philanthropy and design, and, as Mary Watts described in her book *The Word in the Pattern*, the local villagers joined her in the construction and decoration of this Chapel of Rest, which she had planned in a complex symbolic system. The round-headed Norman doorway, for example, 'is decorated with a terra-cotta choir of *Art nouveau* heads of angels – not cast from a single mould but each a labour of love of a single villager following, to the best of his or her ability, models provided by Mary Watts.'[14]

In addition to architectural design, the philanthropic motive led many Victorian women, such as Angela Burdett-Coutts, Adeline Cooper, Octavia Hill and Henrietta Barnett, to formulate policies and housing experiments which prepared the way for the involvement of professional women architects in the public sector in Britain in the twentieth century.[15] Also under the philanthropic umbrella, many impoverished middle-class women found employment relating to architecture by tracing plans and writing specifications. The tasks assigned to women in architects' offices in the second half of the nineteenth century represent the aspirations of women for personal and financial independence through architecture, but they also stand for the limitations of their role and position both in society and in the profession. The copying of architectural plans by tracing, for example, was an essential element of Victorian architectural practice, but it was the least prestigious and most boring job for the most junior member of the firm. It was demanding and required the attention to detail and the neat, repetitive work which were seen as a natural extension of those feminine qualities which were so apt for women's domestic activities, most notably embroidery. Even when women joined together as they did in the Ladies Tracing Society, their marginal position was exploited, since, as a delighted Halsey Ricardo reported to a client, they worked 'at a very cheap rate'.[16]

Women as a source of cheap, often occasional or part-time labour whose presence is a threat as well as an assistance to the male workforce is a theme which recurs in architecture, as in other professions and trades, throughout the nineteenth and twentieth centuries. But in the 1850s and 1860s the liberal reformers of the Women's Movement, led by Barbara Leigh Smith, an artist and founder of a Cambridge college, who set up the Association for the Promotion of the Employment of Women, were more concerned with women's access to paid work in an expanding free market than with the implications of the capitalist system for employed working-class women.[17]

The debates about women's involvement in architecture often centred on their physical limitations. Yet the participation in the building industry of thousands of working-class women in the much more physically demanding work of nail- and brick-making was not seen as problematic or threatening to women's role, because this, in the context of architecture, was defined in middle-class or upper-middle-class terms. The class bias of the nineteenth-century debates ignored the plight of working-class women in the building industry and produced a myopic view of women's capabilities and their potential as architects, blocking women from full participation in the profession, limiting them to decorative or auxiliary tasks.

In the second half of the nineteenth century the continuum of feminist concerns which included the employment of middle-class women also covered women's education, their entry into the professions and the campaign for married women's rights and female suffrage. Of crucial importance from the mid-century was the commitment of English feminists to reform the married women's property law. Inspired by Harriet Taylor's 1851 article on the first women's rights convention in the United States, a nationwide committee was organised and their work culminated in the Married Women's Property Acts, which went through Parliament in diluted form in 1870 and in the full and final version in 1882. Before this date, under common law married women's property, earnings and inheritances belonged to their husbands. As the distinguished jurist Sir William Blackstone explained: 'By marriage the very being or legal existence of women is suspended, or at least incorporated or consolidated into that of her husband.'[18] This 'virtual slavery',[19] which denied full rights and status to women, was the linchpin of patriarchy and the iron fist in the velvet glove of the doctrine of separate spheres that designated a woman's place as in the home rather than in the commercial world, where she could compete with men for jobs and income.

Architecture, unlike painting, sculpture or the decorative arts, was more clearly a 'profession', practised in offices, often organised by partnerships and in firms, with legal obligations to apprentices, clients and builders through legally binding contracts and under the control of local government boards and bylaws. Architects were sued, often in connection with these contracts, and were bound by local ordinances. Since, under common law, married women were not allowed to make contracts or be sued in their own right, they were thereby precluded from many of the professional responsibilities of architecture. These legal restrictions reinforced and heightened the set of underlying negative assumptions about women's role and value that supporters of the reform of the property laws had organised to oppose. As long as women were the virtual property of their husbands, they did not, and could not, act in a professional capacity as the designers of property – property cannot design property. The removal of the legal, ideological and psychological impedimenta by the Married Women's Property Acts, therefore, had great significance for all women, and it had particular importance for the entry of women into the architectural profession.

In the early 1890s leading architects, such as Norman Shaw and W. R. Lethaby, argued that architecture was an art, not a business or profession, and indeed, between the census of 1887 and that of 1891, the classification and status of the architect altered from 'Industrial Class' in 1881 to 'Professional Class' under 'Artist' in 1891. The implication for women of these new perceptions was that if architecture was an art, and art was an area appropriate for women's participation, then architecture was also a suitable activity for women.

The question remained, however, whether women should be allowed full participation in the profession on an equal footing with men or be restricted to those aspects of practice which were seen as expressions of their femininity. Here male supporters from within the ranks of architects, E. W. Godwin, C. H. Townsend and R. Weir Schultz, often did as much harm as good. For example, the Arts and Crafts architect C. H. Townsend's view was superficially sympathetic but exasperatingly double-edged. Citing the divided skirt and the precedent of women decorators who 'have been known to work for days on scaffolds' to counter the often quoted 'difficulty women would experience as regards the inspection of buildings and the necessary mounting of scaffolding', Townsend concluded quite illogically that 'women's work in an architect's office should be "drawing board work", such as ornamental and other detail drawings, competition sets of plans, schemes of colour decoration, and perspective drawings'.[20]

The extension of the ladies' accomplishment of sketching to architectural drafting was part of a process that was gradualist to the point of being counterproductive. Male gatekeepers allowed women out of their domestic sphere and into architects' offices with the ultimate possibility of becoming architects, but it was felt by C.H. Townsend and others that their femininity created problems from which they had to be protected. In fact, this chivalrous view, which dominated thinking about women's role in architecture in this period, circumscribed their architectural activities and blocked them from becoming designers, the most prestigious role in architectural practice. As women's presence would threaten propriety, the dreaded 'commingling of the sexes' could only be avoided by a system of architectural apartheid which physically separated women from men in their own room, and reduced their status and therefore their threat to the established order. In a separate ' "women-clerks" room' she could be set to work as 'a "draughtswoman" ' which was, Townsend wrote, 'an occupation . . . requiring neatness and delicacy of touch, attention to detail, patience and care, [and] is one which would seem at first blush more likely to find its proficients among women than men.' This patriarchal view saw these characteristics as springing from women's femininity and fitting them most naturally and comfortably on to the lower rungs of the architectural ladder.

Today, when women have become professional architects, a similar pattern of discrimination, implemented through the mechanism of sexual division of labour, remains, according to a recent RIBA survey, which showed that women architects can expect to hold fewer positions of power and influence in architectural practices and that they are more likely to earn less than men throughout their careers.[21]

In addition to the more mundane office jobs, the other area to which women were assigned in the late nineteenth century was design for the decorative arts associated with architecture. In *Women and Work*, edited by one of the founding mothers of the

Women's Movement, Emily Faithfull, E. W. Godwin argued convincingly that women should be trained as architects who could design for the applied arts as well as building, and that furniture and decoration were particularly profitable areas for women architect–designers, as they had been for him.[22] However, Godwin's public position was in fact eroded in practice. The work of Beatrice Philip, Godwin's architectural pupil, and later his wife, shows that his argument was applied in his own office, as it was in the profession generally, in its narrowest sense, with Philip painting the decorative panels for Godwin-designed furniture, such as the satinwood cabinet with four painted panels depicting the seasons, 1877, which is today in the Victoria and Albert Museum. There is no evidence that Beatrice Philip designed buildings, and even at a time when the status of the applied and decorative arts was rising and there was much talk of 'the democracy of the arts', the hierarchy of the arts which privileged architecture over decoration made architecture more prestigious, and more financially rewarding, than decoration. Thus, through the repressive mechanism of the sexual division of labour, women were assigned to the 'lesser arts', without the option that male architect–designers had of architectural design.

In addition to decoration, women's experience in the home and their higher moral sense particularly fitted them, it was reasoned, to interior design. Thus the Domestic Revival and the 'Queen Anne' and Arts and Crafts Movements in the late nineteenth and early twentieth centuries helped promote women's participation in the decorative arts and in interior design, as well as, to a more limited extent, in the architectural profession, at the same time reinforcing the cultural stereotype. As interior designers, architectural theorists and writers, women helped develop the late-Victorian cult of the 'House Beautiful'. Books by women proliferated: for example, *The Drawing Room* (1878) by Lucy Faulkner, *The Dining Room* (1876) by Mrs Loftie, *Beautiful Houses* (1882) by Mrs H. R. Haweis and *Suggestions on House Decoration in Painting, Woodwork and Furniture* (1876) by Agnes and Rhoda Garrett.

The Garretts were not only the best-known women designers and decorators of the period but they were also active feminists, campaigning tirelessly for women's rights and 'the struggle "for the successful removal of intolerable grievances" ',[23] as Rhoda's sister, Millicent Garrett Fawcett, called it. For Rhoda, joined by her cousin Agnes, architecture was the original goal, but at first they found it impossible to get taken on in an architect's office. Undaunted, they occupied rooms in a glass-stainer's office and then were formally apprenticed for 18 months to the architect J. M. Brydon, although they were not given any building work there. Their decoration of a house for Agnes' sister, the pioneer doctor

Elizabeth Garrett Anderson, and other projects, including much of the drawing-room furniture at Philip Webb's country house, Standen, established them as leaders in their field.[24]

The Entry into the Profession

Like medicine and the law, architecture achieved professional status in the nineteenth century, most notably through the founding in 1834 of the professional body, the Royal Institute of British Architects. Although women were not admitted for more than 60 years after its establishment, women, as we have seen, worked as architects without RIBA membership or approval. The 1891 census records 19 women architects in England and Wales and five in Scotland, in addition to the women who designed buildings within the 'amateur tradition', who would not have shown up in the census.

In 1898, Ethel Mary Charles (1871–1962) became the first woman to enter the RIBA. Ethel Charles and her sister, Bessie Ada Charles, who became the second woman member of the Institute in 1900, were articled for three years to George and Peto, after being barred from entering the Architectural Association (AA) in 1893. Ethel Charles supplemented her training by doing university extension courses – in which she received distinctions. After completing her time with Ernest George, she worked as an assistant to the Arts and Crafts architect Walter Cave, and travelled in England, studying Gothic and domestic architecture. In June 1898 she sat the RIBA examinations, almost unnoticed, and her name went forward for Associate membership.[25]

A last-ditch stand was made by Fellows who wished the RIBA to continue as an all-male organisation. W. Hilton Nash circulated a paper, which was signed by other architects who believed that 'it would be prejudical [sic] to the interests of the Institute to elect a lady member'.[26] Ernest George nominated Ethel Charles and vouched for her ability and seriousness of purpose. A motion to adopt all proposed new members was put and the vote stood 51 for and 16 against. A few months later the RIBA came within one vote of reversing this decision to admit women.[27]

Ethel Charles practised with her sister, Bessie Ada, and specialised in domestic work (See Fig. 7.1), entering a competition for labourers' cottages and designing houses, especially in Falmouth, such as Gyllyngvase Terrace, 1907.[28] In 1909 she won first prize for a church design from among 200 competitors in Germany,[29] but her knowledge of London architecture directed her attention to the City and commercial building. However, domestic architecture remained the socially sanctioned sphere for women architects and, ironically, the volume of domestic building was beginning to dwindle just as they started to enter the profession. Edwardian England was characterised by a concentration of wealth, population and building commissions in the cities, and large public commissions were jealously guarded by male architects. Alas, Ethel Charles, the first woman member of the RIBA, holder of its Silver Medal (1905), international competition winner and the first woman to address an architectural society in Great Britain, built, with few exceptions, simple, quiet houses, often for women clients, instead of the experimental large-scale projects which she admired. This 'domestic ghetto', in which the Charles sisters and many women architects have since found themselves, limited women's opportunities and reinforced sexual stereotypes; however, it also directed women architects to the most socially useful area of architecture – housing. It is a measure of the different perspectives in the debates surrounding architectural practice today that while many women of the older generation reject domestic architecture for fear of being typecast, and many professional women architects strive for conventional success through the design of public and commercial buildings, feminist architects, with their commitment to women's needs, consciously embrace the stereotype of women as having a special concern for the family and house design.

Although Ethel and Bessie Charles had made a breakthrough into the male domain of professional architecture, few women followed. It made little immediate difference for other women and few joined them in the ranks of the architectural profession. The Charles sisters' struggle shows that at the precise time women were making their entry into the architectural profession, the pressure to maintain the traditional role and position of women intensified: they were refused admission to the Architectural Association (1893), embroiled in battles at the RIBA over entry (1898 and 1899) and involved in confrontations at the AA (1902). All these specific instances of overt discrimination were combined with the daily strain of being outside established practice, swimming against cultural assumptions in a male-dominated profession.

The idea that women were interlopers in the male workplace held sway long after the institutional barriers had been breached at the RIBA. Ideologically, there was only the merest chink in the rigid sexual division of labour which assigned the practice of architecture to men until the conditions of the First World War and the militant suffragist movement combined to force a reappraisal of women's role. Numerically, little impression was made on the profession until the 1930s. The architect Arnold Mitchell expressed the entrenched nature of these attitudes which circumscribed women's activities when he spoke of the 'very serious problem . . . this problem of sex and the woman taking up work which the man up to the present had been accustomed to consider his own separate province.'[30] Fear that women would take jobs, and lucrative ones at that, which had traditionally belonged to men was often heightened by fears of unemployment – male unemployment. 'Architecture, like all professions, is very much over-stocked',[31] R. Weir Schultz reminded his audience at a conference on employment for women at Caxton Hall, London. Looking back on the previous years of her experience, a young woman architect who was optimistic that women would succeed as architects registered the feeling of otherness and the difficulties of getting work in the 1920s:

> There is a certain prejudice against taking women into architects' offices not because they cannot do the work, but because a tendency to jealousy on the part of men is feared. Accordingly the few girl students who start looking for positions have up to now found it rather difficult to get and to keep them.[32]

After the First World War, a new generation of professional women architects emerged in Britain. Although most architectural schools have no records of when they first admitted women, the Glasgow School of Art (c. 1905) and the University of Manchester (1909) are the earliest now known to have accepted women students.[33] Scotland seems to have been more advanced than England in architectural education for women; Edith M. Burnet Hughes was awarded the Diploma in Architecture in 1914 from the Aberdeen Art School, where she later taught (1915–18). The Architectural Association, which eventually produced the most successful group of women graduates, did not open its doors to women until 1917.

In the 1920s less than a handful of women were taken into the RIBA as Associates: Gillian Harrison (née Cooke), Eleanor K. D. Hughes, Winifred Ryle (later Maddock) and Gertrude W. M. Leverkus. It was not until 1931 that Gillian Harrison (1898–1974) became the first full woman member of the RIBA.[34]

In 1928 Elisabeth Whitworth Scott (1898–1972), a recent graduate of the Architectural Association, won the competition for the Shakespeare Memorial Theatre, Stratford-upon-Avon (see Fig. 7.2). Scott's theatre galvanised British women architects, as Sophia Hayden's Women's Pavilion at the Chicago World's Fair had done for American women in 1893. The Stratford Theatre, apart from its obvious importance as the home for Shakespearean productions, was seen as a victory for all women and as evidence of their ability to win and complete large-scale public commissions. Professor A. E. Richardson praised it as 'the first important work erected in this country from the designs of a woman architect'.[35]

Chosen out of 72 entries by a distinguished jury, Scott's design of

1927 looked to new architectural developments on the continent and in Scandinavia and was put up with the greatest care for craftsmanship and materials by the firm that she formed, Scott, Chesterton and Sheperd. The theatre was completed in 1932. Maurice Chesterton disclaimed 'any personal share whatever in the successful design'.[36]

Elisabeth Scott was representative of women architects of her generation. They tended to be eldest daughters or only children, from a professional background, with an architect relative and often building for women clients. She was conscious that she would encounter discrimination.

After the Second World War, like many other women architects, she moved into the public sector, and in the 1960s she worked for the Bournemouth Borough Architects Department on projects such as the rebuilding of the Bournemouth Pier Pavilion Theatre and Restaurant and the Entertainment Hall of the Boscombe Pier Pavilion.[37]

The sexual division of labour, which Anthea Callen describes in her essay, is the repressive mechanism through which architecture is made gender-specific. Architecture in our society is still thought to be an activity more appropriate for men than women, and in spite of improvements in the law and in access to professional bodies and in spite of better educational opportunities for women, women do not have the same options to participate in architecture that men do.

Women's exclusion from architectural practice is a case study in patriarchal control and economic hegemony. The debates which surround women's participation in architecture are highly charged both emotionally and politically, because architecture physically defines the public and private spheres: to allow women access to the design of architecture therefore threatens patriarchal control of spatial definitions, which are essential to maintain the social, economic and cultural *status quo*.

Although the proportion of women entering schools of architecture is rising, women students are met with a set of pressures which induce feelings of inadequacy and isolation. Architectural schools are male-dominated institutions with their overwhelmingly male student bodies and virtually all-male teaching staff (97 per cent). Without female role-models and with an architectural history constructed of male cult-figures, past and present, a precedent for women's architectural practice is still a very real need of women students and architects alike.

This paper has shown that for hundreds of years women have worked as architects in the 'amateur tradition', as conventional, professional architects, and more recently feminist architectural cooperatives have developed a radical client-centred practice.[38]

However, the relationship of women to architecture remains highly problematic; at one end of the design continuum, the image of the architect remains firmly male, and at the other, the women who use buildings have little control over or understanding of their production. The art historical values of innovation and quality which exist in relation to an aesthetic currently known as 'the mainstream' place women's issues and achievements in a nether-world of 'other', while British cities are planned and designed with scant attention paid to the needs of women, especially those in communities where mobility and spending power are restricted.[39]

Women are not, however, inert or powerless. Struggle and the daily life of architectural practice come together. In dealing with clients, for example, issues of race, class and sex are confronted. As the architect Elsie Owusu has pointed out, the expectation that buildings are designed by white middle-class men for white middle-class male clients 'is challenged every time a black woman [architect] walks on site.'[40]

Notes

1 Boys, Jos, 'Architecture', in *A Resource Book on Women Working in Design*, ed. Tag Gronberg and Judy Attfield, London Institute, Central School of Art and Design, 1986, p. 11.
2 'Jagonari Women's Educational Resource Centre', Matrix, 1987. Both Matrix and the Women's Design Service produce information publications, which I have relied on heavily.
3 Fraser, Antonia, *The Weaker Vessel: Woman's Lot in Seventeenth-Century England*, Methuen, London, 1984, p. 108.
4 'Deane, Sir Thomas Manly, 'Sir Thomas Deane P.R.H.A.', *Cork Historical and Archaeological Society Journal*, 1901, p. 152; in the possession of the Deane family.
5 Hussey, Christopher, 'Weston Park, Staffordshire – I', *Country Life*, 9 November 1945, Vol. 98. p. 819.
6 Jourdain, M., 'Shellwork and grottoes', *Country Life*, 11 February 1944, Vol. 95, pp. 242–3.
7 Darley, Gillian, *Villages of Vision*, Architectural Press, London, 1975, p. 47.
8 Hussey, Christopher, *English Country Houses: Late Georgian 1800–1840*, Country Life, 1958, pp. 122–3.
9 'Some points of view we all pursue', n.d., and other archival material, National Monuments Record Office.
10 Callen, Anthea, *Angel in the Studio: Women in the Arts and Crafts Movement 1870–1914*, Astragal Books, London, 1979, p. 22.
11 See, for example, 'Employment for educated women', *Builder*, 30 November 1861; ibid., 2 November 1883, Vol. 44, p. 622; Walker,

Lynne, ed., *Women Architects: Their Work*, Sorella Press, London, 1984, especially pp. 19 and 37.

12 Martineau, Harriet, *Autobiography*, Vol. 2, Virago, London, 1983, p. 231 (originally published 1877).

13 Wood, M. A., 'Memorial to two sisters: Sara Losh's church of St Mary, Wrey', *Country Life*, 4 November 1971, Vol. 150, pp. 1230–1.

14 Blunt, W. S. 'Guide to the Watts Gallery', n. d. Mary Watts detailed the symbolism of her work in *The Word in the Pattern: A Key to the Symbols on the chapel at Compton*, W. H. Ward & Co., London, n.d. (1905?).

15 Darley, Gillian, 'Women in the public sector', in Walker, op. cit., pp. 37–40. See also, Pearson, Lynn F., *The Architectural and Social History of Cooperative Living*, Macmillan, London, 1988.

16 Letter from Halsey Ricardo to a client, 1883, British Architectural Library.

17 Taylor, Barbara, *Eve and the New Jerusalem: Socialism and Feminism in Nineteenth-Century England*, Virago, London, 1983, p. 279.

18 Quoted by Holcombe, Lee, in *Wives & Property: Reform of the Married Women's Property Law in Nineteenth-Century England*, Martin Robertson, Oxford, 1983, p. 25. Before 1882, married women could go to law to obtain their property rights in Equity, but it was an expensive process, thus limiting it to the wealthy. Transactions afterwards were through a trustee, making dealings protracted and cumbersome.

19 Eliza Lynn Linton, quoted ibid., p. 18.

20 Townsend, C. H., ''Women as Architects', *British Architect*, 31 December 1886, Vol. 26, p. viii.

21 'Report from the Women in Architecture Sub-Group', RIBA, January, 1985.

22 Reprinted in *British Architect*, 12 June 1874, Vol. 1, p. 378.

23 Quoted in Taylor, op. cit., p. 279.

24 Moncure, Daniel Conway, *Travels in South Kensington*, Trübner & Co., London, 1882, pp. 166–71.

25 RIBA Nomination Papers for Associate Membership, 1898, British Architectural Library.

26 'The admission of lady Associates,' *RIBA Journal*, 10 December 1898, Vol. VI, p. 78.

27 *RIBA Journal*, 11 March 1899, Vol. VI, p. 278.

28 Drawings by Ethel and Bessie Charles, held by the British Architectural Library, are listed in *Catalogue of the Royal Institute of British Architects C–F*, Gregg Press, Farnborough, 1972, pp. 22–3. The Charles sisters' London address was 49 York Chambers, a block of flats for professional women with communal facilities,

designed by Balfour & Turner in 1892 (illustrated in *Architectural Design*, 1978, Vol. 48, p. 357).

29 Postcard from Berlin organisers to Ethel Charles, 8 May 1909, in the possession of the family.

30 Mitchell, Arnold, *Builder*, 22 February 1902, Vol. 82, p. 181. This statement was made after a talk by Ethel Charles at the Architectural Association which is extensively reported in this article.

31 Schultz, R. Weir, 'Architecture for women', *Architectural Review*, September 1908, Vol. 24. p. 154.

32 *Birmingham Dispatch*, 5 January 1928.

33 Survey of Schools of Architecture, Beeban Morris and Lynne Walker, 1984.

34 *Architects: Women, Biography File*, British Architectural Library.

35 Richardson, A. E., *Builder*, 22 April 1932, Vol. 142, p. 718.

36 *Daily Telegraph*, 6 January 1928.

37 Letter from Bernard Ward, former Chief Architect, City of Bournemouth, to Nadine Beddington, 9 May 1984.

38 See especially, Matrix, *Making Space: Women and the Man-made Environment*, Pluto Press, London, 1984; *Building for Childcare: Making Better Buildings for the Under-5's*, produced and published jointly by Matrix and the GLC Women's Committee, London, 1986.

39 For the radical role that working-class women played in making and assessing housing policy, see, for instance, Swenarton, Mark, *Homes Fit for Heroes: The Policy and Architecture of Early State Housing*, Heinemann, London, 1981, pp. 62, 91–2 and 97–9.

40 Elsie Owusu, talk on design practice at the ICA, 'The Design World: Women on the Cutting Edge', 21 May 1988.

Part Three
Women in Design Production

8
'If You Have No Sons': Furniture-making in Britain

Pat Kirkham

Furniture-making in Britain is, and has been since the Middle Ages, male dominated at the levels of production, design and entrepreneurial activities. Within the various crafts which comprise furniture-making, only upholstery and, more recently, french polishing, have admitted women in any substantial numbers. Women designers have never featured prominently and the majority of firms are run by men.

The expectations of girls and the concept of what is suitable work for females are bounded by myriad assumptions – spoken and unspoken, acknowledged and unacknowledged. The furniture industry is yet another example of the apparently simple and obvious fact that girls and women are capable of a great many things not normally expected of them if they are given the opportunity. In furniture-making, training and career opportunities mainly went the way of boys, but occasionally girls – if they had no brothers to follow their fathers – and widows if they had no adult sons to carry on the business were able to work as furniture-makers.

This essay examines some of the ways in which women have entered the furniture trade and, at the same time as outlining their contributions to it, considers the nature of their marginalisation within it. It covers a broad historical period in order to indicate similarities as well as differences in attitudes over time towards women in the trade, and it indicates how, in particular circumstances, changing social relations tempered notions of 'fitness' and 'suitability'[1] and women proved themselves fully capable of doing what was deemed to be 'men's work'. It focuses on London, particularly in the later stages, because the capital not only constituted the largest single furniture-making centre in the country but was also generally in advance of the provinces in terms of developments in design, manufacture and business practices, at least until the nineteenth century. The focus is also partly for convenience in that it simplifies the analysis of a long historical period and partly unavoidable because so very little is known about women in provincial furniture-making centres in Britain.

Since first beginning research on the modern London furniture industry some twenty years ago, I have kept a file index of women makers, entrepreneurs and designers, but most of the references remain tantalisingly brief. There is sufficient evidence, however, from the late seventeenth century onwards to suggest that women were never totally absent from the trade and that their roles changed over the years. One specific question which intrigued me, together with my growing interest in how and why women were marginalised in some areas of craft and design but not in others, propelled me into pulling together my disparate material. The question related to the opportunities afforded to the daughters of furniture-makers when there was no male heir in the family.

A general discussion related to the gender of heirs took place after Anthea Callen's paper on the sexual division of labour in the Arts and Crafts Movement at a conference on women and design organised by the Design History Society in 1985 (a later version of which is printed in this volume). The roles of May Morris, daughter of William Morris, as designer, embroideress and business woman were the subject of discussion. The question of whether she would have received quite the same encouragement in all those roles within the firm of Morris and Co. had she had a brother was one I felt obliged to raise. Possibly not, seemed to be the answer. Even with someone who distanced himself from so many of the orthodoxies and restrictions of Victorian values as William Morris, it is difficult to argue that children of both sexes would definitely have been treated equally, would have received the same encouragement to design as well as to execute objects, let alone run part of the firm. Would a male child have ended up as a designer/maker of embroidery, a 'woman's craft', or might he have entered a 'male' craft such as furniture-making?

The topic emerged again in my discussions with Ray Hille, one of the few women to run a furniture-making firm in Britain in the half-century after the First World War. Encouraged by her Jewish émigré father, who set up business in London's East End at the beginning of the twentieth century, she not only developed her talents as a designer but also succeeded him as head of the firm. Would this have happened had Salamon Hille had a son? Probably not, was the answer. Yet Ray Hille was thrilled to learn that she followed in the tradition of Catherine Naish, a royal furniture-maker of the eighteenth century who took over her father's royal commission in 1759 because there was no male heir.[2] This was confirmed by recent discussions with Doris Young, designer and managing director of Evans of London, who took over running the family firm after her father's death in 1943. She has no doubt that this only happened because there was no male heir.

The main bulk of this chapter deals with craft and entrepreneurial activities but there is also a small section on women as designers. This leads into the short case studies of Ray Hille and Doris Young, both of whom acted as designers as well as entrepreneurs (though Doris Young much less so than Ray Hille). Together with the section on women and war work, they highlight some of the ways in which the dominant patterns within the furniture trade have been broken through, if not broken down.

The Medieval World

Within furniture-making the notion of capability has often rested on the thorny question of physical strength: were/are women strong enough to undertake the physically demanding aspects of certain furniture crafts? There can be no doubt that in the Middle Ages the woodworking side of furniture-making was arduous. Joiners and carpenters worked in solid wood which was heavy to cut, lift and shape. Indeed, as late as the eighteenth century, certain trade guides commented that youths (and the assumption was that they were male) wishing to become furniture-makers needed to be physically strong. Even in the twentieth century the heavy nature of some of the work was cited by male furniture-makers as a reason why women should not be allowed to enter their craft. Yet hard physical work was not unknown to medieval women: agricultural labour, for instance, was even more physically exhausting and dirty then than it is today. There is no reason to believe, therefore, that medieval women could not have stood up to the physical demands of furniture-making. There is a certain similarity here to the discrepancy between the still-pervasive myth that British coal-mining is too tough and dangerous a job for women and the reality of women working in coal mines in both the USA and the USSR. However, although we know that some women did work as furniture-makers, the evidence, scanty and scattered as it is, does not suggest that men and women participated either in equal numbers or experienced equal opportunities within the trade in the Middle Ages.

Feminist historians have done an excellent job in rescuing the lost world of medieval women. They have shown how the dominant ideology about women, which came through religion and aristocratic power and confirmed women as inferior, was tempered by social reality and particularly by the experience of life in the expanding urban centres which afforded women certain freedoms. They have emphasised that women were 'participant workers in the household unit of production', the main unit of production in medieval Europe.[3] Female producers and retailers were active in a variety of occupations including shipwrights, armourers, bakers, brewers, barber-surgeons, bow-stringers and tanners. Clearly not all medieval women were the saintly maidens of literature and the church, or the anonymous peasants working in the field that popular history would have us believe.

Having established the important part played by women in the medieval economy, however, it is necessary for historians to strike a note of caution. In our enthusiasm to prove women's capabilities by pointing to evidence from the past, we must not overstate the position if the evidence does not warrant it. This is particularly true of furniture-making, where it is difficult to know how far to generalise from a few isolated references to women working, particularly when the evidence relates to different towns in Europe. Some women certainly made furniture, but how many and in what proportion to men is difficult to say. Nowhere do women appear to have worked in the trade in anything like the same numbers as men. A feminist analysis needs to be applied to the evidence in hand even if it leads to the conclusion that women were largely excluded from the areas of work in which we are interested as historians. Indeed, it is not surprising that women should have been marginalised in furniture-making, or any other occupation, given that medieval society was structured so as to exclude women from public and political life. They could not be jurors in courts, serve as borough officials, aldermen and mayors or hold official positions within the manor. The dominant ideology reflected and reinforced the subordination of women: the church encouraged women to model themselves on a Madonna who represented purity, gentleness, domesticity and gentility, while in literature genteel ladies were admired from a distance according to the complicated etiquette of courtly love. Many poor women in the medieval period were denied jobs associated with gentility but nevertheless the ideological importance of gentility in defining femininity partly explains why furniture-making – as opposed to, say, silk weaving – was a male-dominated craft in the more prosperous urban centres. The woodworking side of furniture-making was dirty as well as laborious and could in no way be considered genteel. By contrast, upholstery was considered more respectable. This was partly because the main cost of much furniture lay in the expensive hangings or coverings used: the slightest mistake in cutting and sewing proved extremely costly. It was also a clean craft. There was no dust generated, as with woodworking, and therefore decent clothes could be worn at work without fear of spoiling them. It is clear that by the late seventeenth century more women furniture-makers were associated with upholstery than with any other aspect. This was probably also true for the Middle Ages, but there is insufficient evidence at the moment to bear this out. Sewing was, of course, a skill traditionally taught to girls in the home and therefore it appeared a 'natural' occupation for them to follow. Yet men also worked at upholstery: they learned to cut and sew as part of a craft apprenticeship. Furthermore, in the seventeenth and eighteenth centuries men were the only upholsterers allowed to work with the most expensive materials,[4] and it is very likely that this was a medieval tradition, of the sort that existed within the craft of embroidery.[5]

There were no formal restrictions to women entering any of the furniture-making crafts or any of the guilds which represented them. The origins of the guild system in Western Europe are obscure but, from at least the twelfth century, these collective organisations were the main institutions whereby monopolies over particular crafts were practised: there were strict controls on apprenticeships, prices and wages were regulated and high standards of production were enforced. Women furniture-makers were in guild membership in the English provinces in the reign of Richard II (1377–99) and in 1612 the Upholsterers' Company in Salisbury drew up rules which made reference to sisters as well as brothers. Yet one should not leap to the conclusion that men and women were equal within the guilds, which were very much male institutions. They were run by men, mainly for men. Their language was one of male dominance. Women were allowed to learn a craft by right of *patrimony*, that is by virtue of one's father having been a member of the guild. The London companies were run by *Masters* and few women ever joined the ranks of the Livery (one of the main ruling bodies within each company). 'Brotherhood' predominated; 'sisters' were the exception rather than the rule. The provisions made in most guild rules or charters for widows (not widowers) rested on the assumption that members were male.

Women were mainly involved in the guilds through marriage or birth, acting as *assistants* to their husbands or fathers and thereby supplementing the family/household earnings. Even those few guilds which formally prohibited women from employment made exceptions in favour of wives and daughters. Widows also sometimes carried on the business after their husbands died. Women may have been 'participant workers' in the household economy but their role was defined by their particular relationship to a male furniture-maker. Furthermore, whatever her precise task within the trade, a woman was also expected to run the household as well. Medieval working women did two jobs, just as working women do today.

Some women worked independently of their husbands at their craft or trade. It was customary for the wives of freemen of London and certain other towns and cities throughout Europe to be allowed to work as 'sole merchants' or '*femmes soles*'.[7] In early sixteenth-century London this custom spread to the wives of non-freemen as women became increasingly involved in production outside the home. It was these women who most resembled the small independent male artisan producers. There was one major difference: if a married woman took an apprentice, no matter whether she was a *femme sole* or not, the customs of the City of London decreed that the apprentice be bound to both the woman and her husband, even if the latter worked at a completely different trade and knew nothing of his wife's trade. The regulation ensuring that the husband was absolved of any responsibility for the debts of his wife indicates the independence of the *femme sole*, but it should be remembered that it was introduced to protect the male.[8]

Some of the *femmes soles* may have been women who trained as craft apprentices, but even less is known about this aspect of women's work and training. Some women took on only female apprentices; indeed, the reference to the custom of the City of London requiring that apprentices be bound to the husband as well as the wife applied only to female apprentices. The custom appears to have rested on an assumption that women took on only female apprentices although they did occasionally bind boys. An all-female group of apprentices constructed a particular and different atmosphere in the craft workshop and household, where apprentices lived for the duration of their training from the age of 13 to 21 years. This undoubtedly appealed to many parents and guardians of young girls: they could rest assured that their charges were not in the way of the daily temptations, from general time wasting and lack of concentration on their work to overt sexual relations, that they would have faced in a household which also included male apprentices, whose reputation for riotous behaviour was notorious.[9]

At first consideration it would seem that another reason why parents and guardians preferred girls to be bound with a woman was the latter's knowledge and understanding of the biological and emotional changes associated with adolescence, particularly menstruation. This understanding would have been there, however, had the girl been apprenticed to a married man, because his wife would have been in charge of looking after the apprentices. It may have been that there was also a preference for girls to be taught the details of their craft in the workshop by a woman rather than a man, but the evidence is not clear.

As it was, most women furniture-makers did not learn about furniture-making through a full seven-year craft apprenticeship as most male furniture-makers did. On the contrary, daughters learned about the work as they grew up and wives learned about it after marriage. The guilds recognised the economic necessity of using the 'free' or cheap labour of these women. They also acknowledged that, at a time when life expectancy was not long and death struck indiscriminately, suddenly and frequently, it was necessary for wives or daughters to carry on a business. It was customary in London for this to happen. There is increasing evidence of bequests of tools of the trade from husband to wife in the fourteenth century, as workshops grew in size, and this was to be the pattern throughout the later Middle Ages.[10] This was the changing social reality, noted by historians, which allowed women to step outside prescribed roles – even if for some of them it was only until a son or nephew was old enough to take over the business or they retired from the trade altogether on remarriage.

Although in times of economic expansion the old taboos about what was fit work for women fell away, they were re-constructed at times of economic contraction, as in the fifteenth century, for instance, when male-dominated craft institutions attempted to exclude women from the labour-force.[11] As today, the marginalised position of women made them particularly vulnerable to the ups and downs of the economy. In general, however, the increased opportunities for women to enter the crafts opened up a new world outside the immediate domestic environment and household concerns and brought a new dimension to their lives.

The Seventeenth and Eighteenth Centuries

Major changes took place in furniture-making in England after the Restoration of 1666, when the new craft of cabinet-making was introduced. Trade guides noted that this craft, which produced the sophisticated veneered furniture previously only associated with foreign craftworkers, was 'somewhat laborious' but emphasised that a would-be apprentice needed 'more ingenuity than strength'.[12] Since not even the greatest male chauvinist has denied the ingenuity of women, one might expect more women to have entered furniture-making. This did not happen: indeed, the proportion of women working in the woodworking side of the London trade probably decreased in the seventeenth and eighteenth centuries. This was because the very capitalistic forces which had assisted the entry of women into crafts and trades in the later Middle Ages had created such wealth by this time that the hallmark of the successful tradesman was that his wife did not work either at a craft or assist him in his business. The male success in the world of work was reflected in the relocation of the wife to the domestic sphere – to a supposedly leisured existence.

Little is known of those women who continued to work at the bench. A minute proportion – less than 1 per cent – of furniture-making 'masters' and apprentices were women.[13] The numbers were highest in the 1710s and 1720s and held steady from the 1730s to the 1770s, after which they fell dramatically. Since most women worked in upholstery, it is not surprising to find that 75 per cent of women bound to women 'masters' were in that craft (although this amounted to very few women in all). In general, the fees charged by women taking on apprentice upholsterers were roughly the same as those charged by men. However, what was then the highest fee charged by any London furniture-maker was given to Sarah Goodchild, upholsteress, in 1746 by Thomas Hoare when his son, also Thomas, was indentured for £157 10s.[14] This shows that certain women had equal status to men, although the path to success was more easily reached within the area of upholstery because it was viewed as a domain appropriate to women.

The wives of the poorest craftsmen working on their own continued to be forced by economic necessity to assist their husbands at the bench. Those married to craftsmen who ran larger and more prosperous firms were usually so closely involved in the running of their husband's firms that they were described as 'mistress of the managing part' of them.[15] Management became an increasingly important part of business activity as firms grew in size and complexity.[16] As furniture-makers abandoned their craft work for supervisory and entrepreneurial activities, so too did their wives. It was in this area, rather than as makers, that women played their most significant role within the furniture trade in the eighteenth century.

Many of these women were themselves daughters of craftworkers or tradesmen, brought up in a household which included apprentices and familiar with workshop customs and practices. They helped their mothers run the household and sometimes assisted their fathers in the business. These women transferred skills of management learned in the household – the private domestic sphere – to the public sphere of the workshop. They helped their husbands manage the firm, taking charge of the book-keeping and accounts, as well as standing in for them when they were absent from the workshop. Indeed, the ability of a woman to run the business not only in a husband's temporary absence but in the case of death was something Defoe recommended craftsmen/entrepreneurs to look out for when choosing a wife.[17]

Examples of wives and daughters running a firm can be seen in the royal household accounts of the eighteenth century. Several women appear as royal-warrant-holders, supplying furniture to the Lord Chamberlain's Office, which was also in charge of the repair and maintenance of furniture.[18] These royal commissions were much sought after, not only for their prestige but also because they brought in regular work and income. None of the royal furniture-makers who were female seems to have been an independent *femme sole*. The first woman who appears in the royal accounts after the Restoration is Elizabeth Price, who, in 1685, took over the post of 'Royal Joyner' after the death of her husband.[19] The same post, by then titled 'Royal Joyner and Chair maker', was later taken over by Catherine Naish, who held it for 13 years from 1759, after it had been held by her father, Henry Williams, for nearly 30 years.[20] Women also worked as royal upholsterers. For instance, Sarah

Gilbert took up such a post in 1729 after the death of John Gilbert, her husband or son,[21] while Hannah Farmborough[22] and Lucy Gilroy[23] took over their late husbands' appointments in 1773 and 1783 respectively.

Besides the royal furniture-makers there were other female makers operating in London in the eighteenth century. Sarah Touzey ran a carving firm in Bloomsbury[24] and leading up·holsteresses included Martha Williamson and Sarah Goodchild.[25] Not all of these women were widows carrying on their late husbands' businesses. It has been assumed that the Ann Buck whose trade card (see Fig. 8.1) indicates that she was a dealer in furniture and upholstery in Holborn carried on the business of her husband, Henry Buck, after his death in 1750. A member of the Joiners' Company Livery, Henry Buck was a wealthy cabinet-maker with a workshop in St Paul's Churchyard. Ann appears to have worked independently, however, because not only did she work from a separate address for the nine years before Henry's death but she also ran a different type of firm – he made and sold furniture while she bought and sold it.[26]

One of the better-known examples of a widow continuing a business is that of Alice Hepplewhite, who, two years after the death of her husband, George, published *The Cabinet-maker and Upholsterer's Guide*, 1788, a folio volume of designs from drawings by A. Hepplewhite & Co., which was the largest since the publication of Thomas Chippendale's *Director* in 1754. It proved such a success that a second edition was issued in the following year and a third in 1794.[27]

As early as the 1720s, however, Daniel Defoe commented that some women acted as if they were ashamed to be the wives of tradesmen.[28] This tendency increased as the size and scope of furniture-making firms expanded in the second half of the eighteenth century. Trained craftworkers who ran the larger firms no longer touched the tools of their trade. They were primarily entrepreneurs.

One such was John Cobb, a leading upholsterer of the second half of the eighteenth century, a haughty character who was described as strutting around his workshop 'in full dress of the most superb and costly kind . . . giving orders to his men'.[29] Such a man would have regarded it as a social stigma for his wife to work; she had to pretend she was a gentlewoman, in the manner of their close friends the Halletts. William Hallett was one of the most successful furniture-makers of his day, so successful that in 1747 he bought a country estate formerly owned by the Duke of Chandos, an act which Horace Walpole labelled a 'mockery of sublunary grandeur'.[30] Figure 8.2 shows William Hallett, his wife and family in the ideal situation to which all furniture-makers aspired:

both husband and wife liberated from work and living as country gentry.

The Nineteenth and Twentieth Centuries

One of the major developments in the nineteenth century was the growth of the cheap furniture trade, which supplied an expanding lower-middle-class and respectable working-class market. Beginning in the East End of London in the 1830s, and growing enormously from the 1870s, the 'dishonourable trade' (as it was known, to differentiate it from the quality or 'honourable trade') was characterised by cheap labour, independent masters, small work-shops, an extensive division of labour, hand production, low wages, long hours and a lack of trade union organisation. Cheap goods were not produced in large, heavily mechanised factories – that was not to come until the inter-war years and later – but by human power in highly exploitative conditions.[31]

The overwhelming majority of East End workshops were run by men. A few women worked on their own as independent 'masters' or employed two or three assistants, just as the men did, but these were few and far between. In general, women worked as employees, mainly in upholstery, french polishing and in fancy cabinet-making. Their cheap labour was often undercut by the even cheaper labour of young boys or the 'free' labour of the furniture-maker's own children (girls and boys), who, from about the age of six, were put to doing simple finishing work.[32]

Fancy cabinet-making

There was a distinct sexual divison of labour within fancy cabinet-making, which was also known as cabinet small work. A great deal of this was made for and used by women. Indeed, the word 'ladies' was prefixed to a variety of pieces, such as jewel boxes, dressing-cases, work tables, work boxes, portable desks and writing-tables. Yet the only contribution women were allowed to make was the lining of the interiors of 'cheap luxuries', such as jewel boxes and dressing-cases, with paper, silk, satin or velvet. The women who did this work, which required some skill, were usually the wives of fancy cabinet-makers, but such was the sexual division of labour that the part which required 'greater care and nicety', such as the lining of jewel cases with velvets, was given over to men.[33]

French polishing

Another division of labour based on gender developed later in the nineteenth and early twentieth centuries as increasing numbers of women worked as french polishers. Although there was no difference in the actual craft process carried out by female and by male polishers and they both had to use the same amount of 'elbow grease' when polishing, women generally tended to work on the smaller items, while the very largest pieces of furniture were reserved for men to polish, the implication being that they had greater stamina.[34] The inter-war years saw great changes in this part of the trade, mainly as a result of the introduction of quick-drying cellulose lacquers, which gave a hard finish and were applied by mechanically operated spray-guns. Many polishers found themselves made redundant as the new work was done by less skilled people, often women, in working conditions which were widely acknowledged to be rather dirty, messy and unpleasant.[35]

Upholstery

Women continued to be more strongly represented in the 'soft' side of the trade than in any other. In upholstery a division of labour began to emerge in the early nineteenth century between the two main tasks of stuffing and covering. Both men and women worked as chair-stuffers in the mid nineteenth century, but there was a degree of division in this craft according to gender; the cutting and covering of better-quality items was always left to men. When Henry Mayhew reported on the working conditions of upholsteresses in 1849, he noted that they cut out only the cheaper chintz or holland cases which protected furniture stuffed and covered by male workers.[36] However, women and men both undertook sewing and making up curtains, cases and bed furniture as well as joining together carpet pieces.[37]

Although many upholsteresses were classified as unskilled because they had not undergone any formal training, sewing was traditionally taught in the home and therefore they achieved very high levels of expertise. Its cleanliness and association with the 'feminine' skill of sewing ensured that it continued to be considered sufficiently genteel to be undertaken by women who were 'sober and steady' and of respectable appearance. Henry Mayhew reported that 'there are more old maids employed in the upholstery business than any other.'[38] Many were middle-aged and some were also the widows of upholsterers, but they had one thing in common – they were dependent upon their own wages for their livelihood. The low wages of the East End made that a pitiful livelihood for many of them.

Women and War Work

Just as in the medieval period the dominant ideology concerning women and work shifted according to changes in material circumstances, so in the modern period the two world wars of the twentieth century show most clearly the same process. During the First World War the high rate of male volunteers for the armed forces among furniture-makers ushered in many changes in the trade. Women were brought in as emergency workers and, except for exceptionally heavy work, undertook every process in the trade as and when it was required of them. They also undertook 'war work', such as covering the body and wings of a wooden aircraft with linen.

The official National Amalgamated Furnishing Trades Association (NAFTA) view of women working in the industry was as follows:

> We must act with caution, in the interests of our men, in the interest of the nation, and also in the interests of women, to prevent the sweaters of our trade using the war period, and the plea of patriotism to further their own ulterior motives to secure cheap female labour, to the detriment of the trade, the men employed in it, and the thousands of our members fighting their country's battles in all parts of the world. *One doesn't want these men to come back and find their places taken by women* at one half of the rate. Innovation may be necessary; *women may have to be employed*: but to secure proper safeguards is a duty imposed on us all.[39]

The reference to women working at one half of the male rate is an exaggeration. A national wartime agreement of 1916 between employers and unions fixed women's rates at two-thirds of the male rate for comparable work and also stipulated that women working in furniture-making should belong to an appropriate trade union.

Before the war women had worked mainly in polishing and upholstery, but during it they also worked at cutting and preparing wood as well as at packing and labouring. Some drove the horse-drawn vans and carts in which furniture was moved from shop to shop and finally delivered to the customer. Consequently, NAFTA was forced to change its rules to allow women working at such jobs into union membership – albeit 'emergency membership' for the duration of the war only. By the end of the war, the union as a whole had 3,000 women members, representing over 13 per cent of the total membership – a figure not exceeded until 1943.[40]

Women had proved themselves fully capable of performing all the tasks asked of them, but most did not remain in their jobs after the war. These jobs were taken over by the returning ex-servicemen, who came home expecting a 'land fit for heroes'. Although certain employers had noted the economic advantage of exploiting women's cheap labour, they did not pursue the idea after the war.

At one level they had a forceful union to deal with and it would also have seemed unpatriotic and uncaring to deny work to ex-soldiers, but it went deeper than that. The dominant ideology relating to women and work, particularly the ideas about women's inability to handle demanding physical work that still existed in furniture workshops and factories, together with traditional notions of what was 'men's work' and what was 'women's work', had been set aside rather than effectively challenged. They remained so strong after the war that they overrode any consideration of economic advantage on the part of furniture employers, who never seriously tried to keep women at the jobs they had occupied during the war. Most women also accepted their experiences in wartime as 'exceptional' and either left the industry or returned to their old jobs without giving voice to any protest.

Those women who remained in the trade worked mainly in upholstery and french polishing, with a few in the caning and rushing of seats. One of the unions representing male workers in the latter trade, however, resolved in 1919 to oppose vigorously women's 'intrusion into our shops, and to voice our resentment against their organisation'.[41] This policy, adopted by the United French Polishers' Society was clearly sexist but they justified it by arguing that women were cheap labour and cheap labour brought down the trade as a whole. The society could, of course, have argued and fought for better pay and conditions for female polishers, but instead it chose to actively block their entry into the trade. In 1925 matters came to a head when the UFPS refused to sit on the French Polishers' Federated Committee (the joint committee representing all unions with polishers in membership) as long as NAFTA sent a woman delegate. The latter organisation stood by its decision to have a woman represent their largely female membership. The UFPS replied by refusing to sit with what it called 'the representatives of cheap labour, be it male cheap labour or female cheap labour'.[42] This was one of the issues which kept the two societies from amalgamating until 1969.

The Second World War again saw women take up jobs, including machine sawing, previously done by male furniture-makers. By 1944 one in four workers in the furniture industry was female. Many women who worked as french polishers before the war transferred to aircraft production. They performed jobs such as picking up and putting in tiny screws which were considered suitable for 'nimble female hands' yet classified as unskilled in terms of pay. Some women worked at assembling aircraft on an equal basis as men – equal, that is, in everything but payment.

The influx of women necessitated a change in the way in which both the furniture trade and women were perceived. Furniture factories were physically demanding places in which to work and in wartime women proved that they were up to the tasks before them. This was not only widely acknowledged but also praised, because it was a valuable part of the war effort. After the war, however, there was great pressure on women to return to the home, and certainly to vacate male jobs. Yet even at the height of women's retrenchment in the home in the 1950s and 1960s, female membership of the furniture trade unions remained as high as 15 per cent (as opposed to only 4 per cent in the 1920s).[43] What those women who remained in the industry lost, however, was the right to work at 'male' jobs in machining and assembly work. After the war women went back to their traditional jobs in upholstery and polishing. A few women were allowed to stay on in veneering but, once again, this was because it was considered that female fingers were more nimble than male ones and therefore better suited for the cutting, jointing and matching of veneers.

The changing roles of women during both world wars indicate the extent to which material circumstances affected the ways in which women were regarded in society and opened up new opportunities for them. However, the enduring strength of the dominant ideology must not be underestimated. Set aside for the duration of the war, it emerged only slightly changed and still based on the premise of men's superiority. The opportunities offered by the war were temporary, just as the taking over of her husband's business by a widow in the seventeenth century, until either a son came of age or she remarried, was temporary. Nevertheless, those opportunities did allow women access to areas of work otherwise proscribed and afforded individual women not only an economic livelihood but also considerable satisfaction and fulfilment.[44]

Design

If the historical evidence concerning women and production in the furniture trade is scanty and problematic, then that concerning women and design is even more so. Part of the problem lies in what constituted design before the rise of the professional designer – a long process which began in mid-eighteenth-century London but was still only slowly gaining pace a century later. Furniture was either designed by specialists, such as architects, artists, engravers and others working outside the craft, or by craftworkers trained in traditions which involved a slow evolutionary process of change in form as well as construction. Apart from the few known signed designs by individual designers, the majority of pieces produced since 1750 are of what is known today as 'anonymous' design.

The difficult question is how far this anonymous design was simply a continuous refinement of traditional forms or, as capitalism and sophisticated markets developed, a more complex response to novelty and fashion or a combination of both. We do not know at what stage design took on a more self-conscious role, but in a major world trading centre such as London it must have been from the late Middle Ages at least. Certainly by the late seventeenth and early eighteenth centuries drawing and design were taught as part of a craft apprenticeship to carvers and cabinet makers. Trade guides pointed out that unless youths developed the ability to invent, anticipate or capture the latest trends in style they would never be successful financially.[45] In other words, design was acknowledged as an important element in the selling of objects. Its significance increased until eventually a division of labour emerged between those who made and those who designed.

So where does this leave women? It can be assumed that some of the women who, as has been shown, worked in the furniture trade before the mid eighteenth century also designed furniture. Therefore, they must have been responsible for some (even if it was a small percentage) of the 'anonymous' pieces of English oak and other furniture so greatly admired by collectors today. Beyond that it is not possible to speculate at present.

As a specialised design training, as opposed to a craft training, developed from the second half of the eighteenth century, there is no evidence that women were involved. Indeed, the male domination of this area seems almost complete. It was male craft-trained entrepreneurs such as Thomas Chippendale and John Linnell who took advantage of the new design-teaching at Hogarth's and other drawing academies in mid-eighteenth-century London and who spent part of their professional life as designers.[46] In an attempt to establish themselves in the public eye as designers, certain craft-worker entrepreneurs published pattern books of furniture and ornamental designs in the 1740s, 1750s and 1760s, but, once again, no women were involved.

It has recently been suggested that the designs in the folio of designs mentioned earlier published by A. Hepplewhite & Co. in 1788, two years after the death of George Hepplewhite, might be by his widow.[47] There is certainly no proof that the unsigned designs are by George Hepplewhite, a master cabinet-maker of London;[48] indeed, it is one of history's many ironies that we so venerate a man who is one of the most elusive characters of furniture history and was clearly not one of the leading manu-facturers or designers of his own day. Since his authorship of the designs in the famous Hepplewhite pattern book is open to question, could they have been the work of his widow, Alice, of whom even less is known? Although one wonders why the question has not been raised until recently, there are, unfortunately, no sound grounds for attributing the designs to her – it is certainly not enough to say that the designs themselves are 'of feminine and delicate furniture'.[49] This type of description is commonly used of the light, elegant furniture fashionable in the early and mid-1780s, yet it was not the prerogative of one gender either in terms of design or consumption.

Angelica Kauffmann (1741–1807), the Swiss artist who trained in Italy before working in London, where she became a founder member of the Royal Academy, is often cited as the one woman who was involved in furniture design. Some of her engravings were used as the basis for decorative panels and other painted or marquetry work on furniture, but she does not appear to have designed decoration specifically for furniture,[50] as did a group of male Swedish furniture-maker/designers who lived in London in the 1790s.[51] Kauffman is important in that she was a well-respected artist of her day, but, given the present state of knowledge, we cannot claim that she was a woman artist who designed decoration for furniture, let alone furniture itself.

By the 1860s most of the leading furniture firms employed designers on some basis or another, but none were women. At one level it would appear that the Arts and Crafts Movement, with its rejection of commercialism and its provision of an alternative sphere, ought to have changed all that. The enormous popularity of craft work, particularly from the 1880s, together with the general movement towards the emancipation of women, encouraged greater numbers of women into schools of art and design to study craft subjects.

In chapter 11, 'The Arts and Crafts Alternative', Lynne Walker shows that the number of women designers and designer–makers working within the movement increased greatly in the period c. 1880–1920, but furniture was not one of the main areas affected. Furniture remained problematic because of the question of 'suitability'. Women did not establish workshops which placed a great emphasis on furniture-making or design; there was no female equivalent of Ernest Gimson or Sydney Barnsley whose names today are synonymous with Arts and Crafts furniture.[52]

There were few job opportunities within the trade. This was compounded by workshop practice being seen as the basis of good design at the turn of the century. Links between art schools and local commercial firms were emphasised and the teaching of young workers already apprenticed to a craft became the central focus of design educationalists such as W. R. Lethaby (Central School of Arts and Crafts) and B. J. Fletcher (Leicester School of Art). This meant that women who did not have access to a particular trade through apprenticeship were also denied a training in that area by the schools of art and design.

The Home Arts and Industries Association, founded in 1884 to encourage the practice of handicrafts and morally uplift workers, particularly women, by filling 'empty spaces' in their lives, encouraged the design of furniture, but the women involved mainly concentrated on designing patterns for woodcarving, or designing and executing wood-inlay work.[53] Concentration on decorative work was one way women found of circumventing the constraints upon them. Such work fitted in with a view of woman as both decorative and decorator; the beautiful beautifier of objects and homes. If the decoration of furniture was acceptable for women because of its associations with domesticity and decoration, its associations with the fine-arts gave it respectability and gentility. Some of the women involved in decorating furniture worked independently of men, but others, such as Louise Powell and Kate Faulkner, either worked with men or relied on male relatives or friends for contacts for work.[54] The involvement in craft work of Kate Faulkner, whose gesso decoration on a Broadwood piano was featured at the first Arts and Crafts Exhibition in 1888, for instance, was through her brother, one of the founders of the firm Morris, Marshall, Faulkner and Co., which played such a key role in the Arts and Crafts Movement.[55] A few women trained or teaching in art schools designed decorative items. Margaret Macdonald Mackintosh, for instance, whose own style of design influenced the furniture of her husband, the architect and designer Charles Rennie Mackintosh, designed decorative screens, but few women concerned themselves with furniture proper.[56]

The fine-art associations of the enormously popular craft of 'artistic wood-carving'[57] meant that it was also a 'respectable' area within which women could study and work. The School of Art Woodcarving was established in London in 1879 and within three years had a woman manager and some female members of staff.[58] Standards were extremely high and the school was open to amateurs as well as those undergoing a professional training. Of the latter, men could either go into all-male workshops or teach; once again, there were no commercial opportunities open to women, who could only teach. By the First World War the art and design schools had come nowhere near to breaking out of their established gender patterns. 'Women's Crafts' courses proliferated, but few women were involved in furniture design. In the odd instances where the mould was broken, it was done outside the schools, but only by individuals such as Ray Hille operating in very particular circumstances.

A Case Study: Ray Hille and Doris Young

Showing an early aptitude for drawing and a keen interest in antique furniture, Ray Hille was painting lacquer furniture in her early teens. By 1918, aged 19, she was designing furniture as well as producing detailed workshop drawings.[59] Despite all this, she did not work full-time in the family firm. There was one problem: she was female. It was not thought suitable for a woman, even one as talented as Ray, to run a furniture firm, so she worked as a civil servant. Her father's old age and ill-health meant that she took increasing periods of unpaid leave to manage the firm, but even then it was not expected that one day she would take overall control. However, when in 1932 Salamon Hille decided to retire and sell the firm, he found that the potential buyers would only take a half share and stipulated that Ray should remain because she knew the clients and represented business continuity. Above all, she had design and production expertise. In that year Hille became a limited company under the command of Ray Hille, a young woman in an industry dominated by men at all levels: craft, management and design.

Hille continued to take an active part in running the firm until the 1980s, when, in her eighties, she slowed down – but only a little. A remarkable lady whose story deserves to be told in full detail, in all its glory, she illustrated just how well women could do 'male' jobs when given the opportunity (see Fig. 8.3). So well did she do that job that one of the leading shop stewards at Hille's in the 1950s paid her what was, *in his terms*, a great compliment: she was, he recalled, 'one of the lads'.[60]

Doris Young is another woman who took over and ran the family firm, in this case from 1943. Established by her grandfather in 1868, the business had passed to her father, but there were no male heirs. Doris was one of two daughters and, because she was aware of how much her father wanted a son, she tried to be 'Paddy the next best thing' to a boy.[61] Father and daughter went fishing, just like father and son, and it was on these trips that the young Doris learned a great deal about timber, the furniture trade in general and the family firm in particular. Yet neither she nor her father envisaged her working in the furniture trade. She may have substituted for a son on fishing trips but she was not seen as an alternative heir to the firm. Her entry into the business came about in a much more fortuitous way. Because she was not brought up with an expectation of entering the family firm, she (like Ray Hille) worked as a civil servant, in this case for the Inland Revenue. It was after her marriage and during her child-rearing years that she took an increasingly active part in the day-to-day running of the family firm, beginning with reorganising tax returns and invoice payments. She helped out in the office, particularly with book-keeping, learned about selecting and buying materials and about the organisation of the trade, including trade mills and out-work. She was more than capable of taking over the firm in 1943, when her father died. Her career as a designer is also of interest, not least in terms of gendered design. She has always paid attention to the needs of women as consumers, including the need to keep dusting to a minimum.[62] One of her designs, for instance, was a chair for nursing mothers specially developed for the City of London maternity hospital.[63]

Still active today, Doris Young remains managing director of the firm and is an energetic supporter of the Design and Industries Association (DIA) and design training for the young. She sometimes wonders, as Ray Hille did, why feminists are interested in her work, since she does not consider herself a 'women's libber'.[64]

In conclusion, this survey of women and furniture-making shows the extent to which the trade was male-dominated while not being exclusively male. Parts of it were deemed respectable enough for women to work in, while other parts, such as upholstery and later polishing, had traditions of employing women. The marginalisation of women existed from the Middle Ages, only to increase in the eighteenth and nineteenth centuries. That marginalisation was greater in design than in production, but in neither area were women strongly represented. Where women did break through it was either when general economic circumstances favoured them, as in the case of the two world wars, or in exceptional circumstances which afforded women opportunities not normally open to them, witness the case studies of Ray Hille and Doris Young.

Notes

1 Burman, Sandra, ed., *Fit Work for Women*, Croom Helm, London, 1979.
2 Beard, G., and Gilbert, C., eds. *Dictionary of English Furniture Makers 1660–1840*, Maney & Sons, Leeds, 1986, p. 638.
3 The quotation is from Hilton, R. H., 'Women Traders in Medieval England', in *Class Conflict and the Crisis of Feudalism: Essays in Medieval Social History*, Hambledon Press, London, 1985, pp. 205–15. See also Hanawalt, B. A., ed., *Women and Work in Pre-industrial Europe*, Indiana University Press, Indiana, 1986; Shahar, S., *The Fourth Estate: A History of Women in the Middle Ages*, Methuen, London, 1983; Ozenfant, S., *When Fathers Ruled: Family Life in Reformation Europe*, Harvard University Press, Cambridge, Mass., 1983; Davis, Natalie, 'City Women and Religious Change in Sixteenth Century France', in McGuigan, D. G., ed., *A Sampler of Women's Studies*, Ann Arbor, Centre for Continuing Education of Women, University of Michigan, 1973; and the publication to which most articles on medieval women still refer: Power, Eileen, *Medieval Women*, Cambridge University Press, Cambridge, 1975, with an introduction by M. M. Postan.

I am extremely grateful to Helena Graham for discussing the question of women and work in the medieval period with me and for her helpful suggestions.

4 Campbell, *London Tradesmen*, London, 1747, p. 170. See also Kirkham, Pat, *Furniture Making in London: Craft Design, Business and Labour*, unpublished Ph.D. thesis, University of London, 1981.

5 Parker, Rozsika, *The Subversive Stitch: Embroidery and the Making of the Feminine*, The Women's Press, London, 1984, pp. 98–117.

6 Abrams, A., 'Women traders in medieval London', *Economic Journal*, June 1916, pp. 276–85; Kahl, W. F., *The Development of London Livery Companies: An Historical Essay and Select Bibliography*, Kelley, Boston, Mass., 1960; Reddaway, T. F., 'The livery companies of Tudor London', *History*, Vol. LI, No. 173, October 1966; *Royal Commission on Municipal Corporations*, 1835–7; *Royal Commission on the Livery Companies*, 1884.

7 Postan, op. cit., pp. 10 and 53; Abrams, op. cit., pp. 280–1.

8 Abrams, op. cit., p. 281.

9 Kirkham, op. cit., p. 99, n. 16.

10 Abrams, op. cit., p. 283.

11 Hilton, op. cit., p. 206.

12 Collyer, Joseph, *The Parent's and Guardian's Directory*, London, 1761, p. 150; Campbell, op. cit., p. 172.

13 These figures are taken from the Inland Revenue apprenticeship records in the Public Record Office (PRO) and the apprenticeship records of the Joiners' and Upholders' Companies in the Guildhall Library.

14 PRO IRI/18

15 Pinchbeck, Ivy, *Women Workers and the Industrial Revolution 1750–1850*, Cass, London, 1969, p. 282.

16 Kirkham, op. cit., pp. 154–79.

17 Defoe, op. cit., p. 287.

18 See Beard and Gilbert, op. cit.

19 Ibid., p. 715.

20 Ibid., p. 638.

21 Ibid., p. 338.

22 Ibid., p. 289.

23 Ibid., p. 344.

24 PRO IRI/22

25 PRO IR/18 & 20 and Guildhall Library, Upholders' Company, Apprenticeship Bindings.

26 Beard and Gilbert, op. cit., p. 123.

27 Ibid., p. 422.

28 Defoe, Daniel, *The Complete English Tradesman*, 2nd edn with supplement, 1727; reprinted 1969, Kelly, New York, Vol. 1., p. 287.

29 Smith, J. T., *Nollekins and His Times*, Henry Colburn, London, 1829, Vol. II, p. 177.
30 Quoted in Coleridge, Anthony, 'A reappraisal of William Hallett', *Furniture History*, Vol. 1, 1965, p. 12.
31 Kirkham, Pat, Mace, Rodney, and Porter, Julia, *Furnishing the World: The East London Furniture Trade 1830–1980*, Journeyman Press, London, 1987.
32 Mayhew, Henry, 'Of the fancy cabinet-makers of London', *Morning Chronicle*, 8 August 1850.
33 Ibid.
34 Kirkham, Mace and Porter, op. cit., pp. 9–10.
35 Ibid.
36 Mayhew, *Morning Chronicle*, 16 November 1849.
37 Ibid. See also Anon., *A General Description of All Trades*, London, 1747, p. 215, and Campbell, *London Tradesmen*, London, 1747, p. 170.
38 Mayhew, op. cit.
39 Reid, Hew, *The Furniture Makers: A History of Trade Unionism in the Furniture Trade 1868–1972*, The Malthouse Press, Oxford, 1986, Appendix: 'Women Workers in the Furniture Trade'.
40 Ibid.
41 Ibid.
42 Ibid. See also the journal of the Amalgamated Upholsterers' Union for this period, which is housed at the TUC Library.
43 Reid, op. cit.
44 Interviews with women who worked in the furniture trade in the Second World War, Lancaster, June 1970, and London, March 1987, and also with women who worked in other wartime jobs.
45 Collyer, op. cit., p. 86.
46 Gilbert, C., *The Life and Work of Thomas Chippendale*, 2 vols., Studio Vista and Christies, London, 1978; Hayward, Helena, and Kirkham, Pat, *William and John Linnell: Eighteenth Century London Furniture Makers*, 2 vols., Studio Vista and Christies, London, 1980.
47 Caldwell, Ian, 'Working women in the 18th century', *Antique Collector*, October 1985, pp. 80–1.
48 Beard and Gilbert, op. cit., p. 422.
49 Caldwell, op. cit., p. 80.
50 Ibid.
51 Hayward and Kirkham, op. cit.
52 Comino, Mary, Gimson and the Barnsleys: 'Wonderful furniture of a commonplace kind', Evans Brothers Limited, London, 1980.
53 Callen, Anthea, *Angel in the Studio: Women in the Arts and Crafts Movement 1870–1914*, Astragal Books, London, 1979, pp. 95–136.
54 Ibid., p. 169.

55 See Thompson, Paul, *The Work of William Morris*, Quartet Books Limited, London, 1977, *passim*.

56 Bird, Liz, 'Threading the Beads: Women in Art in Glasgow, 1870–1920', in *Uncharted Lives: Extracts from Scottish Women's Experiences 1850–1982*, Press Gang, Glasgow, 1983, pp. 98–116.

57 It was regarded as sculpture in wood.

58 Callen, op. cit., p. 166.

59 For this and other information on Ray Hille, see Lyall, Sutherland, *Hille: 75 Years of British Furniture*, Elron Press, London, 1981; Kirkham, Pat, *Hille: Profile of a British Furniture Company 1906–1982*, Leicester Polytechnic, Leicester, 1982; interview with author, March 1982.

60 Reynolds, Les, in conversation with author, 17 October, 1987.

61 Doris Young, lecture at the Geffrye Museum, London, 17 October 1987.

62 Doris Young, lecture, Geffrye Museum.

63 The chair was later transformed into a television chair.

64 Doris Young, in conversation with author.

9
Powerful Women: Electricity in the Home, 1919–40

Suzette Worden

Electricity is fundamental to today's generally accepted standard of living in the Western world. Without thinking, we tend to accept the existence of electricity as the most important power-source in our homes and workplaces. It is only a power cut that reminds us of something we take for granted. Just as it is so difficult to imagine a world without electricity today, it must have been even more difficult to imagine the potential of such a resource in the years when electricity was first being harnessed as a power-source. Once the National Grid was built, between the years 1926 and 1935, this became a reality.

At first many people were wary of electricity, so the supply companies and electrical-goods manufacturers had to persuade potential customers that they would be getting a safe service. To achieve this the Electrical Development Association (EDA) was formed in 1919. It initiated advertising and publicity campaigns during the 1920s and increasingly saw women as the main target. Middle-class women were the early targets, but by the 1930s working-class women were also seen as potential consumers. Initially, lighting and water-heating were the main areas for publicity, but later the use of appliances was promoted.

As soon as the possibilities of electricity in the home were recognised, women were drawn into debates on its future uses. As will be shown in this essay, their arguments became part of the general debate on the popular subject of labour saving. Many women were at the forefront of these labour-saving developments, as they were in a position to see the implications of these innovations – their likely economic and social impact. Some middle-class women were also keen to form new groups and organisations in order to influence the ways in which these new resources were to be used. The most significant associations were the Women's Engineering Society (WES), founded in 1919, and the Electrical Association for Women (EAW), a splinter-group of the WES, founded in 1924.

Today the WES is still a viable society and works to encourage women to take up careers in engineering. The EAW, on the other hand, seems to have come to the end of its useful life, after reaching its peak in the 1950s with 90 branches and 10,000 members. After a slow decline it was wound up at the end of 1986. But the contribution it made to educating women in the latest technology in its more dynamic days should not be forgotten.

What concerns us here is the particular interest women had in the development of electrical power and its consequent uses in those early pioneering years. What is most striking, and still relevant today, is the impact of their intervention on the design process itself. Their discussions were never narrowly defined. For them it was as important to discuss the more socially pertinent questions of the day, ranging from smoke abatement to electricity for the working-class home, as it was to discuss detailed design problems. More importantly, both issues were seen to be related. Rather than look only for pioneer women designers, it seems more relevant to articulate the 'anonymous' or collective participation these women achieved, even if this was in the end limited by social pressure to the domestic sphere.

These women looked at the role of technology in society and at its influence over a wide set of values. Such an outlook is still very important for a feminist perspective today. Arnold Pacey writes:

> Technology-practice not only includes innovation, design and construction, but operation, maintenance and use. When, as so often, engineers under-emphasize the latter, one of the positive contributions of a feminist viewpoint might be in stimulating interest in this aspect.[1]

This is an acknowledgment that the areas traditionally considered 'feminine' are worthy of study, but it can also be criticised for assuming that the 'natural' place for the woman is as a consumer. In the context of a history of electricity we need to think of the work of women as consumers as equally important as the work of the inventor of the machines; this allows us to take a broad social perspective across areas not usually related. However, we also need to realise the lack of choice women had over *how* they could become involved. Therefore, any influence they had was a result of making the most of their power as consumers.

Because it was so difficult for women to exercise any control from within the by now expanding industry – although a few pioneers did manage – women seized the only available avenue open to them. They used their traditional domestic role to articulate their interests and thus bring their influence to bear through consumption. In assessing achievements in a wide context, it is possible to see how the two areas of development, production at one end and consumption at the other, were intimately related. Pioneering women involved in the industry and women working in the home were able to gain strength from the mutual support they could give each other through the WES and the EAW.

Electricity had wide-scale implications for industry and commerce as well as for the home. This was an industry with industrial plant and generating equipment as well as a consumer-goods industry with showrooms and related retail services. It had been growing steadily since the 1880s, initially producing power for lighting and then for trams. Manufacturing industries followed this by slowly introducing consumer goods, such as fires, irons, kettles, toasters and vacuum cleaners. Domestic consumption enabled them to spread the load of electricity they had to produce and use the plant to capacity.[2] Hence their increasing interest in the consumer once the initial problems had been overcome.

In the 1920s and 1930s, when electrical supply and its associated industries were growth areas within the British economy, the foundations for present conditions of production and consumption were laid. From 1926 to 1936 the number of consumers increased from just over two million to about eight million, a rise of 300 per cent. By 1936 there were six and a half million domestic consumers, a number that was increasing by three-quarters of a million a year.[3]

Women in Production

Women played an important part in the expansion of the workforce in these industries, which grew to meet the demand. Noting this, Miriam Glucksmann has also described the way in which women's jobs in the emerging electrical industries of the 1920s and 1930s paved the way for the organisation of labour in assembly-line production that was to become commonplace in the 1950s.[4]

In the production of electrical goods, women often contributed considerably to the manufacturing processes. In the 1920s especially, a surprising amount of hand-work went into the production of electrical goods. Initially, this was skilled work, but it was often one of the first areas to be taken over by mechanisation as demand increased.

This is illustrated by looking at light-bulb manufacture, which consisted of a large proportion of hand-work throughout the 1930s. In the early 1920s girls were employed to fix all filaments to their supports by hand for Edison Swan lamp production (see Fig. 9.1). The 1920s General Electric Company's Osram lamp factory, which had developed out of the Robertson Lamp Works, employed over 3,000 workers and had an output of tens of millions of light-bulbs per year, with its main factory at Brook Green, London, and glass coming from factories near Newcastle and Wembley.

Looking at descriptions of production in this factory, it is evident that the women's work in the factory was very monotonous. They were engaged in measuring the tungsten wire and working in the wire-drawing department and they worked in many of the processes where the different parts of the light-bulb were assembled. When putting the filament in the tungsten light-bulbs they used one piece of machinery, a power-pincher. Assembling, exhausting the bulbs to create the required vacuum, capping, filling and testing, and packing were also parts of the production process carried out by women workers. This account of the conditions within lamp production gives an indication of the class differences of these decades and also of women's employment.

This was an industry, with an enormous interest in women as producers as well as consumers, middle class and working class. The following account of the WES and the EAW is an attempt to analyse the problems and appreciate the achievements of those predominantly middle-class women who sought to influence this expanding industry. The WES and the EAW were important communication channels, providing a meeting-ground for these women, so their histories are pivotal.

The Women's Engineering Society

The Women's Engineering Society was founded in 1919 by Lady Parsons, a militant suffragette and wife of Sir Charles Parsons, inventor of steam turbine engines used for generating electricity. Caroline Haslett, the first Secretary and President of the WES in 1939–40, described the first recruits to the WES as

> women for whom the Great War had meant emancipation, women for the most part who by 1920 thought they were now better fitted for life outside the home, and they could no longer be convinced that their sphere should be so restricted.[5]

The early members of the WES were from upper- and middle-class families, often with fathers and brothers in engineering professions. One such member, Verena Holmes, who was President of the WES in 1930–2, had superintended the work of 1,500 women employed in munitions work during the First World War. In 1944 she became the first woman member of the Institute of Mechanical Engineers. Women like her wished to use the experience they gained during the First World War as a foothold into the professions but found they had to fight increasing prejudice during the 1920s. The society gave them a much-needed means of supporting each other.

Caroline Haslett, who was later to become the main driving-force behind the EAW, had also been introduced to engineering through war work, at Cochran's boiler factory in Scotland. She was very typical of the kind of person attracted to the WES in its early years. She also had enormous drive, initiative and dedication and used her ability to bring people together for their mutual benefit within both the WES and the EAW. She was a good organiser and was committed to introducing women to the possibilities of science and ways in which they could make it work to their own advantage. Although committed to household management and a believer in its advantages for women, she also had wider international interests, which were channelled through her work for the British Federation of Business and Professional Women. Her public appointments were numerous; they included being a member of the Council of the British Institute of Management, of the Industrial Welfare Society and a member of the Council and the first woman Vice-President of the Royal Society of Arts. She was Adviser on Women's Training to the Ministry of Labour during the Second World War and then a member of the Ministry's Women's Consultative Council. She was also the first woman to be made a Companion of the Institution of Electrical Engineers.[6]

Women like her suffered loss of jobs and low pay in the 1920s, as a result of men returning from the war, but they continued to support the society with their enthusiasm and hard work. Financially, the society was kept afloat by donations from wealthy society women.[7] The WES gained a certain amount of recognition through its organisation of the conference, 'Women in Science, Industry and Commerce', at Wembley in 1925. They worked with the EAW, the British Federation of University Women, the Industrial Welfare Society, the Institute of Industrial Welfare Workers, the National Union of Scientific Workers and Standing Joint Committee of Industrial Women's Organisations. Sessions covered industry, industrial welfare and factory inspection, commerce and salesmanship, electricity and domestic science. At this point the WES and the EAW were working together to get openings for women to work in industry as scientists, engineers and demonstrators. In later years the EAW was to define its role more sharply and firmly within those areas affecting the home.

Although opportunities in the supply and manufacturing sides of the electrical industry were severely limited, a few members of the WES sought to make whatever inroads they could and encouraged other women to try to find similar employment in power-supply stations or as 'consumers' engineers' repairing appliances in the home. Before the First World War some women had found work in drawing offices, where they participated in the design process. They would have been paid £2 a week instead of the male rate of between £3 and £4.[8] It appears, however, that it was extremely difficult to increase participation in this area because of the fear of job losses by male workers. Electrical engineering was a male-dominated profession. Verena Holmes, who did get into the industry, explained that she was only able to do so because her father was in an influential position and she had a private income.[9] It was just about possible to get into the education system, but to get practical experience through serving an apprenticeship was virtually impossible.

Occasionally, WES members succeeded in gaining the much-needed practical experience. Through the influence of other WES members, Phyllis A. M. Fawssett was able to take first six weeks' vacation work and then a year's apprenticeship at the Edison Swan Electric Company at Ponders End. She wanted to specialise in the design and construction of domestic electrical apparatus.

By the end of the 1930s, however, she finally managed to become a draughtswoman in the lighting section of the Swan Edison Electrical Company.

Another WES member, M. R. Milnes, was fortunate enough to have trained with her father.[10] She started a four-year apprenticeship in 1934 with an electrical supply company, working in an office for the first year and then at the generating station in the second. She learned various fitting jobs: how to drill and tap, bend and shape sheet metal, to do riveting, sawing and filing, and also blacksmithing. She was trained to work on the switchboard as the year progressed. Another six months were spent in a showroom as a demonstrator, where she learned to repair domestic apparatus. This was followed by time on cooker-maintenance in consumers' homes and then work in the showroom again as demonstrator.

Government legislation was another obstacle for pioneering women in electrical engineering. British factory laws as well as the Washington Convention of the International Labour Office forbade the employment of women from 10.00 p.m. to 5.00 a.m. The British government took up the matter through the International Labour Office in Geneva and in 1934 an amendment was agreed by the International Labour Office and the League of Nations, but this only applied to women in management.[11]

The WES adopted this cause and helped to lobby the relevant committees and organisations. At this time trade union and Labour Party sympathies lay with protective legislation, which emphasised internal differences and had split the feminist movement in Britain during the 1920s.[12] Those associated with predominantly middle-class suffrage societies would have been opposed to protective legislation, as it hampered women's right to work. For them the legislation was paternalistic and implied weakness and dependence. The WES had most in common with these women, who were fighting their own immediate discrimination. On the other hand, many working-class women, and those middle-class women engaged in welfare work, saw protective legislation as a means of protecting the rights of women working in sweated trades. For this reason, when the International Labour Office was approached, the arguments for the exemption of women managers was opposed by women representing the TUC on the grounds that it might open the door to night work for all women.[13]

There were few pioneers in the managerial and design side of the industry. Margaret Partridge, an electrical engineer who became a graduate member of the Institution of Electrical Engineers in 1920, formed a company to electrify areas of rural Devon. She was the Managing Director, with Margaret Rowbotham as chairwoman, and Miss B. Shilling, Miss K. Bunker and Miss M. Willis as apprentices.[14] It was their work that had drawn the above legislation to the attention of the WES.

Nora E. Miller was Publicity Manager of the Edison Swan Electric Company and was responsible for the advertising of their products, including Royal Ediswan lamps, Mazda radio valves, commercial lighting equipment, domestic appliances and cables. She saw advertising was a business, not just a dainty occupation for those who wrote nicely or drew rather well. For women wanting to pursue a career in management she advocated an assertive attitude and varied experience at the production end. These women were pioneers, taking on a challenging career, fighting prejudice along the way and setting an example for others to follow. Looking at today's statistics puts their struggle into perspective. In 1984 50 Council for National Academic Awards (CNAA) textile degrees were awarded to men and 581 to women. In contrast, 843 men and 15 women received degrees in mechanical engineering.[15] Assumptions that science and engineering subjects are masculine still need challenging. 1984, Women into Science and Engineering (WISE) year, saw many initiatives to break down these stereotyped images.

Alongside the original aims of encouraging women to enter the hostile world of employment, the WES undertook to consider domestic problems. In 1921 it held a competition for the invention and improvement of devices for labour saving in the home.[16] Entries included a dish-washing machine worked by a hand-pump and independent of water supply, a saucepan with a quick-boiling lid and a floor-polishing machine which did away with kneeling. They hoped to exhibit the entries but found there wasn't enough response. It was this kind of initiative that was to be taken up by the EAW after 1924.

The Electrical Association for Women

In 1924 a group of women recognised the growing institutionali-

sation of the electricity supply and related industries. They wanted
to have an organisation which would bridge the gap between the
supplier and the customers. In June 1924 Mrs M. L. Matthews
presented the idea of the EAW to the Institution of Electrical
Engineers and the Electrical Development Association (EDA),
neither of whom took it up.[17] It was for the WES to support the
idea, which led to the official establishment of the EAW in
November of that year.

Besides aiming to bring together manufacturer, supplier and user,
the association had wider, more idealistic aims. Mrs Matthews
recognised that labour-saving applications ought to be promoted,
but she also spoke of issues beyond the home relating to agriculture,
medicine, housing, health, hygiene and smoke nuisance. Other
founder members, not all women, also recognised the importance
of bringing women into the industry: Mr Llewellyn B. Atkinson, a
representative of the Cable Makers' Association expressed his
agreement at the time.

The EAW's advisory role on electrical consumer goods in the
home, which became its most important function, was scarcely
mentioned. The inclusion of women in all areas of production still
remains an unfulfilled ideal.

In the early days Caroline Haslett, an enthusiastic member of the
WES and later the Secretary of the EAW, saw the potential of
electricity as a help to women's domestic role. Caroline Haslett
considered the EAW primarily a woman's organisation which was
not necessarily there to promote the electrical industry except by 'a
happy coincidence'. The optimistic wish was to extend their
influence outside the normal feminine sphere and achieve close links
with industry. She wrote:

> I do not think the woman's world has yet realised that the
> machine has really given women complete emancipation.
> With the touch of a switch she can have five or six
> horsepower at her disposal; in an aeroplane she has the
> same power as a man.[18]

In 1924 Caroline Haslett attended the first World Power
Conference in London, where she came across Lillian Gilbreth's
ideas and started to think about the application of power to
domestic work. This was followed by her participation in the 5th
International Scientific Management Congress in 1932, when she
became the Chairwoman of a council set up as a result of this
conference. This was COSMITH – the Council for Scientific
Management in the Home. Delegates were sent from this organisation to represent Britain at the domestic sessions of the
International Scientific Management Congresses.[19] In 1951

COSMITH merged with the Modern Home-Making Committee of the Women's Group on Public Welfare.

Labour saving was the popular description of these initiatives. In Caroline Haslett's terms, it was a way of achieving equality. However, this was not its only meaning; it was also equated with other potential goals and became the subject of debates concerning design which continue to this day.

The American writer Christine Frederick is usually considered to be the main exponent of labour saving in this period. She worked within the tradition established by Lillian Gilbreth and, before that, Catharine Beecher, who wrote *The American Woman's Home* in 1869. In this she discussed plans for the model home, where servants would be replaced by the most advanced technology. Although the planning and equipment of the home was to be different, the role of the woman remained as an isolated worker and was not challenged. Christine Frederick's book, *Household Engineering: Scientific Management in the Home*, published in 1920, was based on theoretical ideas of industrial mass-production by Frederick Taylor and Lillian and Frank Gilbreth. 'Taylorism', based on the division of labour, was a logical impossibility for a housewife working alone. Nevertheless, the theory was adapted to domestic work and gained immense popularity. The housewife was expected to 'manage' her own labour 'scientifically', to be executive and worker simultaneously, which was a contradiction of the principle of Scientific Management based on factory production methods. Christine Frederick gave a series of lectures to the EAW in 1927.

Advertisers and manufacturers soon used such ideas to promote their products. Christine Frederick took these ideas to their ultimate conclusion in *Selling Mrs Consumer*, published in 1929. In this she highlighted the way workers were becoming potential consumers for the goods they themselves produced. In recent critical accounts her ideas are portrayed as a sell-out to industry and therefore anti-feminist. Dolores Hayden describes them as

> the final corruption of home economics, representing not women's interests but businesses' interests in manipulating women, their homes, and their families.[20]

At the time the fact that business was to use her ideas to great effect in profit-making was not anticipated. This aspect had nothing to do with emancipating women, which was in fact the intention of Christine Frederick and the feminists she inspired. Dolores Hayden's comments are therefore rather harsh. Feminists of the 1930s never saw her as an 'enemy'.

Generally, the phrase labour saving became the advertiser's

slogan; the promise was of leisure instead of work. But the housewife did not gain more time. Instead, the work changed; higher standards were expected as the housewife was projected into a more glamorous and also a more skilled role. The housewife's cooking and cleaning work were also invested with values that were part of her maternal role too; housework became emotionalised. Women were made to feel guilty if they did not achieve the expected high standards.[21]

Women running homes on their own were encouraged, through advertising, to see an appliance as a replacement for the servant – to be *the* servant. Their work with the appliance was redefined and still had associations with a middle-class servant-employing lifestyle. Labour-saving appliances were thus supposed to replace the servant and solve the 'labour' problem in the home. Two aspects of the replacement of labour – time for leisure and the servant problem – were merged in one phrase.

In addition to this, labour saving became associated with ideas of modern architecture, functionalism and the minimum dwelling through the work of German architects Ernst May, Adolf Meyer and Ferdinand Kramer, who designed housing schemes in Frankfurt from 1925 to 1930 with kitchens designed by Grete Schuette-Lihotsky. Here Christine Frederick's ideas were incorporated into idealistic housing design which catered for a new lifestyle and the ideal person to go with it.[22]

No real distinction was made between labour saved by more efficient planning and the use of machinery and gadgets that made the work lighter or quicker. It was in the interests of manufacturers keen on selling the isolated product to give the credit to the appliance rather than the expertise of the new professional housewife. Put in the advertisers' hands, labour saving ·was used as an enticement to a world of so-called increased leisure through consumption and a passive role.

Members of the EAW, aware of these contradictory problems and not immune to pressure from outside influences, actively tried to influence industry. The EAW contributed to the movement which gave housework a scientific basis and by so doing reinforced women's traditional role within the home. Through a present-day perspective this may be an acceptable interpretation. However, a deeper analysis of the whole movement needs to take into account the way some key members were genuinely trying to enable women to make a choice between roles outside as well as inside the home. It was a positive feminist aim not at odds with one set of ideals within the movement, one that favoured protective legislation, supported welfare provision and, increasingly during the 1930s, argued for a 'new feminism' that emphasised women's special needs.[23]

It is therefore easy to see that there was more to the EAW than the advertiser's slogan. Caroline Haslett hoped that active participants rather than passive consumers would join the society. Yet the very success of their work concerned with the domestic use of electricity in the home is also a reflection of how, in a wider context, social pressures were pushing women back into their more traditional roles. In the early 1920s momentum for the formation of the WES was gathered from the war work women were involved in during the First World War. It was also no coincidence that the establishment of the EAW coincided with Eleanor Rathbone's book *The Disinherited Family*,[24] in which she proposed family endowment schemes as a means to strengthen the family and women's traditional part in it. Her concern with welfare provision for women and children was eventually to become a reality with the introduction of children's allowances in 1945.

In *Women Workers in the First World War*, Gail Braybon shows how quickly the tide turned towards an emphasis on domesticity. Even the Labour Movement accepted that women's place was now within the home. And newspapers like the *Daily Herald*, which had covered all aspects of women's paid work during the war, very quickly focused on domestic issues after the war.[25] The growth of the EAW from 1924 also reflects the speed with which this reversal happened.

Public Service

The EAW flourished and in June 1926 published the *Electrical Age for Women*, which proved to be very popular, showing a profit by 1929 and appearing under the shortened title of the *Electrical Age* in 1932. By 1940 the association had 85 branches and 9,000 predominantly middle-class members. Women MPs and mayoresses were encouraged to become branch presidents in the line of public duty. The work involved was often spoken of in this context. Lady Astor, the EAW's first President and just the kind of person they were looking for, reflected this spirit in her opening address.

> I am proud to have been the first President of an organisation which reflects the practical pioneer spirit of women and their capacity for educational propaganda in new fields. I hope that women will increasingly take this point of view and this spirit into every sphere of industry, commerce and the professions, and that they will succeed in convincing the community that their object is public service rather than personal advancement.[26]

Lady Astor clearly saw the EAW's work in the context of public service, as did most middle-class women who were concerned with the social conditions of the working classes, particularly the working-class woman. As the association developed, its work in this area increased. It was officially recognised in 1934, when, at the EAW's ninth annual conference, called the 'Working Woman's Conference', a resolution was passed stating:

> The time has now come when electricity should be available at an economic rate to the homes of the working people.[27]

A survey of working-class conditions was made and in the same year the EAW published a pamphlet, *Report on Electricity in Working Class Homes*, written by Mrs Elsie E. Edwards.

The EAW was also influential through women working on electricity committees. In some ways this was a recognition of women's importance as consumers by the industry, which by 1937 was earning 36 per cent of its revenue from domestic demand.[28] The extent to which working-class consumers were becoming important is shown by the example of the Borough of West Ham, where in 1934 there were just over 50,000 houses accommodating about 70,000 families, of which 90 per cent lived in houses of less than five rooms and many thousands in two rooms only. Of these, 34,000 were domestic consumers. In 1933 electricity was offered at one penny per unit to slot meter consumers, including the hire of a cooker. General hire charges for cookers were 5s. per quarter. By 1934 1,794 additional cookers were installed, making the borough total 2,630.[29] In the summer of 1934 they were fitting electric cookers at the rate of 50 per week. Out of the 625 suppliers of electricity in the country as a whole, 84 per cent offered assisted wiring schemes, but the figure for hire purchase schemes was less at 76 per cent.[30]

Mrs Hammer, the EAW's first Chairwoman (1924–30), headed the Electricity Committee in Hackney, London, from 1926. A later EAW chairwoman, Mrs Gregory, was also made a member of the West Ham Electricity Committee from 1925. There were many other members working on similar committees all around the country. In Watford, for example, there were two EAW members on the Electricity Committee and the Council Housing Committee had a subcommittee composed of six women, five of whom were members of the Watford branch of the EAW.[31]

These instances of involvement in public welfare were a keen affirmation of the aims of the society where design issues were part of wider-ranging discussions.

Industry and Design: The EAW as Mediator in the Design Process

Design developments of the 1930s attempted to link art and

industry. This was a reflection not only of the preoccupations of both the Design and Industries Association and the Council for Art and Industry but also of a realisation by manufacturers that using the name of an artist was a useful marketing technique. The Council started work in 1934 on the recommendation of the Gorell Committee Report, published in 1932. They wished to see exhibitions used to promote 'good' design and to encourage manufacturers to use the art-school-trained artists as part of a design team, or as consultants in order to improve the design of manufactured goods. Part of this initiative reflected the recognition of a growing new profession – the industrial designer, a professional with a theoretical position as well as practical expertise. In Britain the Society of Industrial Artists, which was founded in 1930, helped to consolidate the designer's position in relation to industry. In the field of appliance design, one or two 'consultants', like Christian Barman, who designed a streamlined iron for HMV in 1934, and Mrs Darcy Braddell, who designed the Kabineat gas cooker for Parkinson's in 1935, stood out.

But these were isolated experiments and were far from typical for the industry as a whole. The EAW's involvement as mediator both reflects this absence of the professional and, at the same time, shows that there could be an alternative – a more collective approach to designing products. In this way consumers, through the EAW, could have a say and fulfil the industry's need for continual improvement and evolution rather than the planning of static and final solutions.

Although Caroline Haslett spoke of the EAW's representing the consumer and its help to the industry as no more than 'a happy coincidence', nevertheless, electrical engineers like Sebastian Z. de Ferranti and Colonel Rookes E. B. Crompton saw the EAW as an important contributor to the industry.

There were instances where the EAW clearly acted as mediator in the design process between industry and the consumer. In 1927, a discussion about electric cookers was organised by sending a questionnaire to all the branches; 11 types of cooker then on the market were investigated. Replies commented upon the need for more runners for shelves, removable enamel linings with moulded corners in the cooker, and grill size. The commentators generally felt that available grills were too small and should be 12″ × 10″. The majority of women answering the questionnaire wanted a separate grill and warming-cupboard as well as stainless boiling-plates flush with the hob. The most convenient height for cookers was seen as 36″ and adjustable legs were suggested. Some manufacturers had taken up these recommendations by 1934.[32] In 1928 a similar investigation was made into the number of socket points needed. Minimum numbers suggested were passed on to the electricity suppliers. This particular scheme was also taken up by the EDA and was an important part of their publicity aimed at getting existing consumers to use more power through appliances as well as electricity for lighting.

Five years later, in the pamphlet *The Design and Performance of Domestic Electrical Appliances* the EAW published recommendations that all cookers should have rounded corners, that the bottom element of the fire, at present switched on from the power plug, should be altered to the top in order to prevent scorching of carpets and that everything possible should be done to overcome the dreadful noise made by vacuum cleaners.

Planning

Even though individual appliances were considered in detail, the EAW was always anxious to evaluate these products in use. They therefore paid close attention to kitchen planning in a more general sense, taking inspiration from American examples. The EAW was very interested in Lillian Gilbreth's work, and a report called *The Kitchen Practical*, 1932, in which the importance of working-surfaces of correct and uniform height, a circular workplace and a planned route were stressed.

In order to popularise these improvements the EAW sponsored a film in 1936. This was called *Motion Study in the Home* and the same theme was used for their annual conference that year. Miss A. G. Shaw of Metropolitan-Vickers and Mr S. E. Britton of the Chester Corporation Electricity Department made the film.[33] It showed the preparation of breakfast for four people using the same electrical equipment, first in a conventional way and then according to a motion-economy plan. The second method showed a saving of energy based on the design of the kitchen linking the three main functions of the room: storage of food and equipment in refrigerator and cupboards, preparation of foods requiring a cooker, working-surface and serving-place and, lastly, cleaning-area at the sink with a supply of hot water.

The EAW was always keen to work with architects and planners and often helped plan show kitchens, show houses and flats. Mrs Edna Moseley, an architect from the Architectural Association and a member of the EAW, designed an all-electric flat, furnished by Heals of Tottenham Court Road, London, at the Bachelor Girls Exhibition of 1930.[34] The EDA paid for its installation and it was estimated that 95 per cent of the 3,000 visitors to the exhibition visited the flat. In February 1936 there was an exhibition of the work of women architects at the Building Centre which included an EAW kitchen.

In 1931 a model of a kitchen was shown at the Housing Exhibition, Central Hall, Westminster, based on real kitchens from working-class flats built by the St Pancras House Improvement Society. The Association estimated the running costs and this was part of the display. In 1934 full-sized kitchens were shown at the EAW headquarters in an exhibition to mark the association's tenth birthday. These included kitchens from the LCC flats on the Ossulton Estate, Somers Town, the Crown Estate Flats, Cumberland Market, and from Westminster, Hackney, Stepney, West Ham, Fulham and Bermondsey. The exhibition showed the layout and design of the actual 8' × 9' kitchens fully equipped with appliances.[35] Posters gave information on the relative costs of running the kitchen for families of different sizes and how much could be done with specific amounts of electricity. Particular attention was paid to the provision of hot-water systems, as this was the most difficult problem housing committees and electrical engineers had to solve for working-class incomes.

The EAW also furnished, planned and equipped a show house designed by the architect Adrian Powell, aimed at the middle-class purchaser.[36] It was planned so that it could be run with or without a maid. It was built in Bristol in 1935 (see Figs. 9.2, 9.3) and was opened with great ceremony on 23 October of that year by the Countess of Westmorland. By the following month it had already been visited by 20,000 people. The annual cost of running this house was estimated at an economical £30, which included heating, hot water, cleaning, fridge, lighting, hire and fixed charges. Reviewing consumption at a later date, it was found to be possible to run the house for an even lower cost of £22 18s. 9d., which included the 30s. per quarter fixed charge and 17s. 6d. hiring charge.[37] The EAW was surprised to receive no criticism of their choice of a modern style for the house, with its flat roof, attached garage and large metal-framed windows. Inside there were built-in fitments and the furniture was supplied by the firm Messrs P. E. Gane Ltd. Mr P. E. Gane was a member of the DIA who, according to the EAW, had a reputation for 'good taste'. The 30' living-room was particularly admired as it provided such a good space for entertaining. Labour saving was not only to come from the use of electrical appliances but also from the fact that there were no metal fittings that required cleaning, no mouldings or dust-trapping pelmets, picture-rails or balusters.

Demonstrators and Saleswomen

Of the activities mentioned so far the EAW was acting for women and predominantly for their benefit within the home. As Caroline Haslett hoped:

way is being made by electricity for a higher order of

women – women set free from drudgery, who have time for reflection; for self-respect.[38]

Therefore, the society continued to consider the wider issues it had raised at its inception and offered assistance to domestic science teachers. From 1927 they had links with the Association of Teachers of Domestic Science and in 1929 a survey of the use of electrical equipment in domestic science centres in schools was undertaken. After 1930 this was followed up by an annual EAW conference for domestic science teachers and from 1933 a diploma for teachers was offered.

Within the constraints of the social climate, the EAW was attempting to help women to achieve employment within the electricity industry. As already mentioned, the founders of the WES had been women emancipated, to some degree, by the First World War. In the 1920s they found their opportunities diminishing. The foundation of the EAW in 1924 is in itself recognition of the expected move of women back into the home. It is in this context that the EAW's initiative on training demonstrators must be seen. This was first thought of in 1927 and their *Report on the Existing Facilities for Showroom Training for Women* was published in 1933. In 1933 the association opened an Electrical Housecraft School (see Fig. 9.4), run by Miss Dorothy Vaughan, which offered help not only to the housewife but also to teachers and those wishing to be demonstrators for the electrical industry. It also awarded a certificate in Electrical Housecraft dependent on examination. If the candidate then worked for another year in a responsible position she could be presented with the EAW Grade One demonstrator's diploma. A salary of 30s. per week could be expected during the training period. Then, if the trainee stayed with the same company, a minimum salary of £2 per week on completion of the course, rising to £3 per week after one year, could be expected. In 1934 there were 177 candidates, 169 of whom sat the exam.[39]

Lord Hirst, the joint-founder, Chairman and Managing Director of GEC Ltd, was a firm supporter of the EAW school. He had the following comments to make in 1932:

I have always seen the value of women's services and recognised the large part women could play in the development of electricity in the home. Long ago I told the Electrical Engineers that what they needed was a body of trained sales women. But it is no use bringing women in unless they are properly trained.[40]

Large firms like GEC were able to put this idea into practice. One of the firm's employees, Mr V. Hindlip Vale, spoke of two types of demonstrator working in the electrical industry. The first group was responsible for demonstrating individual appliances, such as cleaners or refrigerators. They did not have to know much beyond the general details and a persuasive personality was often more useful. Then there were the cooker and laundry-work demonstrators, who were more important, as they had to put over a sound knowledge of domestic science, particularly cookery. Wishing to see more of the latter group, he suggested that supply undertakings should employ a senior member of staff with full domestic science training.

GEC used demonstrators throughout the country. One of them, Mrs Flack, described her work as testing experimental equipment made by the firm to see if the suggested improvements were of real practical use.[41] She hoped her role would bring about real improvements rather than merely act as publicity. She was therefore feeding information back to the manufacturer from the public and playing a part in the design process.

The trade journal the *Electrical Review* also located a need for women to act as household advisers when consumers were having difficulties.[42] This was in an effort to make electricity something people could take for granted and accept without having to be 'experts', something that would simplify their lives rather than make them more complicated, something that was free from the atmosphere of mystery. There were to be no detrimental comparisons with gas.

The EAW published its own handbook in 1934 and this provided a valuable textbook for their courses. It gives a good indication of EAW priorities. There was a great deal of well-explained information on the structure of the supply industry and the maintenance of appliances. It looked at science and technology in as much detail as it did the management of the kitchen, labour saving and cleanliness. By 1935 this handbook had sold 33,000 copies.

The success of this book alone showed that the association had found a real need and was fulfilling an important social function, with the needs of women being kept to the fore. Even though the sexual division of labour in the workplace reflected the expectation that women's proper place was still in the home, the book acknowledged the importance of education in helping women to gain control of the power that was available to them *in* the home.

When looking at the way in which electricity was developed, promoted and exploited in the inter-war years, it is important to see how changes in the design of the home were so closely related to the growth and organisation of the electricity supply and electrical-goods industries. Some pioneering women sought to make an impact on the male-dominated world of the electrical industry and to put power to influence the new industry in the hands of women. The routes they used to do this were through the WES and the EAW. Although the work of each organisation overlapped, they each had their own primary areas of emphasis: the WES worked mainly to keep open employment possibilities that had come about through women's gains in the First World War, while the EAW, in recognising social pressures on women which encouraged them to work within the home, concentrated on the home and those areas traditionally associated with it.

These women were working in response to a traditionally male-dominated industry that was becoming rapidly institutionalised. It is in the light of the strength of this domination that their ideals and achievements must be seen. For this reason the ideals of the WES, although not replaced, were overshadowed by the EAW and its achievements during the 1930s.

The WES and the EAW together hold a fascinating position within a history of feminism for the inter-war period, as the debate over night work expressed the wishes of the pioneers for equal opportunities. The EAW and its wish to bring an understanding of electricity to women in the home incorporated the social reformists within the Feminist Movement. The two associations, taken together, encompass the contradictory sides of feminism.

As already mentioned, the term 'labour saving' covered many different concepts in the 1920s and 1930s. From what we now know of some of these concepts, it is easy to be critical of the EAW and their work by assuming that the women involved allowed themselves to be taken in by the myth of labour saving. Yet when the social pressures against them are acknowledged, some recognition of their positive gains must be made. The kind of work they were doing had many dimensions and alongside an interest and ability to discuss specific design problems, they were able to see these points of detail as part of wider social movements.

Their place within the history of design must therefore be recognised, as they were successful both in influencing the design of products manufactured by the appliance industry and in keeping the woman's point of view visible outside the home. Finally, in the words of Caroline Haslett, throughout the EAW:

> every type of woman found her place; the domestic woman, the girl with a career, the public woman, the leisured woman.[43]

Notes

1 Pacey, Arnold, *The Culture of Technology*, Blackwell, London, 1983, p. 105.

2 Hannah, Lesley, *Electricity before Nationalisation*, Macmillan, London, 1979; Byers, Anthony, *Centenary of Service: A History of Electricity in the Home*, Electricity Council, London, 1981.

3 Political and Economic Planning, *The Supply of Electricity in Great Britain*, London, 1936, p. 76.

4 Glucksmann, Miriam, 'In a class of their own? Women workers in the new industries in inter-war Britain', *Feminist Review*, No. 24, October 1986, pp. 7–37.

5 Haslett, Caroline, *Woman Engineer*, Vol. 5, No. 2, March 1940, p. 24.

6 *The Times*, 5 January 1957; *Electrical Age*, October 1956, pp. 356–9.

7 Lady Parsons, Mrs Wilson, Lady Moir and Lady Beilby were among those who helped the WES in its early years.

8 Drake, Barbara, *Women in the Engineering Trades*, 1919, p. 64.

9 'Careers and openings for women in engineering. A discussion', *Woman Engineer*, Vol. 3, No. 12, September/October 1932, p. 181.

10 Milnes, M. R., 'Introducing the consumers' engineer', *Woman Engineer*, Vol. 3, No. 18, March 1939, p. 280–1.

11 *Woman Engineer*, Vol. 3, No. 20, September/October 1934, p. 317.

12 Banks, Olive, *Faces of Feminism: A Study of Feminism as a Social Movement*, Martin Robertson, Oxford, 1981, pp. 108 and 169.

13 Ibid., p. 169, quoting Lewenhak, Sheila, *Women and Trade Unions*, Benn, London, 1977, p. 212.

14 *Woman Engineer*, Vol. 4, No. 3, June 1935, p. 45.

15 Council for National Academic Awards, *Annual Report 1984–85*, pp. 52–3.

16 *Woman Engineer*, Vol. 1, No. 11, June 1922.

17 Randell, Wilfrid L., *Electricity and Woman: 21 Years of Progress*, EAW and Hodder and Stoughton, London, *c.* 1945, p. 20.

18 Scott, Peggy, *An Electrical Adventure*, EAW, London, 1934, p. 12.

19 Messenger, R., *The Doors of Opportunity*, Femina Books, London, 1967, p. 78.

20 Hayden, Dolores, *The Grand Domestic Revolution: A History of Feminist Designs for American Homes, Neighborhoods, and Cities*, MIT Press, Cambridge, Mass., 1981, p. 285.

21 Cowan, Ruth Schwartz, *More Work for Mother: The Ironies of Household Technology from the Open Hearth to the Microwave*, Basic Books, New York, 1983, pp. 151–91.

22 Burckhardt, Lucius, *The Werkbund*, Design Council, London, 1980, pp. 83–4.

23 Banks, op. cit., p. 171.

24 Rathbone, Eleanor, *The Disinherited Family: A Plea for Endowment of the Family*, Edward Arnold, London, 1924.

25 Braybon, Gail, *Women Workers in the First World War*, Croom Helm, London, 1981.
26 Scott, op. cit., p. 30.
27 Ibid., p. 104.
28 *Electrical Age*, Vol. 3, No. 9, Winter/Spring 1938, p. 357.
29 Scott, op. cit., p. 105.
30 Political and Economic Planning, op. cit., p. 77.
31 EAW, *Annual Report*, 1935; Thompson, Phyllis, 'Women on electricity committees', *Electrical Age*, Winter/Spring 1938, pp. 334–5.
32 Scott, op. cit., pp. 40–1.
33 Messenger, op. cit., p. 79.
34 Scott, op. cit., p. 100. For information on Edna Moseley, see Beddington, Nadine, *et al.*, *Women Architects, Their Work*, Sorella Press, London, 1984, p. 16.
35 Scott, op. cit., p. 100.
36 Worden, Suzette, 'A Voice for Whose Choice? Advice for Consumers in the late 1930s', in *Design History: Fad or Function?*, Design Council, London, 1978, pp. 41–8.
37 *Electrical Age*, Vol. 3, No. 9, Winter/Spring 1938, pp. 338–9.
38 Scott, op. cit., p. 108.
39 *Woman Engineer*, Vol. 3, No. 19, June 1934, editorial.
40 Scott, op. cit., p. 62.
41 *Electrical Review*, 7 October 1932, p. 518.
42 *Electrical Review*, 31 January 1930, p. 193.
43 Scott, op. cit., p. 18.

10
Sexual Division of Labour in the Arts and Crafts Movement

Anthea Callen

We do not, on the whole, find that great opposition is offered by manufacturers to the wider employment of women. Indeed, even with the existing low estimate of the value of women's work, their assistance may be expected. 'There is no reason', says one of them, 'why we should object to employ women. They work for lower wages than men.' On the score of strict justice we may possibly dispute the reasoning of such a view of things, wondering if good work, even if done by a woman, is not worthy of good payment. But we may, nevertheless, accept the position thankfully and while we endeavour to secure the good work, leave for the present the question of its just reward.[1]

The second half of the nineteenth century saw the rise of the Arts and Crafts Movement, bringing with it a new role for women which they readily took up. Although the Arts and Crafts Movement was in many ways socially and artistically radical, at the same time it in fact reproduced, perpetuated and thus reinforced dominant Victorian patriarchal ideology. It recreated in microcosm traditional divisions between male and female roles, which can be seen in the areas of design, production, craft skills, income and management.

As the modern bourgeois ideal of the family came into being in the late eighteenth and early nineteenth centuries, so the modern notion of domesticity evolved. Although hallowed as an almost sacred undertaking and duty for women, at the same time domestic activity was not recognised as real work. It was a labour of love. In a society in which everything was measured in terms of financial profit – especially success and power – women were therefore outsiders, their 'real' work unacknowledged.

Ruskin himself was one of the many writers who eulogised the new domesticity.[2] In the Victorian ideal, woman was the spiritual guardian of the home as a secular temple and a haven within a turbulent mercantile society. This ideal necessitated middle-class woman's exclusion from the productive male commercial world in order to maintain the stability of patriarchal ideology. She provided the 'passive' to give meaning to the male 'active'. She was to be 'a companion, who will raise the tone of [her husband's] mind from low anxieties, and vulgar cares' and 'lead his thoughts to expatiate or repose on those subjects which convey a feeling of identity with a higher state of existence beyond this present life.'[3] The woman's leisure – her exclusion from male-defined work activities – indicated the degree of her man's success and therefore their social status.

This bourgeois ideal of woman, along with the increasing emphasis on domesticity, created a paradigm to which all classes of society were intended to aspire. During the 1840s there evolved the concept of the family wage: in other words, the man's wage, which was intended to support his entire family. While this was, of course, by no means universally implemented, nevertheless the ideal wife's place was considered to be within the home and became, in theory, realisable for the working classes.

By the same token a woman's wages were seen as merely supplementary to the husband's income: 'pin' money. As a result, at no time during the nineteenth century did women's earnings enable them to support themselves adequately. This provoked particularly severe problems for single and widowed women, whether working or middle class. Many women, especially married women, who were obliged to work did so as out-workers – a word which encapsulated both the shift in workplace and in status – taking work into the home in order to fulfil a dual productive role. While superficially reminiscent of the pre-industrial family productive unit, in this new system women were entirely at the mercy of agents and middlemen. These latter frequently imposed harsh deadlines and truck payment, which undervalued both labour and skill. Such out-work was notoriously ill-paid and the hours were excessive; moreover, the women's isolation effectively curtailed any political organisation for improved pay or conditions. This helped to create a cheap labour-force and a reserve 'army' of women which could be called in and then dismissed on economic whim.

The women of the middle classes in particular were raised and educated to embody the ideal of domesticity, their only socially sanctioned career in life was marriage and their training rarely fitted them for work outside the domestic sphere. Yet in fact the opportunities for marriage were decreasing throughout the century, for, as one writer commented in 1872:

> Unfortunately, till it is removed by emigration or some other equally potent remedy, we may never forget the fact that there are too many women in England ... As a matter of fact, we find women in Great Britain outnumbering

men by nearly a million; and we find also, in the face of the marriage theory, that three [million] out of six million adult Englishwomen support themselves and relatives dependent on them.[4]

However, for middle-class women, work, especially paid work, meant a serious loss in social status in which 'lady' and 'work' were contradictions in terms. Leonore Davidoff has cited a typical example of this attitude, dating from 1866:

> My opinion is that if a woman is obliged to work, at once (although she may be Christian and well-bred) she loses that peculiar position which the word *lady* conventionally designates.[5]

The plight of unmarried and destitute gentlewomen became a national concern. In view of the characteristics attributed to ladies, it was essential to find work for them which could be considered 'suitable'. Contamination from the sordid male commercial world was to be avoided at all costs if women were to maintain their role as the haven from that world, and if men were to retain their dominance and authority within it. Thus in both social and economic terms, the reinforcement of a sexual division of labour at all levels of society was essential for the preservation of the very fabric of the society's structure.

Art work was one of the few occupations considered suitable for middle-class women in the Victorian period. Here was a field of employment that appeared to be merely an extension of traditional feminine accomplishments. It would enhance rather than erode the role designated as 'natural' for the Victorian woman, for art work represented only the slightest adjustment of her accepted social position:

> To whom should we so confidently apply for all that concerns the beautifying of home-life as to the *presiding spirit of the home*? Why should not the *instinctive taste and natural grace of woman* be reflected in the hues and harmonies of colour and form on the walls of her rooms, on the curtains arranged by her deft fingers, on the soft carpet beneath her feet, and in the thousand forms of comfort, convenience, or elegance which surround her?[6]

In fact this type of work – although in this context, paid work – was an extension of what Roszika Parker and Griselda Pollock describe as bourgeois women's role in perpetuating aristocratic traditions: 'to be beautifiers, civilizers, orderers in the face of the social mobility and economic instability of a chaotic and threatening world'.[7] At the same time, art work was defined as 'domestic': it would thus not encroach upon the newly formulated male–female labour divisions:

> We may remark, at the risk of repetition, that there is here no question of the introduction of women to new employments, or of the danger of tempting them from their homes . . . All that now concerns us is the question of fitting women to do the work well, *which they already do*, but do badly. In the consideration of new openings in Art-work we do not actually introduce any new element.[8]

This notion that work for women should not disrupt the patriarchal *status quo*, and in particular that it should not remove women from the private domestic sphere, is crucial. As Parker and Pollock argue, it was by labelling certain aspects of artistic production 'domestic', by calling them crafts, that, in the evolution of the modern concept of art, the split between high art and the lesser arts was constructed:

> What distinguishes art from craft in the hierarchy is not so much methods, practices and objects but also where these things are made, often in the home, and for whom they are made, often for the family. The fine arts are a public, professional activity. What women make, which is usually defined as 'craft', could in fact be defined as 'domestic art'. The conditions of production and audience for this kind of art are different from those of the art made in the studio and the art school, for the market and gallery. It is out of these different conditions that the hierarchical division between art and craft has been constructed; it has nothing to do with the inherent qualities of the object nor the gender of the maker.[9]

This hierarchical split can be traced back to Renaissance times, when artists began to shun the practical and manual aspects of their craft in order to raise their social status by identifying themselves with intellectuals. However, significantly, it was with the Industrial Revolution and the rise of the bourgeois family with its acompanying concept of domesticity, that the schism reached completion. So for these Victorian artists, writers and social thinkers who sought humane alternatives to the divisiveness of their society, it is not suprising that pre-Renaissance society as they saw it seemed to offer a charming ideal.

The desirability and popularity of artistic work for middle-class

8.1
Trade card of Ann Buck, 1748
The face is that of Queen Anne,
not of Ann Buck

8.2
William Hallett holding
the plans for his new house,
his wife seated on his left
Painted by Francis Hayman, c. 1748

8.3
Ray Hille's myrtle dining chair
and occasional table, 1948

9.1
Light-bulb manufacture in the 1920s
From the General Electric Company's
The Story of the Lamp, no date

9.2
The EAW show house, Bristol, 1935

9.3
Kitchen of the EAW show house, Bristol, 1935

9.4
EAW's Electrical Housecraft School, 1934

Women participants

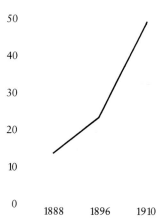

Women designers and women executants

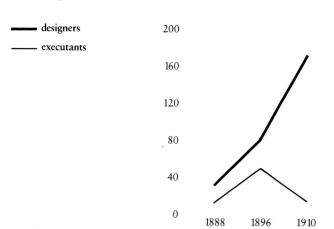

▬ designers
— executants

11.1
Women's participation in
three exhibitions organised by the
Arts and Crafts Exhibition Society

All my own work .

12.1
'All my own work'
Dryad Handicrafts catalogues c. 1922

12.2
'How to use your hands'
Dryad Handicrafts catalogue 1920

BOOKS AND MATERIALS
FOR BASKET MAKING, etc.

SOLD AT

THE DRYAD WORKS

HANDICRAFT DEPARTMENT

42 ST. NICHOLAS ST., LEICESTER

How to use your hands

This leaflet cancels all previous ones.   *DECEMBER, 1920.*

12.3
Dryad summer school, 1921

13.1
The exterior defines the house
Cartoon by A. G. Wise from Anthony Bertram's
The House: A Machine for Living in,
A & C Black, London, 1935

This was built for

this man, so

why build this for

this man ?

This was built for

this man,

so why build this for

this man ?

Plate 2. FITNESS FOR PURPOSE

13.2
Rural and domestic idylls of the garden city
From George Benoit Lévy's
La Cité Jardin, Henri Jouve, Paris, 1904

14.1
A new kind of interior:
the open-plan sitting/dining room

14.2
1950s combination of Functionalism and DIY

fresh ideas for your home

This living-room answers three questions often found in your letters: Does old and new furniture mix? How can family snaps and photographs be arranged to save cluttering tables and piano—save endless dusting too? What is the best way to deal with a few books and ornaments—when there are not enough books for a bookcase and too few ornaments for a special cabinet?

Old and new furniture *does* mix, as this room shows, but there must be a strong colour link between the two. Here the old settee and one chair have been covered to match and a yellow cushion links the settee to another new chair.

Family snaps and photographs, printed the same size, mounted and framed with passe-partout to match, make a very interesting grouping on the wall.

They outline the fireplace and fit round a large picture, adding to their own and the picture's interest by their grouping.

Shelving divided into compartments (built into the fireplace recess in this room) makes a decorative display of a few books and ornaments. The compartments have been varied in height and shape to fit different sized books and frame five different ornaments.

EDITH BLAIR and JOHN LAWRENCE solve three individual furnishing problems with ideas that may serve as starting points for your own redecoration schemes

Camouflaging ugly fireplaces, especially bedroom fireplaces, is a constant theme in all your letters. There are the tiles that won't fit in with new decorating schemes, the yawning gap of the grate behind a gas or electric stove. . . .

The answer is to box in the fireplace with hardboard. Get the board cut to fit by your local timber merchant. Paint the board or cover it with wallpaper (clear varnished for hard wearing). The fireplace will be a really decorative centre of the room without having touched the original fireplace—an important point for those people living in rented accommodation.

We've been asked, by a reader furnishing a room for a growing up daughter, to suggest a bedside shelf arrangement which will both save expense and take the place of a bedside table.

"The room is narrow so it needs very little furniture," she writes, adding, "It has a wall heater so there is no mantelpiece for books or trophies."

In this last sentence we thought we could detect regret, so we show a simple shelf arrangement that serves not only as a bedside table, saving money and space, but as a shelf for books or ornaments (remembering that growing up is just the time to begin collections).

The shelf frames the wall heater and gets rid of that rather bare look wall heaters have. It's also a chance to bring extra colour into the room. Carry a beading on a line with the back of the shelf to the corner and distemper below this and the shelf in a contrasting shade—or use wallpaper, coated with clear varnish for sponging.

33

15.1
Eary 1950s combined kitchen/dining room,
Chippingfield Estate, Harlow

15.2
'Pram-jams' in the Broad Walk, Harlow, 1958

16.1
'A potter's pot-pourri'
From *Dora Lunn, potter:*
papers and photographs
AAD 1/6-1983

16.2
Dorothy Braddell's design for Hope's windows
From *Dorothy Braddell,*
graphic and interior designer: papers
AAD 2364-1980

16.3
Table by lacquer screen, c. 1925
From *Eileen Gray, interior and*
furniture designer and architect:
papers, designs and photographs
AAD 9/67-1980, E1027 Roquebrune

16.4
From *Charlotte Bondy, designer of aluminium foil packaging: autobiography and designs*

16.5
Fabric samples
From *Presage. Paris Fashion Forecast, 1967-8, autumn/winter*

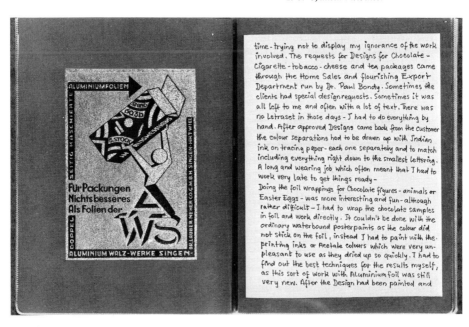

time - trying not to display my ignorance of the work involved. The requests for Designs for Chocolate - Cigarette - tobacco - cheese and tea packages came through the Home Sales and flourishing Export Department run by Dr. Paul Bondy. Sometimes the clients had special design requests. Sometimes it was all left to me and often with a lot of text. There was no Letraset in those days - I had to do everything by hand. After approved Designs came back from the customer the colour separations had to be drawn up with Indian ink on tracing paper - each one separately and to match including everything right down to the smallest lettering. A long and wearing job which often meant that I had to work very late to get things ready -

Doing the foil wrappings for Chocolate figures - animals or Easter Eggs - was more interesting and fun - although rather difficult - I had to wrap the chocolate samples in foil and work directly. It couldn't be done with the ordinary waterbound posterpaints as the colour did not stick on the foil, instead I had to paint with the printing inks or Acetate colours which were very unpleasant to use as they dried up so quickly. I had to find out the best techniques for the results myself, as this sort of work with Aluminium foil was still very new. After the Design had been painted and

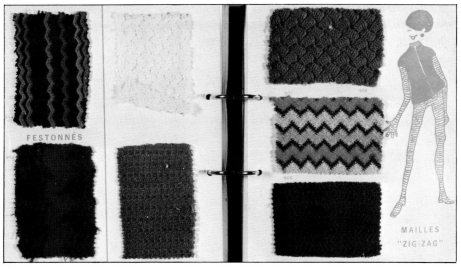

16.6
Two Worth costumes, 1903
From *House of Worth, Paris:*
albums of costume photographs
AAD 1/2-1982

women had been actively fostered as early as 1842 with the establishment of the Female School of Design in London. This government day-school provided design instruction for needy gentlewomen aged between 13 and 30. The influx of ladies into the expanding provincial art schools at this time not only indicated an increasing number of amateur artists but also aknowledged the importance of art for women as part of an acceptable career as governesses and, increasingly, as artists–craftswomen.

The 1870s saw an expansion in opportunities for ladies seeking artistic careers. In art embroidery there was the foundation of numerous institutions for teaching, employment and for selling ladies' work, including, in 1872, the Royal School of Art Needlework in South Kensington, London. In ceramics there were the National Art Training Schools, Minton's short-lived Art Pottery Studio in South Kensington and the growth of the Doulton Lambeth Pottery, which employed almost exclusively lady artists; Howell and James' of Regent Street, London, also organised annual competitions and exhibitions of women's ceramic work. In woodwork there was the foundation of the School of Art Woodcarving in South Kensington. With artistic and technical improvements in colour printing, book illustration became a field in which women's participation was encouraged. The expansion of the market for children's books was especially important, as women were inevitably considered best qualified for this *genre*. In typography and in lithographic illustration, as in most of the male-dominated craft trades, women had to be trained and employed separately in order to avoid direct contact and economic competition with men.

By the time the Arts and Crafts revival was fully fledged, in the mid-1880s, many women were already engaged, if not entirely accepted, in a range of craft and design fields, and their close association with the Movement was therefore quite predictable. The emergence of the Arts and Crafts Movement presented many women with opportunities for otherwise inaccessible practical training in an expanding market. It offered the possibility of paid home-work to those women with family commitments, or those whose social status did not allow them to work outside the home. The Movement gave the relative freedom of freelance work to women faced with punishing discrimination in more traditional professional circles. But while offering women many positive advantages, the Arts and Crafts Movement also insidiously perpetuated the class, sexual and labour divisions inherent in late-Victorian society.

The involvement of women in the Arts and Crafts Movement can be divided into four main categories, which also reflect the broad class divisions within the Movement. First, there were the working-class and agricultural labouring-class women, who were organised and employed in the revival of traditional rural crafts or cottage industries. Ruskin himself was a prime mover in these rural craft revivals. Second, there were the aristocratic, upper- and middle-class women of comfortable means and the appropriate leisure, who were philanthropically engaged in the organisation both of the rural craft revivals and of the artistic training and employment of destitute gentlewomen, mainly in urban centres. Third, there were the impoverished gentlewomen themselves, those ladies forced by circumstances to earn an independent livelihood or augment a meagre one, either by waged art work in an employer's workshop, as out-workers or freelance – usually practised discreetly from the home. The fourth category covers the élite inner circle of, most commonly, educated middle-class women, often related by birth or marriage to the key male figures within the vanguard of the movement.

Most of the crafts undertaken by such women were an extension of Victorian accomplishments and pastimes for ladies. Of those already listed above, woodcarving could be seen as an exception, yet the work was often small-scale, delicate and required very little physical strength. Embroidery and lacemaking were traditionally feminine crafts (although originally practised by both sexes). China painting and book illustration evolved painlessly from the water-colour sketching and drawing so essential to the accomplished lady. Bookbinding, jewellery and metalwork, which required fine detailed work, were also recommended as feminine pursuits.

In certain artistic fields male and female involvement over-lapped, but most were considered masculine or feminine. Thus women were actively excluded from architectural training and practice and many allied trades. Few women made the pots they decorated. Almost no women became wrought-iron workers, founders, stone-masons or plaster-workers. Furniture-making and fine printing were almost exclusively male fields of creativity.

Women were only able to train for bookbinding and metalwork through private, paying classes, as they were prohibited from entry into trade classes at schools like the Central School of Arts and Crafts. The case of Miss L.M. Wilkinson, a pioneer of women's rights who had trained as a bookbinder with Cobden-Sanderson's Doves Bindery and attempted to break the embargo on women at the Central's trade classes in bookbinding in the late 1890s, provides evidence of the discrimination against women in that trade. In a letter to the London County Council regarding Miss Wilkinson's application, W. R. Lethaby, then co-director of the Central, outlined the reasons for her exclusion.

I have now had the opportunity of talking to Mr Cockerell

on the bookbinding matter. He tells me that there is now a strike going on in Glasgow on the employment of women, the point being not any objection to them as such, but that they cut down wages to a vanishing point. He says if a sewer did apply, she would not be admissible beyond the sewing department. He is convinced that putting a woman into the class would break it up in two days.[10]

The sexual division of labour in bookbinding, as in many other crafts, had a clear economic basis as a result of the devaluation of women's work. Only certain tasks were given to women in order to avoid bringing them into direct competition with men, which would threaten male jobs, male status and male wages. The tasks given to women were often the most exacting but also the most tedious and menial, because women were generally thought to be more tolerant of boredom than men. In the bookbinding trade women provided a cheap labour-force as sewers, and it was only in the private binderies, Arts and Crafts workshops or where women set up their own binderies that they could practise all the processes of the craft. In this way both sexual and class divisions were maintained in the broader trade context.

Men only exceptionally associated themselves with the 'feminine' crafts. William Morris was one such exception in that he learned, or rather taught himself, embroidery. But even his involvement was chiefly that of a pioneer, an explorer, and once ancient techniques had been mastered he generally passed the mundane work of execution on to the women of his family and workshop.

Although in its ideals the Arts and Crafts Movement sought to eliminate the split between designer and maker, in many ways it failed. It is significant that the division between designer and executant often represented yet another break between male and female. Nowhere was this so explicit as in needlework. The status of embroidery in particular was high in the Middle Ages, but as Roszika Parker wrote:

> As society 'progressed', embroidery became an almost exclusively female activity, and over the centuries this relationship has been mutually destructive. Embroidery suffered from being characterised as women's work. The same characteristics were ascribed to both women and embroidery: they were seen as mindless, decorative and delicate – like the icing on the cake, good to look at, adding taste and status, but devoid of significant content.[11]

Because of its association with gentlewomen, who were discouraged or excluded from 'unfeminine' intellectual and creative pursuits, embroidery came to be seen as a purely manual skill. However, the creation of designs for embroidery, an activity thought to demand greater intellectual powers, was not eschewed by men. Virtually all the best-known craftsmen of the late-Victorian period made designs for embroidery or lace, which were then executed by women, often their wives or daughters. This supposedly required only manual dexterity – in itself an acquirement which was underrated both because of its links with 'women's work' and because it was ascribed the lowest level in the hierarchy of creative processes.

Jane Burden, wife of William Morris, noted how he became interested in embroidery as early as 1855 and, after their marriage in 1859, initiated her into the craft:

> He taught me the first principles of laying the stitches together so as to cover the ground smoothly and radiating them properly. Afterwards we studied old pieces and by unpicking etc., we learnt much – but it was uphill work, fascinating, but only carried through by his enormous energy and perseverance.[12]

Not only did he teach Jane Burden to embroider, but he seems to have instructed every woman with whom he came into contact in the art. These included Mary Nicholson, who kept house for him at Red Lion Square, where Morris, Marshall, Faulkner & Co. were located in the 1860s; Madeleine Smith, wife of George Wardle, Morris' manager at Red Lion Square; Kate Faulkner, Elizabeth Burden and Georgiana Burne-Jones. The latter four and Jane Burden, with several women working under them, executed embroideries on cloth and silk for the firm.

As soon as the Morris daughters were old enough, they too joined in the collective embroidery work, in the manner of the medieval system Morris admired so much. Henry James recorded in 1869 that Morris 'works it stitch by stitch, with his own fingers, aided by those of his wife and little girls'.[13] The eldest, Jenny, was at this date eight years old, while May was only seven, so their involvement in the craft evidently began at an early age. In respect of the general sexual division between designer and executant, May Morris was an exception. Trained by her father, she took complete charge of the firm's embroidery workshop at the age of 23, in 1885. She wrote and lectured widely, in England and America, on embroidery design and execution, yet her own work is often unfairly dismissed as lifeless in comparison with her father's.

The Morris firm seems to have employed few women in its

workshops, apart from the embroidery section. Contemporary photographs show only one other case, where two women are at work on carpet weaving. Thus, in the main, the Morris firm's activities in which women were engaged divide into two groups: first, members of the family or friends who either helped to run the business and were employed in active production more or less full-time or who, like Georgiana Burne-Jones, served as part-time, and presumably unpaid, helpers; second, the group formed by the unknown number of waged women employees who, under the supervision of May Morris, produced the bulk of the firm's embroideries as well as their ready-to-sew kits.

The employment of women in this traditionally feminine branch of the crafts reinforced a sexual division of labour which was largely repeated throughout the Arts and Crafts Movement as a whole. It is not clear whether May Morris was receiving payment for her work, or if she was simply supported by her father as a member of his family. However, when she was planning to marry Henry Halliday Sparling in the late 1880s, she was forced to experiment with frugal living, which suggests that even at this date she was not earning an independent income from the firm.

> May is away at Kelmscott Manor alone learning to cook & how to live on a few shillings a week. She is bent on marrying without waiting till her future husband gets employment. I have said & done all I can to dissuade her, but she is a fool and persists.[14]

In terms of social status as well as personal self-respect, the question of pay for work is of vital importance. At this time the title 'amateur' was already a derogatory one, and it was applied most often to women and to their work. This is hardly surprising in view of the ideological split between the public and domestic spheres, and of the social unacceptability of paid work for middle-class women. The negative connotations of dismissal and exclusion attached to the title 'amateur' made it yet another weapon in the patriarchal armoury.

The crafts most commonly practised by women echoed both traditional and more recent patterns of sexual labour divisions. Embroidery, lacemaking, china painting, jewellery, bookbinding, illustrating and even woodcarving were all activities which could be pursued *within the home*, often without the need for a special workshop or studio. While this did enable many women to take up craft work, it inevitably reinforced the distinction between the public and private, male and female worlds. It was a situation which in itself often presented the craftswoman with severe problems, as one writer noted (the italics are mine):

It may be that women cannot at once rise to the level on which men stand after ages of culture and conscious freedom; or, more likely that no woman is, or ought to be, able to free herself from domestic duties and associations, which, in their inevitable interruption, render almost impossible the concentration of purpose and leisure of mind essential to high success. We have here a really strong reason against the success of women in any continuous avocation, *especially if followed in the home*. On the master, or on the son of the house, the library or studio door may be closed until opened by himself. But the very nature of her duties makes this impossible for the mistress who manages her own house; while, as a rule, very few mothers have sufficient sympathy with any fixed purpose of work to secure to their girls the same freedom which, as a matter of course, they give to their boys.[15]

In addition, working in the home placed women in a position of physical and psychological isolation not dissimilar to that of working-class women out-workers, except that the latter (for example, in lacemaking) did when possible work in groups to economise on light and heat. Because of family ties or of the need for chaperoning, many craftswomen functioned best in the loosely structured, flexible Arts and Crafts organisations; they tended to avoid production-oriented, tightly-knit workshops. Most of the women active in the Birmingham-based Bromsgrove Guild, for example, withdrew after its removal to Bromsgrove, at which point most of the Guild's 'feminine' crafts ceased.

One of the organisations in which women were most deeply involved at all levels was the unpretentious Home Arts and Industries Association, founded in 1884, which was probably the most influential of all in its nationwide, grassroots dissemination through teaching and practice of the ideals of the Arts and Crafts Movement. It was the organisation which, both practically and ideologically, had the closest links with accepted domestic activities normally pursued by women. It was also the furthest away in the Arts and Crafts hierarchy from the 'master craftsmen'. Work by the Home Arts and Industries Association, shown annually at the Albert Hall in London, was often condescendingly derided as amateurish by critics in, for example, the *Studio* magazine.[16]

It is clear that home-work was the most common way for women to practise a craft in the early 1870s, when a writer noted the lack of craftswomen working in outside studios. Doubtless due to the problems of training and employment of craftswomen in a male-dominated environment, this writer recommended a separate and parallel development of businesses run and staffed by women, where women could also be taken on as apprentices. As well as avoiding ideological conflict, this 'separatist' system side-stepped the problems of male–female competition and of the threat of wage parity or loss of male status. It also eliminated the difficulties of chaperoning women in an exclusively male workplace. This approach to the 'very real difficulties attending the employment of women, in remunerative work of any kind' was detailed by a writer in 1872:

> What seems greatly to be desired is that some women, having first fully qualified themselves by earnest study, should, either alone, or in combination, set up in business, *on strict business principles*, making arrangements for female apprentices, and fairly trying the question of woman's work on its own merits. A few efforts in this spirit, made by wise and competent women, would do more to advance the real interests of women than can be done by all the societies in the kingdom, however well-intentioned, or well-managed . . . As it is, numbers of young women are gathered together in the workrooms of milliners and of drapers, who do their work, and generally in the end marry and settle down in their own homes, not necessarily injured by their businesslife. There seems to be no reason why young ladies might not be so gathered into the workroom of a lady engraver, or designer, and so on, and there be enabled to do work for which they are fitted by natural gift, or by artistic culture.[17]

In practice the training and employment of ladies in an all-female environment bore little comparison to the notorious sweatshop existence of their working-class counterparts. At such institutions as the Royal School of Art Needlework, the ladies were constantly supervised and cloistered in a way appropriate to their station, keeping to a minimum the loss of social status associated with paid employment. Home-work and the need for discretion by a working lady were evidently important factors in creating a sense of isolation among many craftswomen of the middle classes. But a tendency within the Arts and Crafts Movement at large towards male-dominated organisations – reflecting broader social patterns – seems to have reinforced this problem.

The notion of brotherhood so central to the Movement may have its origins in the Gothic Revival and with the Pre-Raphaelite Brotherhood. The trend towards male-bonding, which was apparent throughout contemporary social relations, was the logical product of a social structure which discouraged intellectual and emotional equality between men and women, and restricted social intercourse between the sexes to a narrow, rigid formula. The *status quo* was maintained even among the radical élite of the movement. Take the Morris circle as an example. A letter about Jane Burden written by Henry James to his sister after a visit to the Morris family in 1869 gives an insight into the attitudes to women prevalent at this period:

> A figure cut out of a missal – out of one of Rosetti's or Hunt's pictures – to say this gives but a faint idea of her, because when such an image puts on flesh and blood, it is an apparition of fearful and wonderful intensity. It's hard to say whether she's a grand synthesis of all the Pre-Raphaelite pictures ever made – or they a 'keen analysis' of her – whether she's an original or a copy.[18]

These extraordinary remarks serve to emphasise the degree to which women were distanced and dehumanised as objects of visual display, Jane Burden here being evaluated in terms normally reserved for assessing art objects rather than people. James' comments demonstrate the ideological function of visual representations in mediating the lived experience of, in this instance, Jane Burden as a person. The constructed reality of art displaces real human contact.

Many women in the Morris circle, including Jane Burden herself, were from working-class backgrounds. They found themselves taken up by this group of intellectuals and aesthetes for their sultry beauty and 'earthy sensuality'. Because of class divisions in Victorian society, such women held the appeal of forbidden fruits; yet once conquered, they assumed the status – and, for their men, the taboos – attached to women of the middle classes. Marital sex with women of one's own class was for reproduction, not for pleasure. The Victorian code of morals, here overcast with strains of medieval chivalry, required that any real sensual relationship be abandoned for a remote idealisation of these women. It was evident that sex and marriage were incompatible, as Swinburne so aptly intimated in his letter to Edwin Hatch in 1858, when he said that he liked to think of 'Morris having that wonderful and almost perfect stunner of his to look at or speak to. The idea of his marrying her is insane. To kiss her feet is the utmost men should dream of doing.'[19]

Thus it is no coincidence that so many of the Arts and Crafts guilds – founded upon the Victorian vision of those institutions – were male-dominated or, as in the case of the influential Art Workers' Guild, founded in 1884, exclusively male 'clubs'. Although a Women's Guild was founded in 1907, a minor offshoot of the Art Workers' Guild, it was by then too late for it to fulfil the functions needed in the early years of the Movement: to provide women with a source of mutual support and a sense of common aims, strengths and shared identity. Although in the Guild's separately administered Arts and Crafts Exhibition Society women exhibited alongside men, there was no attempt to integrate men and women in the Guild itself, the powerhouse of the Arts and Crafts Movement, no attempt to institutionalise alternative patterns of male–female labour divisions.

This failure reinforced the sense of 'otherness' experienced by craftswomen; it fuelled the conflict between gender and professional identities to which such women were subject – and thereby reinforced wider Victorian social and work patterns, rather than offering any radical alternatives. So despite its positive aspects, the Arts and Crafts Movement further alienated those women who were faced with the need to reconcile the opposing ideals of lady and work, woman and artist, private and public.

These divisive categories still pose serious problems for women, as contemporary experience and research make clear.[20] Personally, I am not an advocate of Minimal embroidery or Conceptual ceramics, and I cannot agree with those who wish simply to elevate crafts to fine-art status and craftswomen to artist status – this seems neither viable nor desirable as a solution, as fundamentally it changes nothing. Nor do I wish to see domesticity thrown out of the window. Change needs to take place at all levels for it to be effective. What is needed, in my opinion, is continual questioning and reappraisal of the personal and of the political in its broadest sense: self-critical analyses of our approaches to history and the ways rewriting the past can transform the present, of our received ideas and preconceptions of all oppositional categories – craft/fine-art, female/male, nature/culture – and how the construction of such polarised binaries functions to constitute negative 'others' within our patriarchal culture. It is through lack of awareness and understanding of these categories and of their ideological power that we collude in the construction and limitations of our own sexual roles and creative potential.

Notes

1 'Art-work for women I', *Art Journal*, 1872, p. 66.
2 See, for example, his discussion of women's roles in 'Of Queens' Gardens', Section 68, in Cook, E. T., and Wedderburn, A. D. O., eds., *Works*, London, 1902–12, Vol. 18.
3 Ellis, Mrs Sarah, *The Wives of England, Their Relative Duties, Domestic Influence and Social Obligations*, London, 1843, pp. 99–100; quoted in Houghton, W. E., *The Victorian Frame of Mind*, London, 1957, p. 351.
4 'Art-work for women II', *Art Journal*, 1872, p. 103.

5 Letter to the editor of the *Englishwoman's Journal*, Vol. 8, 1866, p. 59; quoted in Davidoff, Leonore, *The Best Circles*, London, 1974, p. 95.

6 'Art-work for women I', op. cit., p. 65.

7 Parker, Rozsika, and Pollock, Griselda, *The Old Mistresses: Women, Art and Ideology*, Rowledge & Kegan Paul, London, 1981, p. 99.

8 'Art-work for women III', *Art Journal*, 1872, p. 130.

9 Parker and Pollock, op. cit., p. 70.

10 See Callen, Anthea, *Angel in the Studio: Women in the Arts and Crafts Movement 1870–1914*, Astragal Books, London, 1979, pp. 189–91.

11 Parker, Rozsika, 'The word for embroidery was WORK', *Spare Rib*, No. 37, July 1975, p. 41.

12 Morris, Barbara, *Victorian Embroidery*, London, 1962, p. 95.

13 Letter to his sister of 10 March 1869; quoted in ibid., p. 97.

14 Jane Morris' letter to Rosalind Howard of August 1888; quoted in Henderson, Philip, *Morris, His Life, Work and Friends*, London, 1967, p. 298. May Morris and Sparling were married in 1890; they were later divorced.

15 'Art-work for women II', op. cit., p. 102.

16 See, for example, Esther Wood on the Home Arts and Industries Association Exhibition, *Studio*, Vol. 23, 1901, p. 106. For more information on the Association, see Callen, op. cit., especially pp. 5–7.

17 'Art-work for women II', op. cit., p. 102.

18 Henderson, Philip, ed., *The Letters of William Morris*, London, 1950, p. lxi; letter of 10 March 1869.

19 Henderson, 1967, op. cit., p. 50.

20 See, for example, Lippard, Lucy, *From the Centre*, New York, 1976; Callen, A., *et al.*, 'A beginning time: Three women artists look at the experience of art college', *Spare Rib*, No. 44, 1976; Parker and Pollock, op. cit., especially Ch. 5; Pollock, Griselda, 'Art, artschool, culture: Individualism after the death of the artist', *Block*, No. 11, Winter 1985–6.

11
The Arts and Crafts Alternative

Lynne Walker

Anthea Callen concluded the previous chapter thus:

> This failure [to institutionalise alternative patterns of
> male–female labour divisions] reinforced the sense of
> 'otherness' experienced by craftswomen; it fuelled the
> conflict between gender and professional identities to
> which such women were subject – and thereby reinforced
> wider Victorian social and work patterns, rather than
> offering any radical alternatives. So despite its positive
> aspects, the Arts and Crafts Movement further alienated
> those women who were faced with the need to reconcile
> the opposing ideals of lady and work, woman and artist
> private and public.

This paper is a sisterly response which aims to adjust that view of
the Arts and Crafts Movement and the women who took an active
part in it, and although there is much common ground, I want to
argue that the extent to which the Arts and Crafts Movement
reinforced Victorian patriarchal ideology is less clear-cut and rigid
than was previously thought and that instead of further alienating
women, the Arts and Crafts Movement provided women with
alternative roles, institutions and structures which they then used as
active agents in their own history.

Most significantly, these Arts and Crafts alternatives provided
opportunities for women's paid employment, which often took
place outside the home, in the public sphere, which in the late-
Victorian period became the new arena for middle-class women
professionals and art workers. In many cases women's Arts and
Crafts design work led to financial and personal independence well
beyond previous experience, enhancing women's position and
status in society in a much more fundamental way than has been
conceded. Instead of alienation, the role of craftworker, which the
Arts and Crafts Movement generated, produced feelings of
competence and satisfaction in women; it did not increase isolation
and 'otherness', as has been suggested. Although the position of
women was far from unproblematic, the improved status of women

within the Arts and Crafts Movement, which dates from the 1890s, was well-established by the First World War, when wartime pressures and the Women's Suffrage Movement combined to make real societal change possible. Thus the Arts and Crafts Movement had prepared the ground, in some quarters at least, for the challenge to the dominant patriarchal *status quo* which came with the Great War. Through alternative patterns of labour and production women in the Arts and Crafts Movement had struck at the centre of the gender–power nexus, the financial dependency of women, to struggle against the Victorian ideology that had restricted them to the private, unpaid world of home and bourgeois respectability.

The social structure of the Arts and Crafts Movement had great implications for women, as Alan Crawford and I found when we surveyed 360 organised Arts and Crafts groups (*c.* 1880–1914) in Britain. We found that the most characteristic organisation of the Arts and Crafts Movement (273 out of 360) was the workshop, which was 'in a basic sense the core of the Movement, where the essential activity was carried on'.[1] We concluded that the Arts and Crafts Movement in Britain was important as an organised response to social needs and was particularly important in relation to women's participation, which highlighted the need to see 'the Arts and Crafts Movement in the harsh light of economic necessity'.[2]

We also argued that the large numbers of women present in Arts and Crafts organisations 'reflected a more fundamental exclusion of middle-class women from paid employment'.[3] What these groups offered – and this was a goal of the Movement generally – was an alternative to the Victorian commercial world, and this was especially significant for middle-class single women.

> condemned to a twilight world without a role in society, often without money, and without a socially sanctioned means of making money. To such people, the possibility of earning some kind of living by making saleable goods at home, or in discreetly anonymised premises, was some kind of lifeline thrown by the Arts and Crafts Movement.[4]

However, the circumscribing nature of the sexual division of labour and its operation within the Arts and Crafts Movement is not in dispute here. Rigid sex roles and sexual stereotypes determined the crafts in which women could participate, and, moreover, the crafts which were thought to express women's 'limited, and "special" feminine capabilities',[5] in Anthea Callen's phrase. Bookbinding, for example, was represented in the *Studio* in 1898 as a natural extension of feminine attributes and endorsed enthusiastically as an appropriate craft for women: 'it is a craft that calls for little heavy manual labour and great patience, with neatness raised to the level of a fine art.'[6] A sexual stereotype reinforced certainly, but women were active agents operating in this specific instance to find employment and creative fulfilment as Arts and Crafts bookbinders. By the 1890s the Arts and Crafts Movement had raised the temperature of artistic production and increased opportunities for women to make money from craft work. For example, the Guild of Women Binders were selling their work through a depot in Charing Cross Road, London, which attracted women from all over Britain. Another writer in the *Studio* praised 'the high-class and original work which women', such as Phoebe Traquair, 'are now producing in the field of book-binding'.[7] The work also, of course, generated income.

A second sexual division of labour existed within the production of the craft object itself: tasks were divided between the male designer and the female maker, and in commercial and trade practice the maker's role was further subdivided with women assigned 'appropriate' menial tasks within the production process. Sewing, as Anthea Callen has shown,[8] was the traditional job for women in the bookbinding trade. However, Arts and Crafts practice was anti-commercial and opposed to trade practices, and it sought to bring the process of designing and making together, giving them equal value. In fact, the holistic Arts and Crafts approach meant that women were not restricted to sexually stereotyped roles in the design process and were free to design the products which they also sometimes made. Women were able to sidestep the restrictive practices enforced by the sexual division of labour in commercial production and found more options, more freedom of expression and, significantly, more financial rewards, through Arts and Crafts alternative practice.

As an index to women's role and position within the Arts and Crafts Movement, the best measure is perhaps the Arts and Crafts Exhibition Society, the central exhibiting organisation of the Movement. They displayed craft work from throughout the British Isles and featured a wide range of work from both men and women, with exhibits from lesser-known figures, provincial designers and amateurs, many of whom were women, as well as exhibits produced in the workshop of the Movement's leading figures, such as William Morris and C. R. Ashbee.

In order to examine the sexual division of labour within the Arts and Crafts Movement three representative exhibitions – those of 1888, 1896 and 1910 – have been studied.[9] The first set the pattern for those which followed; the second took place in the heyday of the Movement; and the last was held in the year which is often cited as the time the Movement died (see Fig. 11.1).

Three questions are crucial here. First, to what extent did women show and sell their work through the central exhibiting body of the Movement? Second, did their participation increase or decline between 1888 and 1910? Third, and most important, was there a sexual division of labour between male designer and female maker and was it broken down or maintained during this period? The evidence supports the view that the Arts and Crafts Movement provided the focal point for hundreds of British women's craft production and sales, that women's participation in the Movement increased during this period, and that the sexual division of labour within the Arts and Crafts Movement tended to break down over the period in question, providing women with access to a wider range of artistic and professional activities.

Using the Arts and Crafts Exhibition Society as an index for women's craft production and a measure of the sexual division of labour within the Movement, the 1888 exhibition reinforced traditional divisions along gender lines in many instances, but there was also a promising flexibility in the system. The predominant activity for women was embroidery, a traditional feminine craft, and the majority of these women were the makers of designs by men. This was particularly true for women married to the male leaders of the Movement – Mrs Walter Crane, Mrs Henry Holiday, Mrs Reginald Hallward and Mrs William Morris (named here as they were normally listed in the catalogue). However, there were an **equal number of independent women embroiderers at the 1888** exhibition who were there in their own right as designers or designer–makers. On the whole, though, women were much less numerous than men at the 1888 exhibition and more restricted to traditional feminine crafts. Notable exceptions were, for example, Agnes and Rhoda Garrett, interior designers who were equally active in the cause of Women's Emancipation and the Arts and Crafts Movement. The Garretts designed a complete interior, which consisted of furniture, metalwork, carpets, wallpaper and woodwork, that equalled the coherence of the work of Morris and Co., which was also on display at the 1888 exhibition. Significantly perhaps, the Garretts' scheme did not include embroidery, which was identified so completely with the Victorian feminine ideal which they were struggling against.

Although many women produced furniture designs, often as part of the Home Arts and Industries Association programme, it has been pointed out that Arts and Crafts women did not make furniture; but then, neither did many of their Arts and Crafts male counterparts, such as W. R. Lethaby, Mervyn Macartney or Ernest Gimson, who gave up chair-making because it was too physically taxing. All Arts and Crafts designers came up against the practical problem that making a craft object is very time-consuming and much less profitable than design.

The 1896 Arts and Crafts Exhibition Society is best known to historians as the exhibition which introduced the work of the Glasgow designers to the English Arts and Crafts Movement. Margaret and Frances Macdonald, whose work was a prominent part of the Glaswegian display, were the paradigm of Arts and Crafts designer–makers: they had established their own craft workshop away from the restrictions of trade practice even before their marriages to Charles Rennie Mackintosh and Herbert MacNair. Like most of the Glasgow contributors, they had connections with the Glasgow School of Art, which, by 1900, had roughly half men and half women in its student population. Art schools, like Glasgow, which imbued their students with Arts and Crafts principles, provided women with the skills necessary to professionalise themselves: with an art-school training women could set up their own workshops, or teach at arts schools or in the state school system.[10]

The revival of craft metalwork, jewellery and enamelling in the 1890s is represented in the new work exhibited by Arts and Crafts designer–makers such as Georgina Gaskin, Phoebe Traquair and Edith Dawson, and the 1896 exhibition also demonstrates women's growing numbers in bookbinding, illustration and stained glass. In addition, it reflects the revival of hand-weaving and appliqué embroidery with exhibits from Maude King and Mary Blount, who helped found and run two of the largest and most remarkable Arts and Crafts groups in the countryside near London: the Haslemere Weaving Industry, where local working-class women wove cotton, linen and silk on handlooms (at a starting wage of 5s. per week), and the Peasant Arts Society, also in Haslemere, which produced appliqué embroidery, hand-woven pile carpets and tapestry carpets.

As Rozsika Parker has pointed out, the impact of one of the Glasgow teachers, Jessie Newbery, who was an exhibitor at the 1896 exhibition, transformed the way embroidery was taught and practised.[11] Embroidery in Newbery's hands was no longer seen as a natural extension of the makers of feminine attributes, but was redefined in Arts and Crafts terms, emphasising the importance of design, simplicity and materials. Stylistically distinctive from the English Arts and Crafts, the work of the Glasgow women at the 1896 exhibition demonstrates how women themselves took an active part in the reinterpretation and professionalisation of a traditional feminine craft, and it also demonstrates the increased breadth of craft and design activities, fuelled by the Arts and Crafts Movement, which were open to women.

Parker brings out the complexity of the problem and argues that Jessie Newbery and Anne Macbeth 'loosened the hold of femininity on embroidery', but at the same time embroidery 'became institutionalised as the province of female staff and girls'. As she points out, 'each new gain for women was accompanied by a new dividing line between male and female territory.'[12] The weight of evidence for the Arts and Crafts Movement in relation to embroidery is analysed by Parker as follows: 'And whatever criticism can be levelled at the Arts and Crafts Movement in terms of sexism and elitism, it was instrumental in raising the standard of hand embroidery and allowing women to recognize the value of their work, not as mere evidence of the femininity which would enable them to attain male financial support, but as something which actually earned them money.'[13]

The broader aims of Maude King and Mary Blount, who both worked jointly with their husbands, were the repopulation and regeneration of the countryside, which was expressed in their quasi-religious philosophy of country life, but the economic imperative for women's work, in this instance working-class women who were employed in their workshops, was often masked or de-emphasised by the statements of Arts and Crafts philanthropists, like the Blounts and Kings, who saw the goals of workshop activities from an idealistic perspective. But from the perspective of the craft-workers it was first and foremost an opportunity to make a living wage in an area which at the best of times provided only seasonal work for women.[14]

By the 1910 exhibition, women's role and position in the Arts and Crafts Movement had strengthened in terms of numbers, and alternative patterns of male–female labour divisions had been established in the crafts represented at the exhibition. Jewellery was the predominant craft for women. Phoebe Traquair, for example, exhibited a silver and gold necklace with an enamelled pendant which incorporated the craft skills that women had taken up in recent years. Previously the jewellery trade had been dominated by men. Although women had traditionally taken part, with the advent of craft jewellery in the 1890s, this became an area which was considered especially appropriate for middle-class women, as the skills required were thought particularly 'feminine'; and, of course, women were its primary consumers. In 1901, Aymer Vallence wrote about women and jewellery in *Studio*:

> The number of ladies who have achieved success in jewellery design proves this, indeed, to be a craft to which women's light and dainty manipulation is peculiarly adapted.[15]

This kind of stereotyping, which saw the work as an extension of the maker's femininity, reinforced the connection between biology and creativity, but at the same time, women worked against the ideological grain by using this craft not as an amateur pursuit but as an area in which they could practise as professionals. Jessie M. King, for instance, made a series of designs for jewellery which were sold exclusively through Liberty's in London. Significantly, jewellery made by women sold very well, as an annotated copy of the 1910 exhibition catalogue in the Victoria and Albert Museum Art and Design Archive shows.

Like metalworking and jewellery, stained glass was another area revitalised by the Arts and Crafts Movement which provided opportunities for women. Traditionally, women were excluded from the stained-glass trade, apart from the occasional freelance commission. However, as we have seen in other areas, the Arts and Crafts rejection of commercialism and its emphasis on the individual designer–craftworker provided an alternative way of working for women.[16] Mary Lowndes, for example, a leading member of the Suffrage Movement, who had trained as a cartoon-maker with the Arts and Crafts designer Henry Holiday, had her own studio in Chelsea from the 1890s, where she made the designs which she then painted on glass in the workshops of Britten & Gilson, the Arts and Crafts firm. This unified Arts and Crafts method contrasts sharply with the strict division of labour in stained-glass production at Morris and Co. Lowndes worked exclusively in the thick, reamy 'Prior's Early English Glass', designing and making both domestic and ecclesiastical work, such as a three-light window at the Church of the Holy Innocents in Lamarsh, which was exhibited at the Arts and Crafts Exhibition Society and illustrated in the *Art Journal*.[17]

How do we conclude this exercise in the application of theory to practice? The three points addressed should now be considered. First, using the Arts and Crafts Exhibition Society numbers, it is clear that women's participation in craft production increased dramatically during the period in which the Movement flourished, and that by 1910 women had achieved virtual parity with men at the most prestigious Arts and Crafts exhibition and at the most important school of art and design (the Glasgow School of Art). Second, by 1896, under the Arts and Crafts banner, women's work had diversified from traditional feminine crafts to include a wide range of activities which were open to both sexes. Stained glass, for example, was a craft which was not an option for women at the beginning of our period (1888), but was very popular with professional women designers by the 1910 exhibition, as the catalogue shows and as the programme of the 'Pageant of Women's Trades and Professions' at the 1909 International Woman Suffrage Alliance makes clear:

Glass Painting has of late years received a great impetus in this country, and women are taking their part with men in the front ranks of the new movement; though it is probable that twenty years ago there was not among artists a single woman glass painter.[18]

Most importantly, by the end of the period there is strong evidence that the sexual division of labour between male designer and female maker had broken down within the Arts and Crafts Movement. The number of women designers taking part in the exhibitions of 1888, 1896 and 1910 showed a continuous increase, and in fact there were five times as many women designers in 1910 as in 1888. The number of women executants, however, was roughly the same in 1910 as it had been in 1888. So far as women are concerned, then, the increase in women's participation was overwhelmingly in terms of designers. By 1910, women were normally designers in their own right, and if they worked as executants it was usually either to make their own goods in an Arts and Crafts way or to work the designs of another woman.[19] This is a finding which challenges the idea that traditional male–female roles were generally recreated in the Arts and Crafts Movement. In the final analysis, the Arts and Crafts Movement, while it may not have won a definitive victory against 'the dominant Victorian patriarchal ideology', did far more than simply reproduce and perpetuate it in a monolithic way. What the Arts and Crafts Movement did was to provide an alternative to the commercial system that excluded women. In the harsh light of economic reality it gave women a role as designer–makers which many of them used to acquire financial independence and personal fulfilment, changing the way women thought about themselves in relation to work and creating the precedent for other women to follow Arts and Crafts ideals well into the 1950s.

One final point about the chronology of the Arts and Crafts Movement can be made in conclusion. Elsewhere it has been argued that the Arts and Crafts Movement did not stop in the period 1910–14 but continued with vigour into the inter-war years.[20] Certainly it seems on the evidence of the Arts and Crafts Exhibition Society that by the time the generation of Morris had begun to die out and even the younger generation of Arts and Crafts men were running out of steam, the women in the Movement were just finding their feet.

Notes

1 Crawford, Alan, and Walker, Lynne, 'Arts and Crafts organizations', a paper given at the Annual Conference of the Victorian Society, 1978.

2 Ibid.

3 Ibid.
4 Ibid.
5 Callen, Anthea, *Angel in the Studio: Women in the Arts and Crafts Movement 1870–1914*, Astragal Books, London, 1979, p. 22.
6 'Bookbinding for women', *Studio*, Vol. 13, 1898, p. 109.
7 *Studio*, Vol. 16, 1899, p. 150.
8 Callen, 1979, op. cit., p. 187; previous chapter.
9 Arts and Crafts Exhibition Society Catalogues, 1888, 1896, and 1910. This is a representative selection of exhibitions; others during this period were held in 1889, 1890, 1893, 1899, 1903 and 1906.
10 Parker, Rozsika, *The Subversive Stitch: Embroidery and the Making of the Feminine.*, The Women's Press, London, 1984, pp. 184–8.
11 Ibid., p. 187.
12 Ibid.
13 Ibid., p. 184.
14 Ibid.
15 Crawford and Walker, op. cit.
16 Vallence, Aymer, *Studio*, Vol. 19, 1901, p. 48. See also Lisa Tickner's excellent *The Spectacle of Women: Imagery of the Suffrage Campaign 1907–14*, Chatto & Windus, London, 1987.
17 Cormack, Peter, *Women Stained Glass Artists of the Arts and Crafts Movement*, catalogue of an exhibition at the William Morris Gallery, London, 1985.
18 'Women workers in the arts and crafts', *Art Journal*, 1986, p. 116.
19 Quoted by Cormack, op. cit.
20 Data compiled from the *Arts and Crafts Exhibition Society Catalogues*, 1888, 1896, 1910.

12
Women and the Inter-war Handicrafts Revival

Pat Kirkham

The spirit and traditions of the Arts and Crafts Movement continued throughout the inter-war years, most notably in the field of amateur handicrafts. The period witnessed an unprecedented boom in handicrafts as they became accepted as a leisure pursuit for thousands and thousands of people, particularly women. The acceptability of amateur handicraft work was based on a change in attitude towards craft as *leisure* as opposed to craft as *work* and also on a breaking down of the hegemonic hold of notions of professional training and individual genius. Amateur craftworkers came from all walks of life. Many handicrafts could be picked up and put down fairly easily and did not demand long stretches of leisure time. Nor were they the most expensive of hobbies, an important factor in the uncertain economic times of the 1920s and 1930s. White-collar and skilled manual workers were well represented in the towns, while in rural areas the Women's Institutes organised a wide social mix of women, many of whom had learned craft work as part of their domestic roles. Although drawn from both sexes, the vast majority of teachers, writers, instructors and students involved in handicrafts were women. The first three categories were professionals but it was at the amateur end, the student/practitioner end of the movement, that women had access to the crafts in an unprecedented way. Open-ended access was a crucial factor; all women had to do to participate was to join a local authority evening class or a Women's Institute.

One problem encountered in discussions of amateur handicrafts is that many people still denigrate some of the types of craft work popular at this time, such as raffia-weaving or papier-mâché work. Whereas crafts such as embroidery or handloom weaving are now deemed worthy of academic study and aesthetic appreciation – and are elevated to 'art' status by some – there still remains a hierarchy within the crafts. The very mention of those at the bottom of the hierarchy solicits a range of pejorative responses formerly directed at embroidery and other 'women's crafts'. This is reminiscent of the way in which within film and television studies soap operas and 'women's films' were once thought too insignificant for academic discussion. These two genres now have their academic respectability;

let us hope that one day all aspects of handicrafts will be considered as worthy of study as any other aspect of material culture.

The problem of the hierarchy, or pecking-order, of respectability within the crafts is exacerbated by the reluctance of art and design historians to study amateur work, which, by definition, is not 'great' art or design. Such élitist considerations need to be set aside for these aspects of popular culture to be viewed as valid in their own right. Rozsika Parker is one of the few art and design historians who examines amateur work but, unfortunately, her excellent and pioneering book, *The Subversive Stitch*, 1984, barely touches on the inter-war period.[1] In terms of pleasure and satisfaction, amateur handicrafts need to be looked at from the points of view of those who undertook them – and oral history interviews leave one in little doubt about the rich rewards they brought many people. This article examines the roots of the handicrafts revival, the widening range of handicrafts undertaken and the participation of women in what was, together with the cinema, dancing and sport, one of the most popular of inter-war pastimes.

The roots of the post-1918 boom in handicrafts activity go back to the ideas of John Ruskin and William Morris, particularly those relating to joy in labour and the need to revive, or at least protect, traditional crafts which were part of a popular cultural heritage.

The particular nature of the inter-war amateur enthusiasm for craft work also depended on a fundamental change in attitude towards the crafts which marks the difference between pre-industrial Britain and the swamping of home, rural and other craft skills by large-scale production, the division of labour, factory organisation and mechanisation. Although historians have over-emphasised the importance of the industrialised and industrialising sector of the British economy in the nineteenth century, and even the early twentieth century, at the expense of other sectors, the century before 1914 saw the working population increasingly losing day-to-day contact with the crafts as *work*, particularly those done in the home or rural areas. Indeed, the very popularity of craft work as a pleasurable *hobby* came about only with its removal from the world of paid work. Once outside that world, it became more accessible to women, who were also largely outside that world of work.

The leap from craft as work to craft as leisure was enormous. The morality of late-nineteenth-century Britain was such that leisure pursuits could not simply be accepted *per se*. Joy in labour alone smacked too much of sheer pleasure. In a society where work was hallowed as morally uplifting in itself, no matter how alienating it might be, leisure also had to have this value placed upon it. The Home Arts and Industries Association, founded in 1884 with the far-reaching aim of recapturing culture as the common property of the people, for instance, hoped to improve the morals of workers as well as improve their handicraft skills.[2]

The association wanted to foster dormant or undiscovered talents and fill the 'empty spaces' in people's lives outside paid work, spaces which it feared might otherwise be filled by drinking, gambling or generally licentious behaviour.

While there was a positive aspect to wanting to fill 'empty spaces' in people's lives (indeed, this theme ought to be a key one in the crafts debate today), we should not underestimate the negative aspect. Fear of what people might otherwise do with their spare time loomed large for those who realised the weight of social discontent in Britain in the years immediately after a bloody world war and workers' revolutions in Russia and Germany. It was argued that handicrafts were character-building: they cultivated resourcefulness, adaptability, initiative, self-reliance and a will to persevere. Social and educational reformers hoped these qualities, as well as the actual activity of handicrafts work, would keep people away from other distractions, be it the public house, the cinema ('mechanised pictures', as W. R. Lethaby disparagingly called it) or class politics.[3]

The teaching of handicrafts in schools would produce a new generation of children less likely than their parents to be tempted by such distractions. This area of teaching developed rapidly in junior schools in the years immediately after the First World War as new educational philosophies, based on the belief that children are innately creative if only given freedom of expression, were put into practice. At the same time as emphasising creativity and joy in labour, however, the teaching of handicrafts remained part of a wider process of socialisation. For girls in particular, it continued to restrain them, to define 'good' behaviour (see Figs. 12.1, 12.2). There was also some differentiation according to gender, which reinforced stereotypical gender roles. Bookcrafts, for instance, were seen as suitable for both sexes while knitting was recommended as a handicraft for girls.[4]

The recognition of children's art and craft work as valid in themselves helped the more general acceptance of non-professional work, whether by children or adults. This was reinforced in the early twentieth century by a growing appreciation of 'primitive', that is, non-European, largely non-representational, art and design. What had formerly been regarded as crude came to be seen as expressive once painters, psychologists, anthropologists, ethnographers and others increasingly recognised the cultural richness of so-called 'primitive' societies in which craft work played an important part.[5] The inter-war years saw a spate of publications, many of which reached high levels of scholarship, which led to a widespread appreciation of non-European craft work in Britain, elsewhere in Europe and the USA. This appreciation of contemporary cultures in which concepts such as 'genius' or 'professional' artist/designer were alien reinforced the arguments of William Morris and his followers in the Arts and Crafts Movement that the monolithic hold of such concepts, and of structures based upon them, had to be broken before art and crafts could flourish freely. Certainly amateur craft work of the type discussed here flourished only when notions of early specialisation, narrow professional training and the isolated individual artist as genius were challenged. Only then were children and women allowed full and free access.

It was not only that women took up craft work on a greater scale than before but also that a wider range was available to them. This expanded rapidly in the early twentieth century, largely because of the impact of the philosophy of W. R. Lethaby, who extended William Morris' concern for the commonplace things of life into an insistence that the very essence of civilisation lay in caring about simple, everyday things.[6] The leading design reformer of the early twentieth century, for him art was simply 'all worthy handicraft', which included not only hand-weaving and basket-making but also cooking, bread-making and 'laying the table nicely'. These latter activities had, of course, been undertaken by women for years and years without anyone considering them as art. Lethaby understood that modern society was too concerned with notions of 'genius' and 'great performers' to appreciate the common things of life. His philosophy elevated the ordinary domestic concerns of women to the same status as oil paintings or marble statues. There was no overnight transformation in attitudes towards such crafts (indeed, the process is still continuing), but Lethaby's insistence on the crucial importance in any civilised society of crafts associated with women gave a new confidence and sense of importance and appreciation to a whole generation of female teachers and students.

One of the organisations which put into practice many of the new ideas about handicrafts was the National Federation of Women's Institutes (NFWI).[7] Needless to say, it found a stalwart supporter in Lethaby, not least because it played a major part in preserving British craft traditions and encouraging new people to take them up. The NFWI was, of course, an all-female institution. The first British Institute was founded in 1915 and the movement quickly established itself nationally. Its ability to foster a cooperative spirit and seemingly cut across class barriers led Harry Peach to liken it to the village guilds of the fifteenth century.[8] All women were not equal within the NFWI, then or today, but, because working-class women often had the greatest craft skills and knowledge, they received considerable attention within the organisation.

The federation's magazine, *Home and Country*, regularly ran articles about 'Women's crafts' – or arts, as Lethaby called them in the articles which he regularly contributed. He went so far as to argue that plain sewing was an art in 'Sewing arts', where he also discussed patchwork, samplers, embroidery, quilt-making and lace-making.[9] This elevation of these activities to the status of art played a major part in generating a new pride in women's crafts which had previously been derided or ignored. That pride was reflected back and multiplied many times over in the exhibitions and other activities organised by local Women's Institutes.

The energetic Alice Armes was the Federation's handicrafts organiser in the inter-war years, when exhibitions were held at both national and local levels. As early as 1917 a small display of NFWI work was shown at the National Economy Exhibition in Hyde Park and there were national NFWI exhibitions in 1918 and 1920. At the local level the Oxfordshire Institutes were particularly active on the handicrafts issue and in 1921 organised a travelling exhibition of hand-work.[10] Local participation was all important if these women were to save crafts from extinction. Even on somewhere as remote as the Isle of Skye the weaving of homespun woollen had almost died out and had to be consciously revived and rejuvenated.

The role of handicrafts in the post-war reconstruction of rural Britain was discussed within the NFWI, but it was felt that most women did not have the time or inclination to develop their craft work on a commercial basis. Instead, attention was turned to establishing a Guild of Learners in 1920 'to assist in bringing the best instruction in handicrafts within the reach of villages' and restoring the best traditions of British craft work.[11] The development of skills and the maintenance of high standards were key objectives: for example, only items of the highest standard, rather than a cross-section of work, were chosen for the National Handicrafts Exhibition which the NFWI held at the Victoria and Albert Museum in 1922. The prestige of the venue indicates the seriousness with which the NFWI approached handicraft work as well as its enormous popularity.

It was relatively easy to agree on standards of quality in production; it was less easy to agree on matters of 'taste'. This in turn reflected class and educational divisions with the organisation. The taste of the well-educated middle-class women who acted as handicrafts organisers conformed to contemporary notions of 'good' straightforward design as represented by the Design and Industries Association, which often used contrasting photographs of objects to show 'good' and 'bad' design.[12] Unfortunately, a great many of the British public, and not a few NFWI members, rather liked some of the items in the 'bad taste' categories. A particular bête noire of art and design reformers was the crinoline lady,[13] in any shape or form, and a furore erupted in Nottinghamshire on this issue. Alice Armes made herself very unpopular with the Nottinghamshire Women's Institutes in the 1920s when she tried to impose her taste on them by refusing exhibition space to a paper nightdress-case in the shape of a crinoline lady. This particular object had been greatly admired by local NFWI members, who were infuriated by Armes' attitude and made it clear that they did not want to see her in the area again.[14]

The range of crafts covered by the Women's Institutes was enormous, embracing more crafts than any other single institution. Classes ranged from shoe-mending to straw-hat-making, from tinkering to tailoring and from basketwork to blacksmithing. This very full and energetic participation of the Women's Institutes in the handicrafts revival could, at one level, have opened up new areas of craft activity for women. At this popular level of the Arts and Crafts Movement, however, it is difficult (certainly at this stage of research) to see any breakdown of the existing gender divisions in the crafts as a result of this activity. While there was an extension of the definition of what crafts were deemed 'worthy' and 'artistic' the very concept of 'women's crafts' appears to have hardened in the inter-war years.

The Women's Institutes never challenged the dominant ideology relating to women's role in society. There were many layers of assumptions about what was 'womanly' that remained unchallenged: Lethaby, for instance, in a foreword to a book on embroidery, recommended '*all girls* to practise the fascinating game of playing with the needle and the pattern book'[15] (the italics are mine). In general, men were concerned with metalwork, woodwork and furniture, whereas women were concerned with all the sewing crafts, knitting, weaving, rug-making, upholstery and leatherwork. There were clearly many, many notable exceptions. Some men knitted and some women made furniture, but the gender divisions generally held true, with some crafts, such as bookbinding and basketwork, appearing 'neutral' enough to appeal to both women and men.

The NFWI was an important and powerful women's organisation but, because it did not challenge the *status quo* with regard to women and crafts, its very strength reinforced, and if anything hardened, the division between those activities undertaken by women and those undertaken by men. The establishment of separate departments of 'women's crafts' in art and design schools also had a similar effect. While their establishment was, at one level, an acknowledgment of the competence of women and their great interest in certain craft areas, at the same time these departments affirmed women's marginalisation, if not exclusion, from others. Suddenly, anything which was not in a department of women's crafts was, by definition, not a women's craft, and vice versa.

Although Glasgow School of Art pioneered many of the artistic women's crafts, such as embroidery, and increased its complement of women staff between about 1895 and 1915,[16] it was other schools which established separate departments of women's crafts. Leicester is a good example of an art and design school which established a special department for women students who were exclusively taught by female staff. The idea of establishing such a department at Leicester School of Art was first voiced before the First World War but it was not until 1917 that it finally opened. It was run by two women, Frances Livingston and Annie Heynes, and they were responsible for teaching 18 students. The only department in the School of Art to be taught by women for women, it was also the fastest growing in the inter-war years. By the end of the 1920s there were 12 full-time staff, who, together with part-time staff, taught over 130 students.[17]

While the department catered for students who hoped to work in local trades and for trainee teachers, it also offered non-vocational training to those who wished to learn how to discriminate between 'artistic and inartistic work and make the best of leisure'.[18] The latter students attended both day and evening classes. The day students were generally married women or others who were not in paid work, while evening students included women who worked in local factories. They all attended because they enjoyed creative craft work. They were taught by the same staff as the day-time vocational students. Creativity was encouraged and students had to make their own original designs for dresses, fabrics or embroidery. Students mostly made articles for themselves or the home. Dressmaking classes were always over-subscribed, with women wanting to make items for their trousseaux, dance dresses and home furnishings.[19] The boom – it almost amounted to a craze – for handicrafts led to a great demand for materials, tools, instruction manuals and demonstrators. Teacher training colleges, junior schools, adult evening institutes, and Women's Institutes were the main bodies generating demand in the 1920s. In the following decade handicrafts were taken up in a major way in senior schools and also in hospitals, with the growth of occupational therapy.[20] The needs of the various institutions and individual craftworkers were met in various ways. The NFWI, for instance, published some instructional leaflets and organised a host of short courses and lectures. Local colleges of art and design also catered for the interested amateur, as did individual artist/craftworkers who offered tuition: Cecile Francis-Lewis, for instance, offered batik lessons in the 1920s at her London studio,[21] while many women learned or perfected their handloom-weaving at Ethel Mairet's workshops.[22] However, the main name associated with handicrafts instruction is Dryad: in inter-war Britain the name Dryad was synonymous with handicrafts. Those who were then schoolchildren remember using the materials while those who taught recall the anticipation with which they awaited each annual Dryad catalogue.

Dryad was owned and run by Harry Peach, a disciple of W. R. Lethaby, who firmly believed in the moral and uplifting values of amateur handicrafts. He also believed that previous attempts to revive crafts at a popular level had failed precisely at the amateur level. Standards had been set too low and he saw one of his missions in life as the raising of those standards. He insisted on good materials and tools for amateur as well as professional craft activities. The story of how the energetic Peach promoted handicrafts and turned Dryad into the world's largest supplier of handicraft materials and publications is told elsewhere.[23] What needs to be noted here is the extent to which women were involved in the enterprise, particularly as writers and demonstrators. The publication of instructional leaflets began in 1920 and books in 1923. The most prolific author was a Dryad employee and former student of Leicester School of Art, Elsie Mochrie, who, in the years between 1923 and 1931, had over 20 publications to her credit, many of which ran into several editions. Mochrie specialised in embroidery, leatherwork and raffia work, while her Dryad colleague, Ivy Roseaman (also ex-Leicester School of Art) specialised in felt appliqué work and raffia work. Another author who worked for Dryad was Ursula Fletcher, daughter of Benjamin Fletcher, Headmaster of Leicester School of Art until 1920 (he then became Head at Birmingham). Joan Reynolds, a former student of the same school, also wrote for Dryad.

Given the instructional nature of the leaflets and books and the popularity of handicrafts in schools, it is not surprising that Peach looked to authors who were teachers as well as practising craft-workers. They included Anne Heynes on patchwork and quilting (Leicester School of Art), Gladys J. Shaw on leathercraft (Birmingham Central School of Arts and Crafts), Lilian E. Simpson (University of Birmingham, lecturer in crafts) and Marjorie Weir on weaving (Bradford College of Arts and Crafts and Examiner to the National Froebel Union), Dorothy Hart on upholstery (organiser of needlework and hand-work, Oxfordshire Education Committee), Louisa Judd-Morris on decorative needlework (Women's Crafts Mistress at Bradford College of Arts and Crafts), Olive Hacking on needlework (London Institute of Needlework and Principal of the School of Constructive Needlework) and Anne Macbeth on rug-making (Glasgow School of Art).

Despite all the publications, the best learning experience for many would-be craftworkers was personal tuition by a skilled worker. Much of the demand for demonstrations and lessons came from Women's Institutes, school teachers and teacher educators. Dryad ran its first, and very successful, summer school in 1921, when about 20 people were taught basket-making, raffia- and small-loom-weaving (see Fig. 12.3). Tuition soon expanded to cover other subjects, including embroidery and leatherwork. Single lessons lasted for one and a half hours but students could also enrol for a group of three lessons or choose courses lasting three days or a week. Dryad Handicrafts staff travelled throughout England and Scotland in the inter-war years. It was on such courses that many women first learned the craft or crafts that would bring them so much creative pleasure for years to come.

Between them, Dryad Handicrafts and the Women's Institute Movement dominated the handicrafts revival of the inter-war years. Neither was afraid to espouse the cause of quality amateur work; indeed, that was the main aim of both organisations. Neither saw the revival as restricted to women or solely concerning 'women's crafts', but because of the sheer numbers of women involved and the types of crafts, such as needlework, knitting and sewing, which were most popular, the main defining markers of the Arts and Crafts Movement in those years were amateur and female participation on a scale never before envisaged. Although complex in its roots and development, the handicrafts revival of the inter-war period represented craft work as a truly popular phenomenon which brought varied pleasures and a great deal of satisfaction to thousands upon thousands of ordinary people.

Notes

1 Parker, Rozsika, *The Subersive Stitch Embroidery and the Making of the Feminine*, The Women's Press, London, 1984.

2 See Willink, W. E., 'The Home Arts Movement', *Transactions of the National Association for the Advancement of Art and Its Application to Industry, Liverpool Meeting, 1888*, London, 1888, pp. 272–5, and Naylor, G., *The Arts and Crafts Movement*, Studio Vista, London, 1971, p. 158. See also Chapters 10 and 11 in this volume by Walker and Callen.

3 See Kirkham, Pat, *Harry Peach, Dryad and the DIA*, Design Council, London, 1986, pp. 70–3.

4 Dryad Handicrafts catalogues *c.* 1924–36, sections on knitting and crochet.

5 Kirkham, op. cit., 71.

6 See Lethaby, W. R., *Home and Country Arts*, Home and County, London, 1923; Lethaby, W. R., *Form in Civilisation: Collected Papers on Art and Labour*, Humphrey Milford, London, 1938

(first published 1922); *William Richard Lethaby 1857–1931: A Volume in Honour of the School's First Principal Prepared by A. R. N. Roberts at the Suggestion of William Johnstone OBE*, Central School of Arts and Crafts, London, 1957; and Rubens, Godfrey, *William Richard Lethaby: His Life and Work*, Architectural Press, London, 1986.

7 For a history of the NFWI, see Goodenough, Simon, *Jam and Jerusalem*, Collins, London, 1977.

8 Kirkham, op. cit.,

9 Lethaby, 1923, op. cit., pp. 45–63.

10 Goodenough, op. cit., pp. 70–2.

11 Ibid., p. 70.

12 See Kirkham, op. cit., pp. 47–69, and Plummer, Raymond, *Nothing Need Be Ugly: The First Seventy Years of the Design and Industries Association*, Blackfriars Press, Leicester, 1985.

13 See Holdsworth, Bruce, 'English Art Education Between the Wars', *Journal of Art and Design Education*, Vol. 3, No. 2, 1984, p. 169.

14 Goodenough, op. cit., p. 72.

15 Waring, Mary E., *An Embroidery Pattern Book*, Pitman, London, 1917, p. vi.

16 Bird, Liz, 'Threading the Beads: Women in Art in Glasgow, 1870–1920', in *Uncharted Lives: Extracts from Scottish Women's Experiences 1850–1982*, Press Gang, Glasgow, 1983, pp. 98–117.

17 Leicester College of Arts and Crafts, *Prospectus*, 1927. See also unpublished thesis (CNAA M. Phil) on the history of the college by Lys de Beaumont, 1988.

18 Ibid.

19 Ibid.

20 See Kirkham, op. cit.

21 I am grateful to Chris Boydell for this reference.

22 See Coatts, Margot, *A Weaver's Life. Ethel Mairet 1872–1952*, Crafts Council, London, 1984.

23 See Kirkham, op. cit.

Part Four
A Place of Their Own

13
A View from the Interior

Alison Ravetz

Women, Class and Gender in Housing

'It's 'aving 'ouses built by men, I believe, makes all the work and trouble', said Arthur Kipps' wife, Ann, at the turn of the century.[1] The sentiment is not misplaced even today. Although women are identified with houses in our society as in many others, throughout history they seem to have had remarkably little to do with house design.

Houses are pre-eminently symbols of public worth and status. A glance at any estate agent's window will confirm that it is the exterior that counts. Interiors are seldom depicted, and then only for 'quality' houses of high value. But it is with the interiors that women are most intimately concerned. Even in the architectural Modern Movement, which broke with tradition in its concern for functional, labour-saving homes, the identification of houses by their exteriors passed without question. So, in Figure 13.1, women do not figure: presumably they are tucked away inside, doing the dishes or ironing the clothes.

There is, of course, a simple and obvious explanation for the phenomenon noticed by Ann Kipps. Scarcely any woman of her time belonged to the design or building professions, and comparatively few do, even now. Sellers, buyers and their agents view houses from the outside, as objects. So, in a different way, does the design professional, who may think about the interior to a greater or lesser extent but who is more concerned with form, façade and site layout. The question addressed here, therefore, is what about the women working in the interiors? Did they make no contribution at all to house design? Or did they perhaps make one that was overlooked?

There is a fast-growing body of feminist research into the relations between women, housing and environments. So far as it relates to the normal built environment, it concentrates on the extent to which this handicaps women, or excludes them from consideration.[2] Another theme that is taken up is that of the atypical or abnormal development, such as the tradition of feminist-inspired settlements and cooperatives.[3] This is more meaningful in an American than a British context, for in the USA feminism was more integrated in society and more effective than in Britain. In Britain, it is possible to trace a movement of cooperative housekeeping, but in the main any contributions that women made to house design had to be from their conventional, subordinate position in society.

The development of housing in nineteenth-century England was strictly related to social class. The evolution of the ordinary urban house was dominated by the Georgian or pre-Georgian terraced house of the urban upper classes. As this was passed down the social scale, it mingled with the small, functional terraced cottages that were built for artisan and sub-artisan populations, many towns having their own distinctive types. The model tenements built for the deserving and industrious poor from the 1840s onwards, although sometimes designed to look like upper-class terraces, provided a different, alien type of dwelling.

The inspiration for house design was provided either by the market – which accounted for the desire to make houses look impressive from the outside and to seem to be better than they really were – or by social policy, which was responsible for building regulations and bylaws. All who aspired to gentility were bombarded, in Victorian England, with information about the precise levels of rent and household establishment they should aim at on their level of income. Wives and daughters, themselves part of a man's 'establishment', must usually have concurred, for the house's status also determined their own access to society, and so to matrimony. Even Karl Marx, living in London in the 1860s, was quick to move to a better house when his precarious fortunes improved, with his daughters' futures in mind.[4]

Such considerations, of course, excluded poor women. Unless they worked as servants for the gentry they were likely to have only part of a house, perhaps even one room or less, as their home. Many of the houses originally built for the gentry as well as other, humbler houses, were subdivided for the poor – a fact that may be overlooked in architectural histories of the surviving examples. For housewives living in such conditions, the greatest possible improvement, as Octavia Hill saw, was to be able to rent two rooms instead of one.[5] Better still if they could have a whole house. Thus, class-determined though the system was, there were also strong gender motivations in moving upwards through the housing stock. This must have served as a powerful barrier to any search that women might otherwise have made for an alternative dwelling type. In housing, as in other spheres of life, women sought improvement through the established class avenues. Only when such an avenue proved a dead-end would they be impelled to think afresh, not along class but along gender lines.

The year 1950 might be taken as a watershed to mark the close of one era and the opening of another, because by then two things of profound significance for women had occurred: the middle-class wife had finally and irrevocably lost her servants and the working-class wife had gained, or was in the process of gaining, a whole house to look after. The two stereotypes that had dominated the Victorian domestic scene had finally bowed out: the mistress of servants and the poor woman living in shared accommodation. Space was left for an apparently new figure, the 'ordinary housewife'. Rich or poor, they were all now multiple role, all-purpose, 'high value-low cost' housewives,[6] responsible for all the material and personal care of other family members, for active consumption in the market and, of course, for housekeeping.

A comprehensive history of the house*wife* has received, if anything, rather less attention than the history of house*work*. Granted, there are certain pools of light: on the married woman factory worker, for instance,[7] and the middle-class mistress of servants.[8] But there seems to be a virtual blank for the prototype of the modern housewife, the woman looking after her own home and bringing up her own family. We might suppose her to be described in the classic *Family and Kinship in East London*, but the view assembled there is compounded of retrospective and romanticised views of working-class life, over-optimistic anticipations of council housing and male, middle-class attitudes on the part of the observers.[9] The Victorian middle-class woman is popularly imagined as a useless, fainting creature; but Patricia Branca's reanalysis of her role depicts her as a pioneer of social, economic and technical change.[10]

Three Nineteenth-century Women

Most Victorians, however, had little general interest or concern for the plight of women struggling with the new domestic role. It was on the poor that male housing reformers focused, and in so far as women were able to play a role in reform, they followed suit – notably, as builders of model cottages and villages.[11] Although it was impossible for women to be legislators, philanthropists, industrialists or professionals, there did emerge three outstanding women reformers who made significant contributions to housing. Thus the heiress Angela Burdett Coutts, using Charles Dickens as adviser and Henry Darbishire as architect, built tenements for the poor at Columbia Market in the East End of London in the 1850s and 1860s. The schemes, and particularly the pretentious gothic market hall itself, apparently enjoyed limited success.[12]

A generation later, Henrietta Barnett founded Hampstead Garden Suburb, in what was then the most fashionable model for reformed housing, that of the garden city. Dedicating her life to the cultural improvement of the working classes in general, rather than women in particular, Dame Henrietta saw the suburb as an extension of her 'settlement' work with Canon Barnett in the East End of London. She appears to have adopted the garden city ideology without question, infused as it was with the paternalism of Port Sunlight and Bournville. It was an ideology in which rural and domestic idylls were fused, as Davidoff and others have shown.[13] The cottage houses and healthy environment of garden cities and suburbs were intended to benefit the family as a whole. Considering how much middle- as well as working-class Victorian wives and mothers had to do with sickness and death, they doubtless would have agreed wholeheartedly with this. The ideal family was considered then, as much later, an undivided whole, although the roles of its members were sharply differentiated. The husband went out to work and returned to till his garden or allotment. The wife meanwhile minded house and children; and both spent their leisure time within the community (see Fig. 13.2). It was a picture that contrasted with the realities of Dame Henrietta's own life, which she had chosen to dedicate to a full-time vocation in the heart of the city, without the handicap of children.[14]

For Dame Henrietta, as for a whole line of women who were involved in the movement as wives, committee members or (in rare cases) professionals, the humanity and social concern of the garden city movement must have seemed to guarantee its appropriateness for women. The movement made some vital contributions to house design, first adopting the socialist-inspired plans of Raymond Unwin and Barry Parker, and later bequeathing them to council housing, through the medium of the Tudor Walters Report.[15] This school of design was the antithesis of the shallow, 'façade' approach to housing mentioned earlier. It tended to design houses from the inside out and was concerned with orientation and outlook, as well as with the optimum use of space. Because of Unwin's strongly held ideological views about the worthlessness of parlours in workingmen's homes,[16] it also involved a debate about the relative importance of the ground floor room, and this was an issue that, as we shall see later, was not allowed to drop for the next 40 years. Although women strongly dissented from Unwin's views on the parlour whenever they were given a public hearing, there is no doubt that his and Parker's work on the planning of the small house addressed itself to domestic labourers and their needs more than any architect had done before.

The third great woman housing pioneer of Victorian times was Octavia Hill, a granddaughter of the social reformer Dr Southwood Smith and the closest female parallel of the male legislator or professional. From the 1860s Octavia Hill worked among the very poor, many of whom belonged to what she called the 'destructive classes'. Her objective was to get them to live more decently by offering inducements such as house repairs, improvements and rewards of various kinds. To this end she became a landlady and agent for other landlords. New houses were of little concern to her, for they were remote from the people she was dealing with. Indeed, she constantly warned of the dangers of providing the poor with accommodation that was too good or too expensive for them. For these and also for ideological reasons she was implacably opposed to the provision of state housing for the poor. Steadfastly refusing to adopt simple, deterministic explanations or solutions, she worked at the interface between people and environments, where cause and effect between 'bad' people and bad environments were ultimately indistinguishable. Her constant refrain was, 'You cannot deal with the people and their houses separately'.[17]

Under the Octavia Hill 'system', through punishment, reward and (one suspects) a degree of moral blackmail, people were expected to become responsible for themselves and to raise their own standards, in surroundings that they themselves learned to value and care for, and which they could afford. Her policy was to make the best of what was there: this seemed, after all, the obvious thing to do, since people could not themselves engineer their own environments.

Easily branded as a political reactionary, Octavia Hill could also be regarded in the rather different light of today's anarchist thought in housing, where control by users is seen as more important than fixed standards and official regulation.[18] Thus, though she could never be called a progressive, she might be termed a radical. She herself likened her work to housekeeping. She was involved with people's most intimate encounters with dustbins, drains, floor-boards, clothes-lines and window-panes. To that extent she may be called the most feminine of all the three nineteenth-century women housing reformers mentioned here. That this was not just a personal foible but had meaning for many people is demonstrated by the enduring success of her distinctive system of management. For, in spite of her own loathing of standardisation and bureaucracy, over the years she trained an army of women helpers and rent collectors, so involuntarily founding a specifically women's profession of housing management. This was the first such profession which a later, male housing profession contended with and eventually absorbed.[19]

Housewives and House Design

Octavia Hill was too bent on getting poor housewives to enlarge the size of their homes by renting a second room to consider how better design might help them in their tasks. One of few who did think along these lines at this time was the illustrious chef Alexis Soyer, but his main concern was with apparatus for cooking.[20] In an abundant Victorian literature on the homes of the poor, there is much talk of sanitary, medical and moral matters, but little or nothing on how their housing helped or hindered women in the domestic tasks they had to perform.

At the other end of the social scale, the mistress of servants had as her object, not the reform of her house, but the question of how to organise the servants so as to get more work out of them. This was also of great concern to men, who paid the wages, but delegated the actual management to their wives. Thus we find that the young David Copperfield admonished his lamentable child-wife, Dora: 'You really must accustom yourself to look after Mary Anne'.[21] By late in the century we find men almost as anxious as women about the threatening demise of domestic service, sometimes coming up with ingenious proposals for labour-saving houses.[22] But it was after the turn of the century, and particularly with the advent of war, that this prospect became an alarming reality for upper- and middle-class men and women alike. One concerned gentleman arrived at the neat solution that his wife and daughters should perform the maids' work, himself meanwhile providing encouragement and labour-saving gadgets.[23]

It was perhaps this strong male interest in getting the housework done with minimum inconvenience to themselves that, more than any feminist inspiration, explains the interest of certain men of the garden city movement in collective housekeeping. 'Co-operative quadrangles' of kitchenless houses were built at Letchworth, Welwyn Garden City and Hampstead Garden Suburb, at the urging of H. G. Wells and the instigation of Ebenezer Howard. Relying variously on professional day servants or tenants' wives to run their common dining-rooms, they were hailed, then and now, as being feminist and revolutionary; but in fact they embodied ideas that had been current for some time. Thus professional catering services and a new profession of 'lady' day servants had been canvassed for some years; and while the removal of individual kitchens does, indeed, seem a revolutionary step, there are ways in which it seems more so today than it did in its own time. The many domestic manuals of the Victorians (of which the renowned Mrs Beeton's is only one) give a clear impression that the kitchen was thought of not so much as an integral part of the family home as a distant cavern from which dinners emerged, with the wife as a nervous intermediary. In the quadrangles, the home (without kitchen) still remained distinguishable and private, with gender divisions unchanged. Ebenezer Howard, who moved into Homesgarth at Letchworth in 1913, congratulated himself, we may remember, on *his wife's* liberation from housework.[24]

Towards the end of the nineteenth century, some of the domestic manuals suggest that middle-class housewives were having to take over the servants' work, and they were admonished to preserve the same standards and routines after the servants themselves had left.[25] At the same time, we know from older women who once worked as servants that they often tried to carry their mistresses' standards into their own homes after marriage. Poor housewives, however, remained overburdened, ignored and inarticulate until, in the years leading up to the First World War and later, in the inter-war period, some educated and politically aware women began to speak up for them. Thus, inspired severally by their Fabian, Liberal, Cooperative or trade union beliefs and affiliations, Maud Pember Reeves,[26] Leonora Eyles,[27] Eleanor Rathbone[28] and Margery Spring Rice[29] described the daily round and labour of the poor working-class housewife. Their work was often supported and researched by the many women's lobbies and pressure groups that by now existed: most notably, for its influence on working-class women, the Women's Cooperative Guild, which had been founded in 1883. Also important for their influence on public opinion and policy were the Women's Industrial Council (f. 1894), which was concerned with the future of domestic service,[30] the later National Council of Women of Great Britain, with its offshoot, the Council of Scientific Management in the Home, and the women's electrical and gas associations.

In so far as they considered the design of the dwellings that working-class wives had to live in, the views of these various individuals and bodies did not always coincide with the conventional wisdom of housing reformers, or with what has since become the received history of housing design. Early in the twentieth century, Maud Pember Reeves felt that scullery houses represented a great improvement for working-class women, as did tenements.[31] In the 1920s, writing as a professional woman purposely living as a poor housewife, Leonora Eyles wrote feelingly of 'all the misery' of housekeeping in a five-roomed house in Peckham.[32] On the eve of the Second World War, Margery Spring Rice considered council dwellings, including council flats, to be the best of all dwelling types. Perhaps the key to the variations was that, as the latter observed, as women were moved into better housing their own standards rose, so that they became more discriminating about things they would never have thought about before. Women's standards were likely to be conditioned by their experience and their growing self-awareness, including awareness of their developing domestic role, in contrast to standards that were 'objectively' derived and imposed from outside.

Many of the accounts of working-class housewives were

concerned with the effects of having to share accommodation. This meant that their multiple tasks might have to be carried out in one small room, which needed constant rearrangement by day and night. One of the greatest problems was the lack of space in which to move around, so that family members had all to get up and go to bed at the same time. Water and waste needed to be carried up and down flights of stairs, and often the only cooking appliance was a broken bedroom grate. Observers of slightly better homes noticed how, even there, there was no space for new appliances, notably those appliances of mobility, the bicycle and perambulator.[33] The former, of course, belonged to other family members, but the latter was first acquired by many working-class wives with the allowance paid to soldiers' wives in the First World War. Prior to reaching this level of mobility, the poor housewife might be literally immured in her home, for apart from the problem of carrying children, she herself often lacked shoes and outer clothing.

Bearing in mind things such as this, it is understandable that the women who commented on early twentieth-century working-class housing, like Octavia Hill before them, did not concern themselves so much with design as with space, housekeeping tasks and standards. As for middle-class housing, two women were unusual in advancing some design suggestions. One was Dorothy Peel, who held a government post in the First World War and was later household editor of *The Queen*. Her long writing career developed from books that took servants for granted[34] to others which argued for improvements to traditional houses, now that the servants had gone.[35] The active Fabian and women's rights campaigner, Clementina Black, published an original design for cluster dwellings with collective facilities intended to be useful to the professional working woman.[36] Neither woman's proposals had any noticeable influence on middle-class housing, which continued to be motivated by class rather than gender considerations.

By far the most significant input of women into house design occurred through the Women's Subcommittee to the Ministry of Reconstruction in the closing stages of the First World War.[37] This was set up by the Minister, Dr Christopher Addison, largely at the urging of a women's movement which was still fresh from its victory with the vote and highly politicised. Labour, Liberal and Cooperative women were involved in the Subcommittee, as well as local suffrage societies, a professional group like the Association of Women House Property Managers, numerous mother and baby welfare groups, and even the typing pool of the Savoy Hotel in London. Probably all those participating would have gone along with the Women's Labour League when it said, 'Women ought to be the housing experts, and consider what they want, and leave compromise aside.'[38]

The brief of the Subcommittee was to visit specimen houses built by the Ministry of Munitions during the war and to advise on various plans for post-war houses for the working classes then being put forward, 'with special reference to the convenience of the housewife.'[39] The members set to work with a will, having efficient officers and experienced campaigners, and they used questionnaire surveys, leaflets, lectures and exhibitions to try to canvass and represent working-class housewives throughout the country. In Sheffield it was claimed that 7,000 such women were reached. The conclusions, put forward in two reports of 1918 and 1919, were that the first priority should be the health of the whole family. In design, adequate space in the dwelling should take precedence over labour-saving devices, and if at all possible, three bedrooms and a parlour or 'best' ground floor room should be provided. Cooking should be eliminated from the traditional kitchen–living-room and transferred to the scullery, where the sink was already placed. There should be a specialised bathroom with a fixed bath and piped water, although it did not greatly matter whether this was downstairs or upstairs, or even whether it contained a wash-hand basin. When considering what would be conducive to labour saving, the Subcommittee stressed fittings and services, rather than appliances. Thus they recommended deep sinks, with a plug and two draining-boards, and wall, floor and corner details that would be easy to clean. Most importantly, they stressed that a hot water supply was essential, while a cheap electricity supply was highly desirable.

The Subcommittee took a deliberate decision to extend its horizons beyond the individual dwelling to the surroundings, for it was impossible

> to treat Housing as a separate matter from Site and Town Planning, and to deal with the modern town cottage as a separate unit. Only through such careful planning can we make a real advance towards building up the communities of the future, whether we are considering their needs from the houswives' and mothers' point of view, or from that of the citizens in general.[40]

Thus the need for children's play space, over and above the private garden, was stressed, and even the comparatively enlightened garden suburb developments were criticised for not paying enough attention to this. To the members it seemed obvious that if the providing societies 'had been organised to a larger extent by women more provision would have been made for the needs of children as distinguished from those of adults.'[41]

Playgrounds, and even social centres, could be argued for on grounds of good health and the promotion of citizenship; but when it came to communal arrangements like wash houses, laundries, holiday homes and public meals services, an interesting gap emerged between the ideals of the Subcommittee and the working-class women they were representing. The former believed that such things would greatly ease the lives of working-class housewives and that 'the solution of many of the more difficult domestic problems will eventually be found along the lines of co-operation rather than in isolated effort.'[42] As things were, however, they regretfully had to conclude that the working-class woman was set against anything smacking of communal arrangements. She had in fact already done more than enough involuntary sharing, as the Labour supporter Dr Marion Phillips noted. Was such a woman's resistance from ignorance, she asked:

> Is it because she is more conservative than any other class of the community? Is it that she is more prejudiced and conventional? Not a bit of it. The truth of the matter lies in a very different direction. Her experience is that the *first* need in Housing Reform is good and sufficient bedroom accommodation. The second is opportunity for cleanliness both for the house and the person. The third is sufficient living room and parlour accommodation to make the social life of the family a real pleasure. Now these are the things she knows she *must have* before she can consider that she has got the right kind of home, and not one of them lends itself immediately to co-operative treatment.[43]

Reluctantly, the Subcommittee respected these scruples and decided that, for the working-class woman for the time being, privacy should be paramount.

The work of the advisory group suggests that women at this time had a very clear idea of what they wanted the house to perform, and why. This is particularly to be seen in the way they fulfilled one part of their brief: namely, a critical scrutiny of plans for post-war, state-subsidised houses published by the Local Government Board. Their numerous and very detailed criticisms of these gave huge offence at the Board, which accused the women of ignorance, invasion of professional (i.e. male) expertise and wild utopianism – as, for instance, in their 'strong opinion, equivalent almost to a demand, that every house should have a separate bathroom with a bath fitted with a constant supply of hot and cold water, ready for use at any hour.'[44] The Board pressured the Minister to suppress the Subcommittee's reports completely. This Addison was unwilling to do; but in the end two parts out of three were suppressed, although the part that was published included their main points of principle.

This episode made it plain that when women did try to intervene in a practical way in house design, even when officially invited to do so, there was a strong hostile reaction. The far more influential housing report of this time was the Tudor Walters Report, where Raymond Unwin, from his now receding socialist past and experience of garden city practice, laid down the design and technical blueprints for post-war public housing.[45] The report, anticipating only a limited number of subsidised dwellings, saw the necessity of taking advantage of the transition that housing standards were already going through, and of providing new standards that would set a model for society. These were not, in fact, intended for the poorest sections of society but, in accordance with the doctrine of 'filtering up', they were to be for the not-so-poor, whose vacated accommodation would benefit all those below them on the housing ladder.

This may help to explain the curiously didactic tone of the report. It reflected Unwin's own thoughts about the futility of putting parlours into workingmen's homes, although it did grudgingly conclude that, since the majority wanted them, they should be provided. The report was deeply concerned with the kitchen area of the house, echoing the Women's Subcommittee in saying that working-class people wanted to remove the cooking function to the scullery, but fearful that in their desire for a parlour people would sanction a recombination of living-room and scullery. Worse still, there was a 'danger' in enlarging the scullery, because families might be tempted to eat their meals in it. After debating this, it somewhat uneasily concluded that

> Perhaps too much weight should not be given to the danger of improper use of rooms, in view of the strongly-marked tendency of working-class families to live in the living-room and to confine the cooking to the scullery.[46]

In spite of making so many assumptions about working-class life, and although the work of the Women's Subcommittee must have been one of its main sources of information (if not the only one), the Tudor Walters Report surprisingly makes no direct reference to housewives. Thus it refers to working-class 'witnesses', but not to women. Nor does it concern itself with housework, like the Women's Subcommittee, or lay anything like the same emphasis on electricity, hot and cold running water, or small but significant details like a double draining-board for the sink.

It might, of course, be argued that the particular bias of the Tudor Walters Report was due to its being more aware of the need for economy and the political realities of the subsidised housing

A View from the Interior

197

that was going to be introduced. In the event, even its recommended standards were considerably higher than what most local authorities built. This included a great many two-bedroomed houses and houses without bathrooms, while only a minority had parlours. At the same time, the three-bedroom 'semi' dominated the new owner-occupied sector between the wars. Typically, this had, downstairs, a small hall with the staircase, two 'reception' or living-rooms and a small working kitchen, or 'kitchenette', as it was commonly called. This was, in fact, the old scullery, now dressed up with words and imagery from Modernism in architecture and aided by ideas from American home economics and household efficiency experts. The builders had, perhaps, their own profit motives for building houses with this internal layout, with compact kitchens; but in its self-containedness, private garden, separate parlour (or 'lounge') and 'labour-saving' kitchen, the spec-built house did in fact come close to the ideal of many women, according to surveys carried out in the 1940s.[47] Together, the new public and private houses of the inter-war years began to transform the twentieth-century housing stock. Both irrevocably departed from the traditional terraced house with attics and cellars.

During this time women continued to be articulate about the reform of house design through a plethora of organisations which included a Women's Committee of the Garden City and Town Planning Association, which was operative from the 1920s, the Electrical Association for Women, founded in 1924, and the Women's Gas Council, founded in 1930. The National Council of Women of Great Britain had a number of satellite organisations, which included a Women's Health Enquiry Committee and the Council of Scientific Management in the Home. This in turn had a Household Service Committee from 1929 and a Research Sub-committee from 1932. The latter concerned itself particularly with kitchen planning and in 1937 it created a model kitchen which toured the country. It continued its work after the Second World War, when it published a critique of the prefab bungalow,[48] and it continued to publish on housework, efficiency and scientific management in the home down to the late 1960s.

During the Second World War, virtually all women's groups in the political parties, and well-established women's organisations like the Women's Voluntary Service (WVS) and the National Federation of Townswomen's Guilds, felt constrained to publish reports on post-war housing. In 1944 the Women's Group on Public Welfare published *Our Towns: A Close-up*, in response to the dreadful urban standards and living conditions that came to light when evacuees were received into comfortable rural homes.[49] A *Housing Digest* prepared for the Electrical Association for Women in 1946 was able to quote from housing reports of 10 different women's bodies, none of which were party political ones.[50]

As in 1918, the government was concerned to incorporate the views of women in its plans for post-war public housing. This was now expected to cater not just for a minority section of the working classes but for a very broad social cross-section of all in need of homes. The new, official, trend-setting report was the Dudley Report, *Design of Dwellings*, which, rather like the Tudor Walters Report before it, was able to register a shift to higher standards, including electricity, gas, and hot and cold running water, all of which were now taken for granted. It also noted that the expectations of women were much higher than before. The report emphasised that 'the housewife is the expert' on the way the house and its rooms were used, and that she must therefore be consulted.[51] Accordingly, it admonished local authorities to make more use of their power to coopt women on to housing committees, which they could do under the 1933 Local Government Act. Of the 20-strong subcommittee which drew up the Dudley Report, eight were women (including a woman architect as secretary) and 17 women's organisations were consulted, out of a total of 57 organisations. They included nine which had not appeared in the 1946 *Digest*.

To obtain its more detailed information about women's needs, the Dudley Report subcommittee did not ask a body of eminent women to represent the voiceless majority but made use of mass surveys. Thus it used the work of a Women's Advisory Housing Council, which surveyed thousands of housewives in towns and villages, and more thousands of young women in factories and the forces. The Society of Women Housing Managers also carried out mass surveys on council estates, and local women's groups were consulted by many city councils. Besides confirming that women, when asked, were enthusiastic about the ideas for post-war housing that were being circulated by architects and planners, these surveys conveyed to the subcommittee the notion that house design should hinge around the housewife's work patterns, particularly the rota of family meals. This led them to the conclusion that there must either be room to eat in a larger kitchen, or a dining recess in a through living-room adjacent to the kitchen. In the illustrations the wife was depicted as cooking or serving meals, while the husband was either cleaning shoes or being waited on. It is fair comment, therefore, that 'women's views were seen as important but only in their capacity as housewives.'[52]

While it is outside the timespan covered by this essay, it is of interest to note that the Parker Morris Report, which appeared in 1961, reviewed and set new, improved, official housing standards and adopted quite a different attitude to women. The Report took cognisance of the four million working wives, and it considered the layout and use of rooms from the point of view of the family and the individual rather than the housewife. Concerned with growing leisure time and affluence, it emphasised the proliferation of household appliances, which husbands and other family members would use, as well as the wife. A different climate for women at this time, and one not necessarily in their own interests, is reflected by the fact that only 10 women's organisations gave evidence to the Parker Morris Committee – less than one-fifth of the total.[53]

Conclusion: The View from the Interior

This brief review suggests that it is not strictly true to suppose, with Ann Kipps, that women were not involved in house design. Their input was quite large, especially in the period between the wars, although in many ways it never surpassed the peak reached with the Women's Advisory Housing Subcommittee of 1918. At that time, however, the male establishment closed ranks when women threatened to become involved in any direct or practical way. The policy, which was clearly seen again at the time of the Dudley Report, was to *consult* women and to design *for* women as housewives. One risks being inaccurate and simplistic, however, in supposing that this limited and patronising approach necessarily alienated women. The evidence suggests, on the contrary, that women themselves agreed that houses should be designed for housewives. At first this was largely because of the preoccupation with the working-class housewife. Reformers and campaigners like Rathbone and Eyles, and the many women's bodies giving evidence or publishing reports, agreed that the first concern was to provide houses that would enable working-class mothers to rear healthy families and perform their housework more efficiently. It was, to a large degree, a case of middle-class women prescribing what they thought was best for working-class women, and they did not make any distinction between the housewife and her family: they assumed their interests were identical.

This helps to explain why, with occasional isolated exceptions, there was no campaign among women to promote alternative and distinctly feminine or feminist house designs, and how the most available model, that of the garden city movement, was taken over. At its most basic, this offered the first priority: a self-contained house with privacy. Later, as the small twentieth-century house evolved, in both public and private sectors of the market, it gave women some of the conveniences they wanted. These eventually extended beyond the space and basic utilities stipulated by the 1918 Women's Subcommittee to more specialised, technological devices, which were welcomed by virtually all women activists and women's organisations in the belief that 'labour-saving' kitchens would both lighten the drudgery of working-class wives and enable middle-class wives to fulfil their multiple roles without servants. Any fallacy inherent in this idea did not begin to appear until after 1950, when women had experienced their mechanised isolation and found that it seemed mysteriously to make them subject to guilt, depression, and a 'problem that has no name'.[54]

While this was the main course of development, a much more muted interaction between women and their domestic environments escaped notice. This had in fact come to light, without comment, in the 1918 Women's Subcommittee's surveys among working-class women and it was brought out clearly and systematically by a Mass Observation *Enquiry into People's Homes* in 1943. Based on a questionnaire of about a thousand housewives in different parts of the country, this differed from other wartime surveys in canvassing opinions about actual, existing homes, rather than asking loaded questions about people's post-war expectations. The report found a high degree of 'acceptance of conditions as they are'[55] – so much so, that women evidently experienced difficulty in distancing them-selves from their houses in their responses. Thus one woman 'never thought of disliking the place where she lived.'[56] Mass Observation found this surprising and disturbing, especially when it came to questions of neighbourhood, where they found housewives completely uncritical, their views being 'bounded by its physical characteristics, its shops, its mass entertainments – notably the cinema – and the neighbours.'[57] The report concluded that 'to an extent unbelievable to those who have not investigated it, many people are passive-minded, letting things be done to them, hardly thinking of what they could get done, if they would co-operate with their neighbours and fellow citizens'.[58]

Did this mean, then, that women in general were hopelessly apathetic about the environments they lived in? Apathy is likely to have played a part, although, apropos of the quotation above, it is worth remarking that the great attraction of the cinema for women was that it offered warmth, escape and, above all, inaccessibility to others, for a short while.[59] Where houses were concerned, Mass Observation had to concede that women were not without discrimination. They showed a 'very detailed interest in and innumerable ideas about the home and its possible improvement.'[60] These related to the long-established ideals of privacy and space, showing that women had clear ideas about what rooms they wanted, how many, and for what purposes. This led Mass Observation to conclude that 'normal working-class citizens want from their house an expression of independence, autonomy, control of life.'[61]

It appears, therefore, that the women in question viewed their houses subjectively as the arena and instrument of their own social and working roles. This stance is not all that far from the Octavia Hill approach. It is also compatible with the findings of those observers who found that a variety of dwelling types and design could suit women, given differences in their background housing experience and current needs. To the insights of those mentioned above might be added the Leeds women canvassed by the 1918 Women's Subcommittee, whose preferred house type was remarkably like the more solid, traditional Victorian terraced houses of that city.[62] Because of this subjectivity, and also because of the great flexibility of many aspects of housework, there were, for women, no absolutes. Given space, privacy and the basic services, any type of dwelling would have things in its favour and could be adapted to changing family needs.

It is not surprising, therefore, that Mass Observation was able to record very high degrees of satisfaction with different types of dwelling. Between 84 and 86 per cent of informants liked their homes when these were council houses, council flats and 'Modelville' (i.e. Bournville) houses. The kitchen was a strong determining factor, and it is significant that 90 per cent of those in new (council) flats liked their kitchens.

It was, if anything, harder for women to say what their ideal house would be than to pass judgment on their existing one. This might be partly out of a sense of realism – they knew they would never have their dream home – and partly, perhaps, because it was difficult to project needs and routines, so carefully tailored around their existing habitat, into a future one that had not been experienced. Negatively, they could imagine the benefits of relieving drudgery through plumbing and bathrooms; positively, it was more difficult to say what benefits more rarefied innovations might bring. Added to this, standards and even terminology were changing fast, so that Mass Observation found 'there is great confusion in the public mind about the homes they could have and should have. On a few points there is mental chaos.'[63] At the end of the day, however, nearly half the sample would have liked a small house with a garden, although as many as 21 per cent gave 'here' as their free choice.

Thus the view from the interior expressed by housewives reflects a highly personal relationship with their homes. The view was subjective, but it did not follow that it was irrational. This was difficult for those who worked professionally in housing to comprehend. Designers and policy-makers had to treat houses as objects, and even the women campaigning for better housing had to adopt the same 'objective' stance if they were to be heard in the public arena. Inevitably, all such 'operators' fastened on to physical, quantifiable standards, seeing reform also in physical terms: in design, fittings and materials, rather than other aspects.

Such aspects could have included reform in women's access to housing, in housing costs (cleaning and furnishing costs as well as rents), or innovations in the organisation of domestic labour. The women speaking from the interior did so because that was their place; but any effect this had on house design was merely oblique and confirmed their housewife's role. That there might be objective lessons to be read from their subjectivity was something that would not easily occur to anyone who had not shared their place.

Notes

1 Wells, H. G., *Kipps*, 1905.
2 'Women and the American City', *Signs*, special issue, 5.3, Spring 1980; Wekerle, Gerda R., Paterson, Rebecca, and Morley, David, eds., *New Space for Women*, Westview Press, Boulder, Col., 1980; Matrix, *Making Space: Women and the Man-made Environment*, Pluto Press, London, 1984.
3 Hayden, Dolores, *The Grand Domestic Revolution: A History of Feminist Designs for American Homes, Neighborhoods, and Cities*, MIT Press, Cambridge, Mass., 1981; Pearson, Lynn F., *The Architectural and Social History of Cooperative Living*, Macmillan, London, 1988.
4 Kapp, Yvonne, *Eleanor Marx*, Vol. 1, Lawrence & Wishart, London, 1972.
5 Hill, Octavia, *Homes of the London Poor*, Macmillan, London, 1875.
6 Oakley, Ann, *Housewife* (cover design), Penguin, Harmondsworth, 1976.
7 Hewitt, Margaret, *Wives and Mothers in Victorian Industry*, Rockliff, London, 1958.
8 Branca, Patricia, *Silent Sisterhood: Middle-class Women in the Victorian Home*, Croom Helm, London, 1975.
9 Young, Michael, and Willmott, Peter, *Family and Kinship in East London*, Routledge & Kegan Paul, London, 1957.
10 Branca, op. cit.
11 Darley, Gillian, *Villages of Vision*, Architectural Press, London, 1975.
12 Tarn, J. N., *Working-class Housing in 19th-century Britain*, Architectural Association Paper No. 7, Lund Humphries, London, 1971.
13 Davidoff, Leonore, l'Esperance, Jean, and Newby, Howard, 'Landscape with Figures: Home and Community in English Society', in Mitchell, Juliet, and Oakley, Ann, *The Rights and Wrongs of Women*, Penguin, Harmondsworth, 1976.
14 Barnett, Henrietta, *Canon Barnett, His Life, Work and Friends by his Wife*, 2 Vols., Murrary, London, 1918.

15 Local Government Boards for England and Wales, and Scotland, *Report of the Committee . . . in Connection with the Provision of Dwellings for the Working Classes* (Tudor Walters Report), Cd. 9191, HMSO, London, 1918.

16 Unwin, Raymond, *Cottage Plans and Common Sense*, Fabian Society Tract 109, 1908.

17 Hill, op. cit., pp. 102–3.

18 Ward, Colin, *Housing: An Anarchist Approach*, Freedom Press, London, 1976; Turner, John F. C., *Housing by People: Towards Autonomy in Building Environments*, Marion Boyars, London, 1976.

19 Brion, Marion, and Tinker, Anthea, *Women in Housing: Access and Influence*, Housing Centre Trust, London, 1980.

20 Ravetz, Alison, 'The Victorian coal kitchen and its reformers', *Victorian Studies*, XI, 4 June 1968.

21 Dickens, Charles, *David Copperfield*, 1849–50.

22 Layard, George Somes, 'The doom of the domestic cook', *Nineteenth Century*, 33, February 1893; Stevenson, J. J., *House Architecture*, II, Macmillan, London, quoted by Franklin, Jill, 'Troops of servants: Labour and planning in the country house 1840–1914', *Victorian Studies*, XIX, 2 December 1975.

23 A Survivor, *Life Without Servants or, the Rediscovery of Domestic Happiness*, Mills & Boon, London, n.d.

24 Hayden, op. cit., p. 231.

25 *Beeton's Houswife's Treasury of Domestic Information*, Ward Lock, London, n.d.

26 Pember Reeves, Maud, *Round About Pound a Week*, Bell, London, 1913; Virago, London, 1979.

27 Eyles, Margaret Leonora, *The Woman in the Little House*, Grant Richards, London, 1922.

28 Rathbone, Eleanor F., *The Disinherited Family: A Plea for the Endowment of the Family*, Edward Arnold, London, 1924.

29 Spring Rice, Margery, *Working-class Wives, their Health and Conditions*, Penguin, Harmondsworth, 1939; Virago, London, 1981.

30 Butler, C. V., *Domestic Service: An Enquiry by the Women's Industrial Council*, London, 1916.

31 Reeves, op. cit.

32 Eyles, op. cit., p. 25.

33 Rowntree, B. Seebohm, *Poverty: A Study of Town Life*, Nelson, London, 1901.

34 Peel, Dorothy Constance (Mrs C. S.), *The New Home*, Constable, London, 1898; *Marriage on Small Means*, Constable, London, 1914.

35 Peel, Dorothy Constance, *The Labour-Saving House*, Bodley Head, London, 1917; *The Art of Modern Housekeeping*, Warne, London, 1935.

36 Black, Clementina, *A New Way of Housekeeping*, Collins, London, 1918.
37 Ministry of Reconstruction Advisory Council, *Women's Housing Subcommittee*, First Interim Report, Cd. 9166, HMSO, London, 1918; Final report, Cd. 9232, HMSO, London, 1919; McFarlane, Barbara, 'Home Fit for Heroines: Housing in the Twenties', in Matrix, op. cit.
38 Quoted in McFarlane, op. cit., p. 28.
39 Ministry of Reconstruction, 1918, op. cit.
40 Ministry of Reconstruction, 1919, op. cit., para. 56.
41 Ibid., para. 61.
42 Ibid., para. 66.
43 Phillips, Marion, 'Co-operative housekeeping and housing reform', *The Labour Woman*, V, 22, February 1918.
44 PRO, *RECO I* (in Files of Ministry of Reconstruction Women's Housing Subcommittee, 1918–19, in Public Record Office, London).
45 Local Government Boards, op. cit.
46 Ibid., para. 89.
47 Mass Observation, *An Enquiry into People's Homes*, Murray, London, 1943.
48 Women's Group on Public Welfare, Subcommittee on Scientific Management in the Home, 'Report of an inquiry into . . . the temporary prefab bungalow on the household routines', *Sociological Review*, 43, section 2, 1951.
49 Women's Group on Public Welfare (with National Council of Social Service), *Our Towns: A Close-up*, Oxford University Press, London, 1944.
50 Association for Planning and Regional Reconstruction, *Housing Digest: An Analysis of Housing Reports Prepared for the Electrical Association for Women*, Art and Educational Publishers, London and Glasgow, 1946.
51 Central Housing Advisory Committee, *Design of Dwellings*, HMSO, London, 1944.
52 Matrix, op. cit., p. 74.
53 Ministry of Housing and Local Government, *Homes for Today and Tomorrow* (Parker Morris Report), HMSO, London, 1961.
54 Friedan, Betty, *The Feminine Mystique*, Gollancz, London, 1963.
55 Mass Observation, op. cit., p. 5.
56 Ibid., p. 68.
57 Ibid., p. 208.
58 Ibid., p. 208.
59 Eyles, op. cit., p. 117.
60 Mass Observation, op. cit., p. 4.
61 Ibid., p. 159.
62 PRO, *RECO I*, File No. 623.
63 Mass Observation, op. cit., p. 5.

14
The Designer Housewife in the 1950s

Angela Partington

It is commonly accepted that consumption has become part of 'women's work' since shopping and other time-consuming tasks, such as childcare, have replaced 'productive' labour, such as the cultivation and preparation of food and the making of clothes. The processes of industrialisation have meant that production has shifted from the home to the factory, and mass-produced goods require mass-consumption.[1] Recently, especially in the field of media studies, it has been acknowledged that to consume is not to absorb passively but to contribute to the process of making meanings.[2] Also the notion of the gendered consumer has become increasingly important in feminist cultural analysis.[3]

But what is involved in women's consumption (on behalf of the family as well as herself) has tended to be taken for granted rather than investigated. Shopping itself requires a wide range of social skills and expectations, involving a series of ritualised exchanges. But perhaps more important, the choice and use of commodities involve an extensive and constantly changing repertoire of knowledge and desires. Exactly how, and under what circumstances, women consume goods and services is crucial to the ways in which meanings are articulated in feminine culture.

The 1950s saw a sudden acceleration in the rate at which British women acquired new consumer skills, partly because there was a flood of new commodities (especially from the USA) which had been 'held back' by the war, and partly because the government's reconstruction programme included the resocialisation of domestic labour. Women were being encouraged to reassume the roles of wife and mother with a new fervour and enthusiasm as part of their patriotic duty in the 'battle for peace'. The welfare state was set up partly to support and maintain the family as a social institution and as an economic unit, following the disruptions of wartime.[4] What must be stressed, though, is that these roles were to be different from the way they were before the war. The consumption of new goods and services became part of the housewife's expanded job-description.

The concept of 'home management', which had been deployed in the USA since the thirties, became current in the language of women's magazines and those professional groups with an interest in improving the efficiency of the housewife: for example, doctors, psychologists, educationalists, scientists and designers. The discipline of home management was concerned to demonstrate

> how the breakdown of domestic tasks could lead to more efficient housework. Diagrams of movements in the kitchen, after the manner of F. W. Taylor's analyses of labour in the factory, indicated supposedly optimum kitchen layouts. The analogy between the home and the factory . . . was strengthened by frequent references to the kitchen as a workshop and to domestic appliances as tools.[5]

Running a home and rearing children was to be a scientific operation, which would supposedly give the housewife new status and importance. But analogies and references to factories notwithstanding, the effects of home management were to reposition women as consumers not producers as most of them had been during the war. Home management demanded the consumption of 'better-designed' equipment and furniture, such as kitchen utensils which resembled catering equipment and stools which looked like a painter-and-decorator's ladder. It demanded the consumption of totally new kinds of interiors (see Fig. 14.1).

> In the pursuit of efficiency, in the lightweight furnishings, the easily movable rugs, the flushed doors and recessed cupboards, the interior conforms to a set of outside standards that were intended to make the home the basis of the nation's welfare. In this sense, flush doors, for example, introduce a set of political values into the home: what is considered to look best in the home is what enables the housewife to fulfil her role of caring for workers and children most efficiently.[6]

Women were not only expected to consume but to consume *in a particular way*. Women's magazines played an important part in educating women to do so in a disciplined and 'responsible' way, exercising restraint and 'good taste' by choosing well-designed (i.e. useful, efficient) goods. Although the emphasis on commodities was, if anything, less than in women's magazines today, with rather more fiction and fewer advertisements, where attention *was* paid to new goods on the market it tended to be heavily informative and educational. The visual layout often resembled a trade catalogue. Many features were meant to 'test' housewives on their ability to 'choose wisely' and there were regular 'shopping guides' informing the reader of what was available in the shops and offering advice on what to look for. This training was justified on the grounds that it 'saved' the housewife time, energy and money by telling her what the 'best buys' were. The editors of women's magazines were inclined to address their readers on behalf of the government (though they also directly opposed its policies on occasion)[7] and, in these exhortations to consume properly, we can see how women's desires were being channelled, regulated and controlled.

British designers wanted to promote Functionalist principles and Modernist theories because they gave weight to the claim that good design could rationalise and standardise production by eliminating waste and improving efficiency. Functionalist design is based on the theory that the function of an object should determine what it looks like – 'form follows function'. Principles are that function determines the choice and handling of materials, that the object should be easy to manufacture and that decorative visual features should be eliminated. It is a design aesthetic opposed to 'styling', maintaining that the object should not be housed or encased in a decorative or symbolic exterior but should be stripped of all unnecessary trappings so that it signifies its function and nothing else. In British design, European Modernism was modified by references to classical or traditional styles (e.g. Georgian, the vernacular), but there was a clear movement away from ornate and/or organic-shaped forms which encased the object towards simpler, 'uncluttered' and geometric-shaped forms which were part of the object.

During the 1940s institutions were set up for 'the encouragement of better design', such as the Design Research Unit and the Council of Industrial Design (now the Design Council), and professional design accrued prestige and status. Post-war reconstruction created a boom-time for architects, planners and designers, and in 1951 the Festival of Britain testified to the extent of their power. By prioritising utility and efficiency, designers were able to exert control over women's desires, transforming them into needs and requirements which could be met by a well-designed home.

What is of interest to feminist design history is whether women did dutifully carry out their new task of consumption by choosing, buying and using designed commoditites, *as they were intended* to by these powerful and predominantly male groups (the government, the media, manufacturers, designers). If not, why not?

Electric fires which won the approval of the professional design community were those which 'did not pretend to be anything else',[8] that is, they were not 'disguised' or camouflaged as a piece of furniture. Most early electric fires had imitated coal or log fires, but this was immoral and dishonest, according to Functionalist principles.

This morality implicit in the idea that a fire should not be used for anything but heating a room reiterated and took further the manufacturers' assumptions about the housewife's needs. Notions of the 'functional' and the 'practical' have a universalising effect, reducing the varying circumstances of specific situations to a single aspect, reducing a constellation of desires to a simple set of needs. By assuming that an object has one function and that it is obvious what that function *is, has been* and always *will be* to everyone, regardless of social and/or economic distinctions. Functionalism assumes rather a lot. In the fifties its influence and the aspirations of the welfare state were mutually supportive. Both attempted to transform domestic space into an object of surveillance and control, to intervene in domestic labour, to plan and regulate biological and social reproduction. Their images of the electric fire articulate the post-war ideal of the machine-like home, smooth-running, scientifically operated, everything in its proper place, efficient and tasteful.

Not surprisingly, because of wartime shortages, women were enthusiastic in their purchasing of new goods (by the end of the fifties, 4 out of 5 families were the hire-purchasers of goods worth £1,000 million) but not all were to satisfy practical needs. Commodities were put to all kinds of uses which were dependent on social circumstances representing all kinds of desires, relations and obligations. For instance fireplaces continued to be used for the display of trinkets, ornaments and pictures which worked as documents and records of important family events (births, marriages, holidays, school outings, etc.). Through this symbolic use, women could experience and manipulate a range of emotions by moving, removing or adding to their collection. Features requiring labour-intensive maintenance (brass fenders, iron grates, wooden mantelpieces, ceramic tiles) continued to embody attitudes towards housework ranging from pride to anger, from pleasure to frustration. Fireplaces continued to be used as the central decorative focus of a room, and as a family gathering-place, with all its possible connotations of loyalty and affection, confrontation and bitter irony. All these meanings and more could be produced, depending on the particular ways women chose and made use of fires. Women also used fires differently depending on their class and ethnic positions. For instance, a woman may have wanted to cook over a sitting-room fire sometimes, use it to dry clothes if she didn't have a back garden or yard, or use it to burn rubbish. The distinctions *between* women, and the ways in which their different economic and social circumstances determined their expectations and provided them with knowledge, tended to be glossed over in the designers' glib moralising.

Women used fires, as they did all commodities and cultural

objects, to assert and celebrate their femininity. In choosing and making use of a fire, women displayed and exercised tastes which were specifically feminine. As consumers their skills were expanding in relation to a whole range of cultural forms, of which the designed object was only one and a relatively new one at that for most women. For instance, in the fifties the film melodrama was very popular with women audiences, in many ways continuing the tradition of the 'woman's picture' from the thirties and forties and anticipating television soap opera. The repertoire of knowledge and understanding demanded by and invested in these films was the same as that which came into play in the use of designed objects, therefore the pleasures of both were interdependent. All kinds of attitudes, beliefs and feelings about men, children, families, work, responsibilities, friends, anxieties, problems and aspirations had to be addressed by the films to make them meaningful and valuable to women. Likewise with the designed object, so the idea that it was just to heat a room, to sit on, to cover the floor, to store clothes, or whatever, is absurd and says more about the designer's self-image than it does about the female consumer's needs.[9]

Ironically, women's desire to consume meant that they were just as likely to work outside, as well as inside, the home, in order to be able to afford new goods. Possibly this is one of the reasons why modern designs of domestic appliances which made them look like factory equipment proved so unpopular. Since many women were actually spending their days in factories it is perhaps not surprising that the later designs, in which the machinery was completely hidden in a smooth elegant plastic casing, were much more successful.[10]

The electric fire is only one example of a commodity which was misappropriated by women in the fifties. Chairs, for instance, were being designed as if sitting down was the only use they had, whereas the female consumer was using them to represent her relations with friends, with husbands and children, with inlaws and with herself, by discriminating between colours, shapes and textures and by demonstrating the consumer skills she had acquired in a variety of contexts and situations. She used all designed objects to make meanings; the fact that these objects also had ostensibly practical functions was irrelevant.

By treating the commodity as a more or less expressive unity, depending on the imagination and innovation of the designer, or as the designer's 'solution' to a practical problem, design history invalidates other meanings and devalues women's culture. By examining how commodities signify at the much more 'superficial' level at which the consumer places them in relation to other commodities, investing them with value as a way of identifying herself as a social being, we can recover some of these meanings and legitimate women's knowledge.

Women's consumption of designed objects in the fifties was profoundly equivocal. 'New ideas' in design, which usually embodied Functionalist principles, were well represented in women's magazines. For instance, there was an emphasis on arrangement, planning and management as necessary for 'saving' time and energy and 'making space'. Built-in cupboards and shelving were promoted, as were wall-to-wall carpets and 'clever' use of wallpaper to 'create' height and width. The housewife was invited to think of a room as a functioning space, and therefore to make it 'work' as a designed totality by boxing in fireplaces and using colour 'schemes' to link objects together (rather than simply choosing your favourite colour for new curtains you had to make them 'go' with the rest of the room) (see Fig. 14.2). There was also an emphasis on 'dual-purpose' rooms and 'multi-purpose' furniture which extends, folds or converts, which helped to promote the idea of the home as a 'machine for living in'.[11]

But very often the deployment of these ideas ran contrary to the ideals and principles they were supposed to represent. For instance, there was a strong emphasis on do-it-yourself, which was in some ways a continuation of the 'make do and mend' war years, and this tended to demystify professional design as a kind of glorified homemaking. The housewife was expected to rely on her 'fashion sense' and other skills she already had, since putting a room together was often compared with putting an outfit or a meal together, which somehow undermined the preciosity of design theory. The need to combine old and new furniture if the room was to have a 'designed' look resulted in a blatant camouflaging and faking, by decorating, recovering or disguising old pieces to make them 'go' with new ones. The need to arrange things systematically and prevent 'clutter' often resulted in an outrageous formality beyond the boundaries of 'good taste'. Also, modern designs were referred to as the latest *fashion*, undermining functionalism's pretensions to be beyond 'style' and anticipating its obsolescence. The virtues of furniture or equipment which enabled the housewife to be more hygienic or efficient were often referred to ambiguously, because the housewife knows that there is no such thing as 'saved' labour or time, since it is always spent on yet another chore.

The female consumer of the 1950s, then, was not the 'happy housewife heroine' of feminist mythology, passively and blissfully acquiring mass-produced goods and oblivious to her material conditions of existence. Even if designed objects did represent patriarchal ideologies for designers and manufacturers, they were invested with other meanings and values by female consumers. Consumption was a form of consent to the position which was being allocated to women, but far from being a suspension of knowledge[12] it was the basis of women's knowledge of their own economic and social position in post-war circumstances.

Although I am putting forward women's misappropriation of commodities as evidence of resistance, I am not suggesting that this was a form of spectacular or subcultural deviancy, understood as a withdrawal or refusal of consent.[13] There was nothing self-consciously rebellious or romantically transgressional in this misappropriation. However, because it required consent it has remained largely unrecognised as resistance by feminists. Because women consumed readily and took pleasure in their consumption, they have been condemned as the owners of unraised conscious-nesses; but it is precisely through consuming that feminine knowledge was articulated. Women paid 'lip-service' to legitimate notions of 'good taste' (responsible consumption) while their pleasures in consumption were inevitably 'improper' and irrespon-sible, because as a dominated group women could not isolate the practical functions of objects from the social contingencies and circumstances of everyday life.

The ideal of responsible, regulated and controlled consumption was a utopian image promoted by powerful groups with economic and ideological interests invested in seeing women as domestic labourers, as the means of biological and social reproduction (childcare), as supporters and maintainers of workers, as an emergency and back-up labour-force and as a huge market for consumer goods. In failing to consume 'properly', working-class women, in particular, resisted all this. Feminine taste remained hopelessly incompatible with the 'good taste' promoted by professional designers. Women's resistance to this ideal was not an obviously political rejection or refusal of attempts to position and dominate them,[14] but rather a surplus product of those attempts, an inevitable failure of the dominant groups' ideal.

Yet feminists have persisted in assuming that women's consumption is a passive form of unconditional and total consent to their subordinate role, and even look on the female consumer with contempt. The fifties is thought to be an all-time-low in terms of feminist history. But if we take women's consumption seriously as an active and positive force in the production of feminine meanings and values, it is a period of intense conflict and contestation, using domestic space as the site and object of gender politics. Needless to say this struggle continues, and remains largely unrecognised.

As well as suggesting a particular approach in design history, one which acknowledges the pleasures of consumption as well as those of form and which takes into account the meanings produced by the (usually female) consumer as well as by the (usually male) designer, this also has implications for feminist design practice. Women's desires and knowledge are for women to use in their assertion of themselves as a gender-specific group with particular (subordinated) economic and ideological interests, therefore it is not in their interests to reduce those desires to a set of universalised 'needs' which can be conveniently met by the same old Functionalist principles with a few modifications here and there. The Functionalist concepts of 'utility' and 'usefulness' are not neutral or objective, and the notion of design practice as providing 'practical solutions' to 'practical problems' also embodies dominant values. Both have been deployed as part of the strategies of dominant groups in their attempts to subordinate and control women.

Yet feminist strategies in design have so far centred precisely on modifications of Functionalism,[15] in an attempt to improve the conditions under which women live and work. But the effects of this are to make the housewife more efficient (it is well known that the introduction of 'labour-saving' equipment has coincided with an increase in the average amount of time women spend on housework),[16] and it does nothing to intervene in the reproduction of gender relations. Rather than trying to solve women's problems by designing the perfect kitchen, which is impossible anyway, feminist designers should be exploring the ways in which femininity is celebrated through women's use of commodities.

Notes

1 See Oakley, Ann, *Housewife*, Penguin, Harmondsworth, 1974; Bland, L., *et al.*, 'Women "inside and outside" the relations of production', in CCCS, *Women Take Issue*, Hutchinson, London, 1978; Schwartz-Cowan, Ruth, 'The "Industrial Revolution" in the home: Household technology and social change in the 20th century', *Technology and Culture*, No. 17, 1976.

2 See, for example, Myers, Kathy, 'Towards a theory of consumption – Tu: a cosmetic case study', *Block*, No. 7, 1982; Hebdige, Dick, 'Object as image: the Italian scooter cycle', *Block*, No. 5, 1981.

3 Examples include Kuhn, Annette, 'Women's genres' in *Screen*, Vol. 25, No. 1, 1984; Mattelart, Michele, *Women, Media, Crisis*, Comedia, London, 1986.

4 See Bland, *et al.*, op. cit.; Winship, Janice, 'Nation Before Family' in *Formations of Nation and People*, Routledge & Kegan Paul, London, 1984; Wilson, Elizabeth, *Women and the Welfare State*, Methuen, London, 1977.

5 Forty, Adrian, *Objects of Desire: Design and Society 1750–1980*, Thames and Hudson, London, 1986, pp. 216–17.

6 Ibid., p. 118.

7 Ferguson, Marjorie, *Forever Feminine*, Heinemann, London, 1983. See also Winship, op. cit.

8 Forty, Adrian, 'The Electric Home', Unit 20 of Open University Course A305, *History of Architecture and Design 1890–1939*, 1975.

9 Indeed, much of the so-called Functionalist design exemplifies a formalist aesthetic, so that although objects 'looked' functional they were often less practical than traditional designs, and sometimes very difficult to manufacture.

10 Forty, 1986, op. cit., pp. 217, 219.

11 Often quoted dictum, from Le Corbusier, influential exponent of European Modernist design.

12 It tends to be assumed, in the field of cultural analysis, that when a subordinate group offers consent to a dominant group, they forfeit knowledge of their conditions of existence ('false consciousness'). But consent is invariably given partially and conditionally, and may always be withdrawn.

13 As is suggested by commentators on youth culture, for example, Hebdige, Dick, *Subculture: The Meaning of Style*, Methuen, London, 1979.

14 Although in the late forties women openly opposed the implementation of welfare policies, see Winship, op. cit.

15 Examples range from the efforts of the Women's Labour League in 1918, see Forty, 1975, op. cit., to the solutions put forward by Matrix in *Making Space: Women and the MAN-made Environment*, Pluto Press, London, 1984.

16 See, for example, Oakley, op. cit., p. 7.

15

Inside Pram Town: A Case Study of Harlow House Interiors, 1951–61

Judy Attfield

Harlow had its 40th birthday in 1987. In the early 1950s it was like a frontier town, with unpaved roads, few amenities, one street-light and no history of its own. No one felt the disorientation of newness more than the first young women who moved into Harlow in its pioneer days, when the roads were 'nothing but mud, mud, mud . . .'[1] and so 'choc-a-block with prams' that they called it Pram Town.[2] They didn't see the move away from London as a cosy retreat to a rural setting, although most of them came from overcrowded living conditions in rented rooms, small flats or shared family houses. The familiar areas they knew as home only offered them uncomfortable living conditions after the war. So, leaving the security of extended families and the communities of inner London to brave the discomforts of a new town was the only way they could secure a new house of their own.

At first many women suffered from a form of depression often referred to in the vernacular as 'New Town Blues'. In one town the number of women admitted to hospital with a diagnosis of neurosis was 50 per cent above the national average.[3] Critics who advocated a denser, more urban type of planning than the low-density 'prairie planning'[4] used in Harlow were quick to cite prairie planning as a contributing factor, suggesting that it led to isolation caused by the great distances between neighbourhoods and the centres for services and amenities.[5]

> I knew a lot of women that moved down here . . . we all moved together and some of them suffered terribly with depression and loneliness, although there was a better sense of community then than there is now . . . We had to start our foundation again . . . we were the ones, the women were the ones that was left to cope and adjust, harder than any of the men . . .[6]

Having children helped many of the young women of Harlow feel more at home. It was motherhood which brought them out of the isolation of their houses and into contact with each other as they tramped over the mud fields pushing their large prams to the shops and the baby clinics before the roads were made up.

I don't think I can honestly remember that anybody didn't like Harlow for any other reason than mostly missing their family and it was nearly always Mum. 'Cause you must remember that we were all quite young. It wasn't the same for the men. There was the pub just down the lane at Glebelands called The Greyhound and quite a few men went down there and had a game of darts and a pint.[7]

In looking at the impact of design on the lives of women in the new towns, two important debates can be identified. The first centres around the control of space and how, through planning and the design of the house, it placed women in the home. The second, most easily discernible in the way tenants furnished the interiors of their houses, centres around the conflict between popular taste and the establishment's official 'good design' values, which it sought to impose on the public. Much to their consternation, architects found that their intentions for tenants' furnishings, in accordance with the rules of functional modern design, which disallowed traditional period styles or ornament, were totally ignored.

The plan for Harlow was based on the picturesque rural English tradition,[8] which considered architecture one of the aesthetic ingredients in the natural landscape. The New Town Movement, from which it stemmed, had originated with the concept of the garden city, formulated by Ebenezer Howard in 1898.[9] This attempted to embody a synthesis of political, moral and economic ideals based on the principles of nationalisation of land, decentralisation and community. Harlow was just one of a number of satellite towns planned to provide for overspill from London after the Second World War. The model for the ideal 'community' was the pre-industrial settlement or village.[10] Harlow's equivalent was the residential neighbourhood, which, unlike the medieval village, deliberately separated the public male domain of work – industry, trade and commerce – from the private female domestic world. Women's place in Harlow was unquestionably in the home. In spite of precedents in housing design to accommodate communal domestic work, such as kitchenless houses with cooperative housekeeping units,[11] there is no evidence that any such arrangements were ever envisaged here.

The reconstruction period launched a whole series of government reports and plans for the design of post-war Britain and took advantage of the austerity conditions of war to control the design of furniture and textiles through the Utility scheme. This was first implemented in 1943 in the hope that it could impose 'good design' ideals on the public by regulating the use of scarce materials and labour through rationing and statutory designs. The establishment's view is evident in Jeffrey Daniel's heroic description of the principles of Utility:

> The Utility scheme, although born out of necessity, was inspired by ideals of social justice based on a fervent belief in the perfectibility of man in society that is Neo-classicism's chief philosophic legacy, and its creators thought of it in those terms.[12]

Without an understanding of dominant cultural values it is not possible to explain why the dictates of 'good design', which designers thought would solve the social problems of housing, had nothing to do with how women related to the design of Harlow – its layout and their houses – nor why they furnished and designed their homes so differently.

The conflict between popular taste and the official 'good design' movement is usually characterised in conventional design history as the 'failure of Modernism', in which the professional design establishment blames itself, as it did in the fifties, for failing to educate the public to 'raise its standards' of taste and choose good/modern design.[13] More recently, since post-Modernism, the attack has been levelled at Modernism itself, for failing to incorporate vital human values or to fulfil its promise of effecting social reforms. But blaming the designers and planners or the modern aesthetic itself fails to take account of differences – in ways of looking, speaking or in the design process – from any position other than that of the professional design establishment.

'Back to Front and Inside Out'[14]

The design concept, introduced in post-war housing, of placing the working area of the house in the front was, significantly, advocated by a woman – Elizabeth Denby,[15] an influential adviser on working-class housing:

> . . . workers and children have a surfeit of communal life during the day. Not so the women. While the living room should face west or south on to garden or balcony, with utmost obtainable privacy from being overlooked or overheard by others, the kitchen, the workshop, should look on to the street, so that the woman can join, however indirectly, in the life of the neighbourhood . . .[16]

This revolutionary design idea broke the traditional correlation of 'front' with public display of status, which placed the non-working, leisure area of the parlour or front room, with its window drapery and ornaments, on show to the street. It is a good example

Inside Pram Town
217

of the climate among post-war designers who favoured rational principles and innovation as a means of doing away with social pretensions. But they did not acknowledge anything problematic about a captive housewife marooned in her kitchen, passively catching glimpses of the outside world from the strategically designed windows but unable to participate actively in it. This isolation, however, was very real to women in Harlow, who, at home on their own during the day, looked out through their windows only to see blank expanses of landscape, devoid of familiar landmarks or human activity.

> When I used to look out of the window, I couldn't see a thing . . . I thought I was the only person on earth . . . It took me years before I classed this as a home. I loved the house and I was proud of it, but if ever I thought of going to Walthamstow, I was always going home, 'cause that's where my roots are, was . . . I was always going 'up home' to see Mum and Dad . . . It made us feel very emotional, we felt very much alone. I felt as if I'd been thrown right out of a nest, although I was 28 when I came here. It took a great deal of time to accept it, although I loved it and common sense told me I'd done the right thing.[17]

Most Harlow houses contained an open-plan 'larger living-room', often running from front to back, rather than the two separate reception rooms (dining and lounge) typical of the inter-war, middle-class, spec-built, suburban semis so disliked by Modernist architects. Some of the earlier houses, such as those built on the Chippingfield estate, combined kitchen with dining-room (see Fig. 15.1), but none of them had parlours or front rooms of the type found in the nineteenth century in London terraced houses familiar to Harlow tenants. Much confusion was caused by the disappearance of the wall separating the front room, traditionally kept for best, from the more private, everyday back of the house. The sense of dislocation was reinforced in estates like Chippingfield, where the 'back' or service door was positioned next to the 'front' door on the public façade facing the street.

To young women negotiating the newness of unfamiliar surroundings, traditional values embodied in the metaphor of 'front' must have had a significance totally different to those held by the young architects and designers trying to create a new concept in living.

A Place of
Their Own
218

I had this cretonne and I made them [the curtains] myself. The front had to match, didn't matter too much about the back. This was going back to my mother's day, of course.

The front of the house always had to be matched upstairs and downstairs. And [for] the front door's one, I crocheted lacy curtains.[18]

The parlour and all its trappings symbolised for the designers of the new society all that was anathema to the modern view. The rather abstract concept of space was considered crucial in the fifties, as *Design*, the magazine produced by the Council of Industrial Design, reported:

> Focus on space, a key word, space that gives freedom. Destroy the distinction between rooms. The home is subservient to life in the home. Banish the cold formality of front parlours that attempt to impress callers – then stand unused, to collect dust . . . Push back the wall, bring the kitchen in, dissolve divisions that separate life into compartments . . . Allow freedom to change and space to move.[19]

A censorious account of 'mistakes' made by tenants appeared in a 1957 review of 'Furnishing in the new towns' by *Design* magazine.

> They fight shy of open-plan living . . . there is a strong tendency to shelter behind net curtains. Large windows are obscured by elaborate drapes and heavy pelmets, by dressing table mirrors and large settees. Corners are cut off by diagonally placed wardrobes and sideboards. By careful arranging and draping, the open plan houses are being closed up again, light rooms are darkened and a feeling of spaciousness is reduced to cosy clutter . . . in achieving cosiness they are completely at variance with the architects' achievements in giving them light and space.[20]

From fairly early on, net curtains appear to have been a bone of contention between tenants and architects. The pages of the *Harlow Citizen* feature complaints from architects about 'windows heavily shrouded in net curtains' and from tenants that 'privacy is one of the things held in low regard in the town from the planners' point of view'. It reported the advice given by a doctor to a woman he diagnosed as suffering from Harlowitis: 'Buy yourself net curtaining for every window in the house, shut yourself in for a week and forget the place ever existed. It will do you a power of good.'[21]

In the Harlow houses with an open-plan living-room, the stairs appeared to become the separating agent between private and public (display) areas, as Mr V. H., a former supervisor for the Sheraton group, which opened the first furniture shop in Harlow, in the Stow shopping precinct, noted:

> There wasn't much money about in those days . . . They always bought for the bottom half of the house and didn't matter so much about the top half . . . they had a nice new home and they wanted to impress their friends, who didn't necessarily go upstairs . . . the bedroom was last.[22]

To anthropologists such as Erving Goffman, 'front', or external façade, is a metaphor for display to an audience, so that 'back', or interior, becomes the less formal area where the individual can seek refuge, relaxation and 'drop *his* front' (my emphasis).[23] It is the separation, or boundary, which gives the two areas their definition. But what we also have here is a quite specifically male point of view. This is only made clear when we read critical feminist accounts of literature on the home, such as discussions in Davidoff et al of these meanings using a gendered perspective:

> The underlying imagery is the unacknowledged master of the household looking *in*, so to speak, at the household . . .[24]

Mrs D. S. made a similar point. Having described how she finally felt 'this is my domain now' about her house in Harlow after many years of adjusting to her move from Walthamstow in 1951, she described how her husband felt about the house:

> 'As long you're behind the door, I'm at work all day so it doesn't make any difference to me where I am as long as I've got a comfortable place to come home to.'[25]

Could it be that people were not interested in the status value of their houses in the way that was generally imagined? For women it was their place of work – their view was from the inside.[26] Was the Harlow house in the 1950s really perceived by its inhabitants as a public statement of status, and if so in what ways was this class-and gender-specific? Much of contemporary literature on housing, based on Functionalism, dismissed the parlour as outdated and 'difficult to use',[27] a result of ill-considered design. Could it be that the display takes a different form and that what is being displayed is also different from the previous period?

Raymond Unwin's opinion that emulation of the middle class was the sole factor governing the popular preference for the parlour in 1918[28] was generally still held by the designers of the 1950s.

However, recent feminist history of housing uncovers a different reason for the importance accorded to the parlour in the First World War reconstruction period. It shows that as a result of women's attempts to have their views taken into account on the design of housing, the government set up a Women's Housing Subcommittee in 1918 to report on the 'housewife's needs'. The conclusions were based on interviewing working-class women and on an intimate knowledge of their living conditions. They included a recommendation for a parlour, because of the need for women to have a room where they could relax and escape from unfinished work.[29]

The practical nature of women's views on housing design was confirmed by my interviews with women in Harlow, particularly those who moved into Harlow in the early 1950s. Mrs C. S.,[30] for example, liked the stairs in her new two-storey house because 'you could put the children to bed [knowing] they were away from the noise and we knew they would have a good night's sleep'. Another woman commented on the large size of the hall because it was big enough to fit the pram, while Mrs C. E.,[31] one of the first people to move into the Chippingfield estate in 1950, saw no objection whatsoever to having the 'back' door next to the front door. It was noticeable that it was in fact a man who attributed what was probably his own dislike of the working and main entrance doors being side by side to 'the housewife'.[32] In Mrs V. Ta.'s case, her husband's preference prompted them to move to an estate with the more conventional gabled roof and 'proper' back door.[33] This does not necessarily prove anything; and it is more than likely that functional reasons are given for preferences which are just as motivated by symbolic needs. Nevertheless, it is significant that the responses I received from women whose opinions I sought on what they valued most about their houses were weighted on the side of use. Yet there was also a strong element of display, which can't be reconciled with the separation that is usually made between function and display.

It is understandable that Harlow's first residents were uncritical of their new houses because they were such a change for the better, compared with the cramped conditions they had had to endure during the war – living with family or in rented rooms, in small flats over shops or converted requisitioned property, sharing bathrooms and toilets with other families. Many of them felt they had 'come up in the world with these houses'. Mrs C. E., who had lived in a Nissen hut, compared the difference 'moving from purgatory to heaven . . .'[34] This is not to say there were no difficulties in adapting to the unconventional open plan, or any of the other design innovations introduced into people's lives by the new town concept. Mrs D. S.,[35] whose poignant account of her loneliness and sense of isolation is quoted earlier, explained her greatest problem rather incredulously: 'Funnily enough I couldn't get used to the *newness* of things.' This in a time, just after the war, when there was a craving for new things after a long period of having to 'made do and mend'.

Although most Harlow houses were designed along the lines of open plan, there was an awareness on the part of the architects of the preference for separating the dining area from the rest of the living-room, and provision was usually made for the fitting of folding doors or curtains between the two spaces. Some of the later developments, such as Hookfield (1966), actually provided two separate rooms.[36] From a lifetime's experience working for Harlow Corporation Architects Department, Mr A. M. was well placed to see both the way open plan was received by the tenants and the way architects reacted to tenants' ideas of interior decoration.

> Every architect thought that after his house had been built ... it should be furnished as he thought it should be ... Of course, that didn't happen. At one time we used to be very conscious of the interior decoration. We'd pick the wall colours, the ceiling colours, the colour of the doors ... fairly early on we came to the realisation that we were utterly wasting our time because no matter what we put on the walls ... no sooner had people gone in, they couldn't even wait for a year to pass ... they'd paper them direct with some of the most awful wallpapers. And you'd throw your hands up in horror. Then you'd get the house where there was the do-it-yourself handyman who'd put up all these sort of shelves and divisioning walls and change doors ... despite the fact that they were renting housing ... Right from the beginning people did things themselves ... They wouldn't be allowed to change fireplaces and things like that but a lot of them did it surreptitiously ... Architects, especially if you're working in mass housing, have got to try and design a basic framework in which people can do their own thing, because they're going to do it anyhow.[37]

Although there were some attempts at experiment and the town built the first housing towerblock in 1950, on the whole most of Harlow's housing was designed along conventional lines of two-storey terraced houses and low-rise flats. Perhaps that is why Le Corbusier, champion of modern urban high-rise housing, refused to visit Harlow during his stay in England for the Congrès International d'Architecture Moderne (CIAM) in 1951.[38]

Pride, Polish and Screw-on Legs

The furnishing and equipping of the house played a vital role in the transformation of house into home. In the early fifties the most important factors determining choice, apart from differing tastes, were cost restraints and availability of goods. Rationing of furniture ended in 1948, but the Utility scheme continued to operate until 1952, with more freedom in the design allowed as long as certain specifications and cost limits were adhered to. Even with fewer restrictions, though, most Harlow inhabitants had little choice. There were still severe shortages, which made it difficult to obtain new furniture even when the money was available. Houses were often furnished with a mixture of pieces inherited from families and bought second hand as well as new. Hire-purchase schemes offered by retail furnishing shops made it easier to buy new, though it didn't allow much choice either. Mr V. H., the Sheraton supervisor, said:

> You didn't have to sell furniture, it was just a matter of being able to supply it . . . We used to do hire purchase and cash but the vast majority of our business was hire purchase . . . we worked everything out over a two-year period, with something like a 10 per cent deposit . . . They bought a suite for 39 guineas and paid ten shillings a week or whatever it was. They bought what was going in the shop at a price they could afford . . . It's difficult to realise today how hard it was for families then to maintain a front room with a three-piece suite, dining-set and television, all on hire purchase.[39]

Under the circumstances it was impossible to produce the kind of interior which architects would have approved of – even had Harlow residents had the same values – as Mr A. M., the Harlow corporation architect, remarks:

> I've seen houses of young couples where there was a genuine interest . . . in modern stuff but it wasn't necessarily integrated. You'd probably find one or two nicer pieces of furniture that were quite modern and then on the floor you'd find the most awful blooming design of carpet which would ruin the whole thing.[40]

The lighter, more 'contemporary' style of furniture was taking over by the 1950s but the traditional matching suites or sets continued to be sold, in spite of attempts by designers to introduce the modular 'unit' furniture advocated by the Modern Movement:

pieces that could be bought singly and built up into groups. When the Utility scheme was discontinued in 1952, cost and quality controls were lifted. Much of the industry adapted its production to cater for the lower-income market, to the detriment of quality and design. The smaller, lighter style of contemporary design was used to economise on material. The Harlow branch of Sheraton's consistently made the record sales figures for the group, but without any particular effort to improve standards. In fact, the make of furniture a shop chose to sell was often determined by the manufacturer who gave the best discounts.

Many women I interviewed were able to recall in great detail the acquisition of their first pieces of furniture and equipment. The three-piece suite was accorded great importance. Mrs C. S. bought her Utility suite in 1945:

> It was a beautiful suite . . . solid and very, very comfortable. I'll always remember, it was green, uncut moquette with a sort of Alexandra rose pattern on it in beige.[41]

Mrs D. S. still has her french-polished walnut bedroom suite, consisting of two wardrobes, a chest of drawers and dressing-table. Purchased in 1951, it was her first piece of non-Utility furniture. She paid £50 for it, having earned 'fantastic money' making gliders during the war, and the price must have included the luxury purchase tax in force at the time.[42]

Another tenant recalled the colour scheme of her hall and living-room and the arrival of her first fridge, acquired in 1957:

> We had a blood-red wallpaper on one wall and grey up the stairs. That was the height of fashion. When we managed to save up, we bought this long carpet . . . grey with red and black dashes all over it . . . Nobody else had a refrigerator round here . . . I felt sick with the excitement of it. I had refrigerator coming! And there it was – splendid in its packaging and ice-blue inside. It looked beautiful. I'd really arrived.[43]

The beauty she exclaims over had little to do with the official 'good design' rules, although for all we know the fridge in question may have been a model on show at the Design Centre. Opened in 1956, the Centre exhibited to the public the Council of Industrial Design's approved selection of designed products – provided the manufacturer agreed to pay for the privilege.

The observation made by one of Harlow's architects that the ways people furnished their houses 'were not expressions of taste but pride of ownership', perfectly illustrates the elitist criterion which requires taste to be value-free. It is sustained by the assumption that someone with taste is in command of specialised knowledge about how to discern beauty from abstract form, and therefore how to put together a scheme so that the elements make a cohesive or integrated whole. This concept can afford to disallow any association of beauty with so-called vulgar materialism because it speaks from a privileged position. Pierre Bourdieu uses this definition in his critical analysis of taste,[44] showing how it works as a vehicle for class distinctions: it separates the I-know-what-I-likes from the I-know-what-to likes.

Bourdieu's class analysis of taste helps to put the design establishment's criteria into a social context which allows criticism of dominant cultural values that are not normally questioned. This type of analysis can show how all tastes fit within a hierarchical framework with 'high' taste as dominant and therefore the measure by which the others are judged. It can be applied to the front/back debate and explains why the tenants' choice to use net curtains caused so much official disapproval and appeared at the time to be so transgressional. But how does this help to acknowledge women's work as a contribution towards the design of the home?

We need to go back into that fifties interior, where functional and leisure areas blur into one, where front and back no longer meet neatly in the middle but on the stairs, and consequently the confusion caused by the lack of definition between public and private spaces which women experienced in a totally different way to men. Particular pieces of furniture offer themselves as good examples of the type of display referred to in Veblen's now classic *The Theory of the Leisure Class*, in which certain social groups identify themselves in terms of status through 'conspicuous consumption', according to a hierarchical system of emulation.[45] The glass-fronted display cabinet, for example, used for best china and ornaments, was still in evidence in the fifties. The fact that the Utility furniture scheme excluded a china cabinet but included a bookcase in its range of furniture types gives an indication of the official line. Even when it was discarded because it was considered out of date or because of lack of space, its contents were kept and displayed on open shelves, over pelmets and on any other available surface. A more modern 'token parlour substitute', which doubled storage with display was the sideboard, incorporating an illuminated cocktail cabinet with rise and fall action and a full range of fittings and accessories. A furniture buyer was reported in the *Cabinet Maker* as saying, 'I wonder how many times the average purchaser uses the cocktail part of the sideboard and how long the vogue will continue',[46] while a second-hand furniture dealer from Harlow commented, 'The strange thing was that people couldn't afford

cocktails or any of the other drinks that went with it . . . Whenever
you saw one of these things, it never had anything in it, so how the
fashion caught on I don't know.'[47] Although tempting, it would be
too easy to surmise that the only significance of the empty cocktail
cabinet is the importance given to display as opposed to function in
the 1950s. After 1957 the changes in consumption had a lot to do
with the marketing of domestic products through novelty and
design styling. But all the same, the customer was still largely in the
hands of the retailer.

> One of the things about the Harlow houses was that
> people took great pride in them. They may not have had
> much but what they had they looked after . . . the women
> spent years giving the furniture a high polish.[48]

> We were the homeworkers . . . We had to get on and make
> the best of everything that we could. That was taking
> pride in what you'd got. Everything was polished.[49]

'Pride' and 'polish' cropped up in tandem time and time again
during interviews. They seemed to go together particularly in the
fifties, when people still expected to buy things to last a lifetime.
Women's pride in their work to maintain their homes through the
care and arrangement of its furnishings appeared to be associated
with a sense of pleasure which, though associated with display, was
also intimately connected with work. Therefore it is necessary to
consider the way in which the interiors were used, to get away from
the static concept of taste as something that recognises only features
which are supposedly inherent in the form of the object.

Bourdieu's theory of 'habitus'[50] is helpful in explaining the way
in which individuals form their identity through their relationship
to a group or class by means of sets of shared attitudes and tastes.
These lead them to choose a particular repertoire of furnishings,
food and clothes, recognisable as the 'life style' so beloved of the
marketing world, which uses the concept in styling products for
particular target groups. Bourdieu's view of goods as 'cultural
capital', however, is highly generalised and cannot be applied
indiscriminately to any historical period. The conditions of
austerity experienced by the women of Harlow were different from
the more affluent consumer society of the sixties, or the
sophisticated market fragmentation of today, in which groups like
yuppies, dinkies (double-income, no kids) and woopies (well-off
older persons) can be identified. Bourdieu's theory also cannot deal
with the way in which artefacts or designed goods can be made to
articulate meanings other than those intended by the designers.[51]
Jean Baudrillard's critical analysis of taste and consumption[52]

moves beyond the limitations of Bourdieu's consideration of taste as a set of unchanging fixed preferences into which everybody can be slotted according to their social status. Baudrillard discusses consumer goods in terms of meaning; in observing how objects are arranged, used and cared for, it is also possible to account for social mobility and changes of meanings over time:

> A given class is not lastingly assigned to a given category of objects (or to a given style of clothing): on the contrary, all classes are assigned to change, all assume the necessity of fashion as a value, just as they participate (more or less) in the universal imperative of social mobility. In other words, since objects play the role of exhibition of social status, and since this status has become potentially mobile, the objects will always simultaneously give evidence not only of an acquired situation (this they have always done), but also of the potential mobility of this social status as such objects are registered in the distinctive cycle of fashion.[53]

Meaning in this context loses all value because anything can mean almost anything, with no reference to history, experience or use; it is posited on status as the concept against which other meanings are constructed. This is not to deny that the relationship between signifiers and signified is arbitrary, but seeing that does nothing to explain how meanings can be changed.

Baudrillard specifies polish as an aspect of 'fanatic housekeeping', which 'corresponds to the demand to surpass the strict necessity of use towards an appearance – an imperative of cultural promotion',[54] In declaring housekeeping to be 'neither true labour nor culture' he typifies the male-dominated ethos which trivialises and invalidates women's work and domestic cultural production. While both furniture and money were in short supply among Harlow residents in the early fifties, pride and polish were used to construct meanings. But by the beginning of the sixties the consumer society was in full swing and second-generation Harlow tenants like Mr and Mrs T., who set up house in 1961, were less traditional than their parents, more affluent and very fashion conscious:

> I can remember the three-piece suite – it was uncut moquette, grey and mustard . . . we had a purple carpet . . . an orange wall . . . it was very modern. Mum and Dad didn't think it was up to much. I think it's awful now – some of those things we had . . . my father-in-law made us a cocktail bar . . . with white quilting on the front, and it

had sort of Formica marble contact stuff on top . . . And everything had those screw-on legs. We bought a Pye radiogram and that had black screw-on legs as well . . . Once we couldn't afford any wallpaper so George painted the wall white and we got saucepan lids, even the dustbin lid, and with a black pen he drew circles and triangles all over this white wall. That looked fantastic and everyone said, 'Oh God, he's so artistic'. He's a butcher! We used to sit down and think up all these ideas . . . We loved furniture . . . that's all we used to do, walk around looking at furniture . . .[55]

There is little doubt that display as well as function played a part in the way Harlow tenants furnished and cared for their houses. They were making the places their own through the use of design. The way many chose to take possession, metaphorically speaking – because at the time housing was still rented from the Corporation – was to invest their own values, often knowingly in contravention of the approved official line. This involved replacing permanent fixtures, such as fireplaces, with models of their own choice, closing off open-plan areas and furnishing in reproduction style in spite of propaganda to throw away 'bulky white elephants'. Windows designed by architects to let in light were veiled behind Venetian blinds and layers of curtains, topped with double pelmets and an array of ornaments. Through the appropriation of privacy by the concealment of the interior from the uninvited gaze, people took control of their own interior space and at the same time made a public declaration of their variance from the architects' design.

A Woman's World Revealed

In 1956 the local paper was reporting 'Harlow's new problem' as 'the booming birth-rate', with more than 1,000 prams 'on the road' at shopping rush-hours causing 'pram-jams' (see Fig. 15.2). In the early fifties the Harlow Development Corporation refused applications from firms which depended on employing large numbers of women, on the grounds that married women with young children (who formed the largest part of Harlow's female population) should not go out to work. However, the huge demand from women themselves soon caused the Corporation to change its approach. 'One firm alone stated that it has a waiting list of 250 women hoping to obtain employment.'[56] The need to get out of the house was as strong a motivating force as the extra income.

The question of whether or not married women should go

out to work or stay at home and look after the family, has always been a vexed one. But many young married couples in the New Town find that the comparatively high rents and the high cost of living make it necessary for the wife to work in order to supplement her husband's income. There is also the problem of furnishing the new house and since the restrictions on hire purchase, this has become even more difficult.[57]

It was mainly ladies night in Harlow Parliament on Friday when the motion that 'Day nurseries are a direct incitement to women to go out to work rather than stay at home and look after the children' was defeated.[58]

Married women are going out to work in ever-increasing numbers . . . They find that housework alone no longer keeps them happy. They need the stimulus and interest of outside work, and in fact many women grow quite neurotic if they are deprived of it.[59]

In 1961 41 per cent of the adult female population in Harlow was working.[60] The official figures might not actually reveal the full picture, because there were many, like Mrs V. Ta., who 'never did go out to work as such.'[61] But she took in lodgers, did paid domestic cleaning, minded children and later took up market-research interviewing. This way she always managed to be 'at home for the children'. Even when her youngest son was 16, 'I always was at home before him, always; so that they hardly knew I went.' For many women of her generation, 'work' was not a term they could identify with because it referred to what the men did when they left home in the morning to earn the family wage. Although most of those I interviewed did some sort of paid work apart from housework, they spoke of their earnings as 'pin money', 'pocket money' or 'for the extras', referring to the money in terms of what they were saving it for: 'a carpet', 'the kiddies' school holidays', 'a refrigerator'. Their sense of identity was not formed through their occupation in the way that their husbands' was, but through their relationships as wives, mothers, daughters and friends. The work they did at home was not perceived as 'work as such' because it was done in the home for the family.

I really enjoyed the company . . . the atmosphere and the girls I worked with, they were all so nice . . .[62]

The lack of value given to domestic work is an issue which has been widely discussed in feminist cultural critiques and social histories, where housework has been named as 'one of the most important sites of women's oppression'.[63] Nevertheless, many of the findings have not been taken into account by the mainstream or by disciplines like design history. The concept of 'labour saving', however, is familiar to design history, where the issue of domestic work has been raised in relation to the design of housing and domestic appliances. But on the whole it tends to be discussed around the mythical 'housewife' stereotype, involved in some 'gross self-deception' in an unconvincing 'pretence that housework was not work'.[64] It is quite easy to fall into this trap by using only advertisements as sources of reference rather than drawing directly on the experiences of women themselves. The fact that women may not have called the labour they carried out 'work as such' does not mean that they were unaware or ashamed of doing it, though they were probably only *too* aware of its low social status. The prejudice which has surrounded domestic work has been associated with 'women's work' in general and can be traced back to the time when middle-class or respectable women did not work but had servants to do the housework.

The application of science, whether in the design of housing, kitchens or appliances for helping with housework, is only part of the labour-saving story.[65] So far, case studies have served mainly to demonstrate the strength of gender and class divisions, in the home and in society at large, by showing how the concept was used to exploit women through the marketing of domestic appliances and power like gas and electricity, but did not necessarily make the work any easier. It was also used as a device for cost-cutting in the name of rational, modern house design during the inter-war period, reducing the size of the kitchen to an impossibly small kitchenette.[66] What is often not given enough importance is the feminist campaign which started in the nineteenth century to professionalise domestic work and to raise its social status, pay and conditions. The 'wages for housework' campaign and the transformation of housework into domestic science or household management were strategies adopted to elevate the status of women from servants to paid workers with a recognised skill. In *Democracy in the Kitchen*, Mrs H. Ellis wrote *c.* 1890:

> Every Englishman's home may be his castle, but we know well enough that the castle as at present constituted always has one or two feudal slaves in it, the wife or the 'slavey' or both, and it is difficult to tell the one from the other.

She was not alone in advocating the formation of municipal bakehouses, kitchens and dining-halls run by professionals. Other feminists suggested the design of kitchenless houses served by public restaurants, laundries.[67] More recently, feminist architects have advocated a degendered, flexible, adaptable and therefore more equal order of spaces inside the house, rather than the conventional hierarchy of rooms which keeps women in their 'place'.[68] There are others who have sought to enhance and celebrate the work conventionally and contentiously termed 'women's work', reserving the domestic space and particularly the kitchen for females.[69]

Some of the most radical criticism of role and 'place' enforcement through gender identity has come from developments in semiotics and psychoanalytic theory, which have identified language and other forms of representation, such as imagery, as the most powerful devices through which social and sexual identity are produced. This knowledge can explain why marketing uses ideas such as 'labour saving' to sell products to a Mrs Consumer stereotypical housewife. The fact that the products appealed to women is indisputable but the degree to which women were actually coerced by such stereotypes is highly debatable. We are on safer ground if we look at the whole question from the receiving end and let the women speak for themselves, taking into consideration the specific circumstances of how design affected their lives.

Veblen has generalised on the way particular social groups identified themselves through taste, but he casts women in the role of the vehicle for conveying their husbands' status through a 'display' of leisure typical of the Victorian ideology of domesticity:

> In the lower middle class there is no pretence of leisure on the part of the head of the household. Through force of circumstances it has fallen into disuse. But the middle-class wife still carries on the business of vicarious leisure, for the good name of the household and its master ... The leisure rendered by the wife in such cases is, of course, not a simple manifestation of idleness or indolence. It almost invariably occurs disguised under some form of work or household duties or social amenities, which prove on analysis to serve little or no ulterior end beyond showing that she does not and need not occupy herself with anything that is gainful or that is of substantial use ... There goes into these domestic duties such solicitude for a proper combination of form and colour, and for other ends that are to be classed as aesthetic in the proper sense of the term ... If beauty or comfort is achieved – and it is a more or less fortuitous circumstance if they are – they must be achieved by means and methods that commend themselves to the great economic law of wasted effort.[70]

Veblen wrote the above in 1899, but 60 years later Hugh Casson still found it necessary to ridicule the popular assumption that:

> Having Taste is woman's work. For a man to possess it, in England at least, is generally considered to be not only undignified, but unmanly and therefore suspect . . . Beauty in masculine eyes is really defensible only when viewed as an investment. It is tolerable at week-ends or in retirement – where, like a dangerous animal, it can be caged in a golden frame or behind a glass-fronted book-case, and tamed by one's wife, the traditional sub-contractor for cultural activities.[71]

Behind the notion that woman is the 'sub-contractor for cultural activities' lies the assumption that the main contractor is man, who sub-contracts the less important work because he is too busy getting on with the important things in life – the economic imperatives out there in the real world of work. Women are left at home to get on with taste and consumption, using their so called 'natural' gifts, 'the woman's touch'. It is as if they are born with good colour sense and do not have to learn it, together with all the other skills necessary to do housework. Much of this can still be seen to apply today, but before looking further into the myth that what women do is not real work, or that women are incapable of being practical, we need to look at the relationship between gender and class identity in the specific case of Harlow new town in the fifties.

Paul Oliver described the 'first generation' moving into suburban semis during the thirties as

> a new breed, unknown to Veblen and unstudied by his successors. They were carving out a new kind of home and family-centred life, which was, in truth, 'neither town nor country', and hence not fitting into the stereotypes loved by planners and sociologists alike. An argument developed in the Victorian era may not be all that appropriate to the period between the wars, when the suburbs were more intent on developing their own culture than on mimicking another.[72]

Harlow was 'neither town nor country', it was not based on home ownership, nor was it a suburb or garden city. In the early fifties it didn't quite know what it was. Meanwhile planners argued over density levels and high- versus low-rise housing and critics were already writing about the 'failure of new towns', both architecturally and socially, because they had not managed to produce the Reith Committee's utopian vision of a 'truly balanced community' which would integrate all the social classes. In 1953 new-town dwellers were described by Sir Henry Wells, chairman of the Commission for the New Town, as 'vaguely and without knowing it, middle-class aspirants'.[73]

Dorothy Peel's solution to the unsatisfactory design of houses described in her book *The Labour Saving House*[74], written in 1917, was to have a woman architect. This, less than 20 years since the admission of the first woman into the architectural profession, was obviously not as daring an idea as suggesting that men might share in the housework:

> Having houses built by men makes at least a great part of all the work and trouble, for my own experience . . . of architects points to the fact that they are concerned to provide you with a house which looks charming and which may be stoutly built, but that such details as the make of the bath, the size of the service lift, the position of the kitchen range, and arrangement of the cupboards, house-maid's pantries, and so forth, concern them not at all . . . Men, as a general rule, do not have to keep house, neither do they have to do housework, thus it is not surprising that such details as these escape their notice.[75]

At the other end of the social scale, but in roughly the same period, Robert Roberts recalls, in *The Classic Slum*, 'the struggle for the acquisition and display of objects . . . [of] prestige', and wrote of his father's great pleasure at guests' admiration of the family possessions, particularly 'the opulent show of bric-a-brac on the overmantel'. But it was at his mother's insistence that a cast-iron bath was installed.[76] These examples may seem rather removed from Harlow, but they were echoed in the ways that the women in particular, among those interviewed, valued the practical and working parts of their houses. This was also extended to their 'tools of the trade' – their household appliances. Yet at the same time there was a keen interest in display. When a decentred, gendered view of history is taken,[77] the classic middle-class correlation between women, leisure and display is disturbed. The display seemed to be more to do with what women were not allowed by convention to call their work. It was this that they were proud of and eager to display:

> I was fortunate in having a washing machine . . . it was a boiler and it had a handle on the top . . . It did some marvellous washing – they licked these automatics into cocked hats. You certainly had to work it, you stirred it up, and it had a wringer on the top, and you had to rinse things, but the washing was beautifully white and clean.

> You put your washing on the line on a Monday . . . and
> you were proud of your whites. They were blowing in the
> breeze and everybody could see them.[78]

'You certainly had to work it' is seen as an advantage over the automatic type of washing machine. There was a sense in which the machine didn't take over the job but left the credit to the person who worked it. Only if we take Veblen's theory of the leisured class literally, rather than as an explanation for the way in which the dominant class distinguishes itself from other groups, can we accept that women were self-deluded enough to believe that what they did all day was not work.

Because women in Harlow were expected to form their feminine identity through the display of leisure, it would seem they found another way to make their *work* conspicuous. There is no product in housework: it only 'shows' when it is *not* done. The signs which announce its efficient completion are more to do with excessiveness – high gloss and shine, brilliant whiteness, non-functional furnishing and collections of ornaments.

We have seen how 'pride and polish' went together, how lacy curtains and the whites on the line had a special significance for women because they represented their work. The communicative strength and power of these symbols explain why they were stolen to give meaning to otherwise meaningless products: for example, why the symbol of a line of brilliant white washing was used to such effect in marketing detergent, a commodity which in the fifties was new and unknown.

The process of meaning-making is usually discussed from the other end by looking at advertisements, where women are made to appear passive, having the work done for them by products and appliances. This method relies on a closed system which insists that meaning lies *within* the text,[79] the design, the image, so no reference can be made to where it comes from. If we can see meaning as not fixed but historically determined, it is also possible to see that the same object can mean different things to different groups at different times.

> People worry about what type of coffee table they're going
> to have, if it don't match with something else – but that's
> not happiness.[80]

Mrs D. S. said this looking back at the time in her twenties when she first came to Harlow and having a new matching bedroom suite in french-polished walnut was important to the making of her home. The comment shows she understands how meanings are rooted in people's experience and not in *things*, where they are made to reside temporarily through human intervention.

Where no allowance was made for Harlow residents to participate in the design of their environment, it was soon appropriated.
Modernity has been unjustly blamed for a whole gamut of evils.
The 'stealthy privatisation' of the new towns since 1979, according
to John Cunningham, threatens to condemn them to a footnote in
history:

> The Tories' philosophy sounds too straight to fault; it is
> simply that the Government wants to make the new towns
> as much like old towns as quickly as possible . . . Their
> success – in planning and social terms – is almost an
> embarrassment to the British, who traditionally are
> immobile, hooked on historical architecture.[81]

This study of Harlow has been an attempt to record a part of its
history which gives credit to the women pioneers who helped to
make it into a home and a community, and transformed New
Town into Pram Town – a place they could call their own.

Notes

1 This quotation, like others used here, comes from a series of taped
interviews with residents and persons involved in the early days of
Harlow. The interviews were carried out in 1982 and 1986 and are
now housed in the New Town Record Centre, which can be visited
by appointment with the Study Centre Officer, Town Hall,
Harlow, Essex, CM20 1HJ.
2 The term 'pram town' was first used by the national press in 1952,
when 35 live births per 1,000 population were recorded in Harlow,
twice the national average (source: 24th Annual Report of the
Harlow Development Corporation, March 1971, and *Harlow
Citizen*, No. 142, 13 January 1956).
3 Nicholson, John H., 'Two generations of new towns', *Social
Science Quarterly*, Winter 1967/8.
4 Richards, James Maude, 'Failure of the new towns', *Architectural
Review*, July 1953. In this article Richards attacked the new towns
for their lack of urbanity: 'the Reith Committee, on whose report
the New Towns Act was based, had in its mind a picture of a
scattered garden-suburb type of town . . . If by urbanity we mean
the sense of being part of a built-up community, then no one
standing in a typical neighbourhood of a new town, taking in the
vast deserts of roadway verges and pavements rimmed with little
houses dwindling acre by acre into the far distance, can say that the
new towns, however successfully they may contribute towards the
housing shortage, are, as attempts to create new urban communities,

anything except a failure.' For an account of the architecture of the welfare state, see Frampton, Kenneth, *A Critical History of Modern Architecture*, Thames & Hudson, London, 1980, pp. 262–8.

5 Nicholson, op. cit.

6 Interview with Mrs D. S., November 1986.

7 Interview with Mrs V. Ta., November 1986.

8 Pevsner, Nikolaus, *The Englishness of English Art*, Penguin, Harmondsworth, 1984, pp. 173–92. (First published by the Architectural Press, London, 1956.)

9 Howard, Ebenezer, *Garden Cities of To-Morrow*, Faber and Faber, London, 1946. (First published in 1898 as *Tomorrow: A Peaceful Path to Real Reform*.)

10 Davidoff, Leonore, l'Esperance, Jean, and Newby, Howard, 'Landscape with Figures: Home and Community in English Society' in Mitchell, Juliet and Oakley, Ann, *The Rights and Wrongs of Women*, Penguin, Harmondsworth, 1976, pp. 139–75.

11 In 1909 Ebenezer Howard constructed 'Homesgarth', 32 kitchenless apartments in a Cooperative Quadrangle at Letchworth. See Hayden, Dolores, *The Grand Domestic Revolution: A History of Feminist Designs for American Homes, Neighborhoods, and Cities*, MIT Press, Cambridge, Mass., 1981; see also p. 205 above.

12 *Utility Furniture and Fashion 1914–1951*, exhibition catalogue, Geffrye Museum, 1974; see also Russell, Gordon, *How to Buy Furniture*, The Council of Industrial Design, 1947.

13 MacCarthy, Fiona, *A History of British Design 1830–1970*, London, Allen & Unwin, 1972, p. 93.

14 This quotation is taken from a report in the *Harlow Citizen*, 1 February 1957, on a discussion at the St Paul's Women's Fellowship in which the 'benefits and drawbacks of Harlow' were discussed. 'Benefits . . . were good, clean homes and healthy atmosphere for their children. The main drawback, they all agreed, was the architecture of the houses. Those were described as being "back to front and inside out" but none of the women wanted to leave Harlow.'

15 Denby, Elizabeth, 'Plan the home', *Picture Post*, 4 January 1941, p. 21.

16 Ibid.

17 Interview with Mrs D. S., November 1986.

18 Interview with Mrs V. Ta., October 1986.

19 'Focus on British design', *Design*, No. 121, January 1959, p. 33.

20 'Furnishing in the new towns', *Design*, No. 98, February 1957, p. 43.

21 *Harlow Citizen*, 15 July and 22 July 1955.

22 Interview with Mr V. H., September 1982.

23 Goffman, Erving., *The Presentation of Self in Everyday Life*, Penguin, Harmondsworth, 1980.

24 Davidoff *et al.*, op. cit., p. 154.
25 Interview with Mrs D. S., November 1986.
26 See 'A View from the Interior' by Alison Ravetz in this volume.
27 Chapman, Dennis, *The Home and Social Status*, Routledge & Kegan Paul, London, 1955, p. 58.
28 Quoted in Matrix, *Making Space: Women and the Man-made Environment*, Pluto Press, London, 1984, p. 29.
29 Ibid.
30 Interview with Mrs C. S., September 1982.
31 Interview with Mrs C. E., September 1982.
32 Interview with Mr J. D., August 1982.
33 Interview with Mrs V. Ta., November 1986.
34 Interview with Mrs C. E., September 1982.
35 Interview with Mrs D. S., November 1986.
36 Interview with Mr A. M., September 1982.
37 Ibid.
38 Ibid.
39 Interview with Mr V. H., September 1982.
40 Interview with Mr A. M., September 1982.
41 Interview with Mrs C. S., September 1982.
42 Interview with Mrs D. S., November 1986.
43 Interview with Mrs V. Ta., October 1986.
44 Bourdieu, Pierre, *Distinction: A Social Critique of the Judgement of Taste*, Routledge & Kegan Paul, London, 1986, pp. 11–96.
45 Veblen, Thorstein, *The Theory of the Leisure Class*, The Modern Library, New York, 1934. (First published 1899.)
46 *The Cabinet Maker and Complete House Furnisher*, London, The Cabinet Maker, January 1953.
47 Interview with Mr D. B., September 1982.
48 Interview with Mr V. H., September 1982.
49 Interview with Mrs V. Ta., October 1986.
50 Bourdieu, op. cit., p. 77.
51 Forty, Adrian, *Objects of Desire: Design and Society 1750–1980*, Thames & Hudson, London, 1986, p. 7.
52 Baudrillard, Jean, *For a Critique of the Political Economy of the Sign*, Telos, St Louis, Mo., 1981.
53 Ibid., p. 49.
54 Ibid., p. 45.
55 Interview with Mrs B. T., September 1982.
56 'Harlow trade council report', *Harlow Citizen*, 8 January 1955.
57 *Harlow Citizen*, 27 January 1957.
58 *Harlow Citizen*, 18 January 1957.
59 *Harlow Citizen*, 4 October 1957.
60 White, L. E., 'The social factors involved with the planning and development of new towns', unpublished paper given at UN round table, 1964.

61 Interview with Mrs. V. Ta., November 1986.

62 Interview with Mrs I. M. B., October 1986.

63 Arnold, Erik, and Burr, Lesley, 'Housework and the Appliance of Science', in Faulkner, Wendy, *et. al.*, *Smothered by Invention: Technology in Women's Lives*, Pluto Press, London, 1985, p. 161.

64 Forty, Adrian, 'Housewife's aesthetic', *Architectural Review*, No. 969, November 1977, p. 282.

65 See Chapter 9 by Suzette Worden in this volume for a historical account of the labour-saving movement.

66 Unit 20 of Open University Course A305, *History of Architecture and Design 1890-1939*, 1975, p. 52; Roberts, Marion, 'The Fireside and the Kitchen: Domesticity and Rationality in Twentieth Century British Family Housing' in Langdon, Richard, ed., *Design and Society*, The Design Council, London, 1984, pp. 93-7.

67 See note 11 above; Roberts, Marion, 'Private kitchens, public cooking', Matrix, op. cit., pp. 106-19.

68 See Torre, Susana, 'Space as Matrix, Making room: women and architecture', *Heresies 11*, New York, Vol. 3, No. 3, 1981, p. 51.

69 Maglin, Nan Bauer, 'Kitchen Dramas', in ibid., pp. 42-6.

70 Veblen, op. cit., pp. 81-2

71 Casson, Hugh, 'Beauty and the beast: a matter of taste' *Observer*, 1 March 1959, p. 11.

72 Oliver, Paul, Davis, Ian, and Bentley, Ian, *Dunroamin: The Suburban Semi and Its Enemies*, London, 1981, p. 190.

73 Wells, Sir Henry, 'Postwar victory' in 'New Towns Supplement', The Times, 25 September 1968.

74 Peel, Dorothy, *The Labour Saving House*, London, John Lane The Bodley Head, 1917.

75 Ibid., p. 30.

76 Roberts, Robert, *The Classic Slum*, Penguin, Harmondsworth, 1983, p. 34.

77 See Judy Attfield, 'FORM/female FOLLOWS FUNCTION/male', Walker, John A., *Defining Design History and the History of Design*, Pluto, London, 1989.

78 Interview with Mrs V. Ta., October 1986.

79 See Partington, Angela, 'Conditions of a feminist art practice', *FAN (Feminist Arts News)*, Vol. 2, No. 4, 1987, pp. 13-15.

80 Interview with Mrs D. S., November 1986.

81 Cunningham, John, 'How the new towns will be a footnote in history', *Guardian*, 10 April 1985, p. 17.

Appendix: Women at the Archive of Art and Design

Meg Sweet

The Archive of Art and Design (AAD), a section of the National Art Library of the Victoria and Albert Museum, is housed at 23 Blythe Road, London W14 0QF (tel: 0171-603 1514). It collects, conserves and makes accessible the archives of artists, designers, design societies and companies concerned with the promotion, manufacture and marketing of art and design products. With a particular emphasis on the twentieth century, it covers a wide range of design areas including textiles, fashion, furniture, stained glass, arts and crafts, ceramics, graphics and book illustration, architecture, metalwork and jewellery, interior design and industrial design (see Figs. 16.1–16.5).

Some major archive groups where women are the creators

AAD 3-1977 Helen Megaw: designs, papers, correspondence mainly in connection with the Crystal Design Project for the Festival of Britain. 1945–62.

AAD 1-1979 Edith Crapper: artwork, business records, biographical material and tools used by this illustrator and miniaturist. 1922–57 and n.d.

AAD 2-1980 Dorothy Braddell: day books, watercolours, designs for advertisements and exhibition displays. 1920s–60s.

AAD 9-1980 Eileen Gray: architectural drawings, glass negatives of houses and furniture, working papers and notebooks, correspondence. 1913–37 and n.d.

AAD 5-1981 Rosemary Grimble: pen-and-ink drawings, some used to illustrate books and articles. C. 1950–80.

AAD 7-1981 Sue McKechnie: research papers on aspects of the Derby porcelain trade, including gilders and painters. 1970s.

AAD 5-1982 Catherine Lucas: research notes on the history of costume C. 1970.

AAD 1-1983 Dora Lunn, potter: notebooks, correspondence, autobiographical material, photographs, press cuttings and MSS. of short stories. 1899–1950s.

AAD 7–1983 Charlotte Bondy (*née* Schmidt): autobiographical notes, designs for and examples of wrappings and advertising in aluminium foil. C. 1925–36, 1984.

AAD 14–1984 O. Bayles: floral designs for textiles. n.d.

AAD 10–1986 Bertha Sander: drawings and designs of costume, textiles, furniture and interiors, correspondence, samples, published material, photographs. C. 1916–36.

AAD 6–1987 Rita Gooday: album of photographs of textile designs. 1920s–30s.

Some major archive groups where women are the intended clients

AAD 5–1977 Lilley & Skinner Ltd: albums of advertisements and brochures, mainly for shoes. 1909–62.

AAD 5–1978 *Commission Européenne de propagande pour la soie*: annotated photographs of silk clothes. 1970s.

AAD 9–1979 John French: fashion photographs, correspondence, press cuttings. C. 1948–65.

AAD 1–1982 House of Worth: albums of annotated photographs of fashions. 1895–1939.

AAD 11–1983 Jean Stehr, 'designer of ornamental hair works': albums of hair styles. C. 1893–1901.

AAD 2–1984 Opitz albums of jewellery designs and photographs. Late nineteenth century.

AAD 5–1984 Maison Arnold annotated fashion drawings. 1920s–30s.

Notes on the Contributors

Juliet Ash teaches the history and theory of fashion design at Ravensbourne College of Design and Communication. She is co-editor with Lee Wright of *Components of Dress: Design Marketing and Image Making in the Fashion Industry*, Routledge & Kegan Paul/Comedia, London, 1988, and co-author with Elizabeth Wilson of *Chic Thrills: A Fashion Reader*, Pandora, 1992.

Christine Boydell is senior lecturer in design history at the University of Central Lancashire, Preston. She studied design history at Manchester Polytechnic and completed a postgraduate diploma in the history of art and design at Birmingham Polytechnic. In 1992 she completed a Ph.D. on Marion Dorn.

Jos Boys is a researcher and journalist specialising in issues concerning women and the built environment. She was a founder member of Matrix, feminist architects, and was also involved in setting up the Women's Design Service, a resource centre on design issues affecting women. She teaches architecture at De Montfort University, Milton Keynes, where she is researching a Ph.D. on the the relationship between social processes and design processes.

Cheryl Buckley is Reader in design history in the Department of Historical and Critical Studies, University of Northumbria, Newcastle upon Tyne. Currently she is co-writing a book on *Fashion, Gender and Representation*. Earlier publications on women and the pottery industry include *Painters and Paintresses: Women Designers in the Pottery Industry 1870–1955*, The Women's Press, 1990, and 'Made in Patriarchy: Towards a feminist analysis of women and design' in V. Margolin (ed), *Design Discourse, History, Theory, Criticism*, University of Chicago Press, 1989.

Anthea Callen is Chair of the Association of Art Historians and senior lecturer in the history of art at the University of Warwick where she is also Dean of Arts. Her most recent publication is *The Spectacular Body: Science, Method and Meaning in the Work of Degas*, Yale University Press, 1995.

Zoë Munby studied design at Manchester Polytechnic and went on to do research into the history of Lancashire textiles. She works as a tutor-organiser with West Mercia District of the Workers' Educational Association.

Angela Partington completed her Ph.D. at Birmingham University in 1990, and is lecturer in design and cultural history at the University of West of England, Bristol. She has published a number of articles concerning the relationship between women and visual culture, and is currently writing a book on twentieth-century British design, to be published by Manchester University Press.

Alison Ravetz, Professor Emeritus of Leeds Metropolitan University, studied English and Archaeology at Cambridge and London. She is author of *Model Estate* (1974), *Remaking Cities: Contradictions of the Recent Urban Environment* (1980), *The Government of Space: Town Planning in Modern Society* (1986) and *The Place of Home: English Domestic Environments 1914–2000* (1995). She has a daughter and two sons and lives in Leeds.

Meg Sweet was archivist of the Archive of Art and Design of the Victoria and Albert Museum at the time the appendix was compiled.

Lynne Walker is a historian based in London. She is currently, writing a larger history of British women and architecture, funded by a grant from the Royal Institute of British Architects.

Suzette Worden completed a Ph.D. thesis on 'Furniture for the Living Room: 1919–39' in 1980. Since then she has lectured on the history of design at the University of Brighton. She is co-author with Jill Seddon of *Women Designing: Redefining Design in Britain Between the Wars*, University of Brighton, 1994. She was also joint curator of a travelling exhibition of the same name. She is currently engaged in a research project on 'Quality Educational Software for Design History' in the Rediffusion Simulation Research Centre at the University of Brighton.

Lee Wright is a lecturer in the history and theory of design at the University of Ulster in Belfast. Her most recent research concerns vernacular traditions in American design.

Index

00734082e